Education That Matters

How Strong Moral Principles, Literacy and Patriotism Will Save Public Schools

Myrna J. Sanner

WESTBOW
PRESS®
A DIVISION OF THOMAS NELSON
& ZONDERVAN

WestBow Press books may be ordered through booksellers or by contacting:

WestBow Press
A Division of Thomas Nelson & Zondervan
1663 Liberty Drive
Bloomington, IN 47403
www.westbowpress.com
1 (866) 928-1240

ISBN: 978-1-5127-7375-0 (sc)
ISBN: 978-1-5127-7377-4 (hc)
ISBN: 978-1-5127-7376-7 (e)

Library of Congress Control Number: 2017901323

Print information available on the last page.

WestBow Press rev. date: 02/23/2017

Contents

Dedication

Education That Matters is dedicated to all colleagues who share my passion for quality education. I am so very grateful to the many students and families who showed kindness to me both in and out of the classroom. Your co-operation, understanding and encouragement gave me the determination to research and write about quality education.

Education That Matters is dedicated to my many friends and family members. Without their help and encouragement, this book would never have been possible. They listened to my voice when I became discouraged and shared their enthusiasm and determination that I must complete the project. I especially thank my husband, Dean, who spent countless hours listening to me elaborate on my ideas and made so many positive suggestions. It is also dedicated to my daughters, Michelle and Elizabeth, who have shared our adventures in Japan, in our travels throughout the world, and the many other events that have made each of us who we are. In addition to my two daughters, I express my appreciation to my friend, Linda, and sons-in-law, Tom and Chris, for their opinions and support. Watching my five grandchildren mature and exhibit high moral principles, set academic goals, and practice patriotism fills my heart with pride and gives me hope for all children.

This book is also dedicated in loving memory of our son, Richard Dean Sanner, Jr. who passed away on September 24, 1985, when he was only sixteen. He and the spiritual inspiration of my God and Savior, provided guidance in choosing the moral principles that are so important when giving hope and love to our youngest generation.

Preface

I have been asked: "Why an ordinary public school elementary teacher and an ordinary wife and mother would write *Education That Matters: How Strong Moral Principles, Literacy and Patriotism Will Save the Public Schools?*" My answer is that I have always had a passion for quality education. In addition, I have had the opportunity of listening to teachers who educate the rich and the poor; who instruct the literate and the illiterate, who face children who embrace the American culture and those who do not; who impart knowledge in private schools and public schools; who teach in the inner city and in rural areas. I have listened to families that home school, those who attend alternative schools and those who value only a private school education. I have listened to families that have immigrated to the United States and families that have lived in the United States for centuries. Reading newspapers and magazines, and listening to the news, have kept me current with the social and political policies and issues that affect education. Everyone seems to be thirsting for a better understanding of why public education is failing to provide a quality education.

Education has been my passion for over 50 years---as a student, parent and teacher. During the past five plus decades many political policies and reforms have been implemented. In 1963, Dr. Martin Luther King gave his "I have a Dream Speech" and in early 1964, President Lyndon Johnson declared a "War on Poverty." Soon after, the Civil Rights Bill was passed; the Elementary and Secondary Education Act and Head Start had their inception. The 50th anniversary of these historical dates, the lack of student progress and the "burn out" of teachers warrant the necessity of *Education That Matters.*

I have watched the United States' international test score ranking in language arts and math decline. I have watched the moral values and social skills of young children deteriorate. Respect, manners, a strong work ethic, kindness and responsibility are some of the social skills that are lacking in many students. Virtues of honesty, fairness, compassion, loyalty, spirituality, and love, are expected of society; however, some families, politicians, and others feel that a moral code should not be expected of them. Students no longer value the English language and patriotism seems to be something in the past. Citizenship is often desired; however, the refusal to integrate into the American culture and resistance to learning the English language are all too prevalent. Bullying, gangs, violence, drug abuse and other lawless behaviors have crept into the hearts and souls of the youth. All of these practices and behavior have contributed to the decline of student learning.

According to The Constitution and the Bill of Rights, public education is the responsibility of the state and local governments. During recent years, the federal government has gradually crept (sometimes taken giant steps) into the public schools in the name of political correctness and social justice. Federal reforms and mandates have caused many schools to "water down" the academic curriculum. In some cases, a double standard, which chooses "winners and losers", has been created in the name of social justice. The Common Core advocates uniform learning goals and a "one size fits all" approach. Many of these reforms and practices conflict with individual learning goals and are dividing the public schools.

Far too many students graduate from high school without the communication skills necessary for employment, the military or college. Far too many students fail to observe the positive behavior code, lack a moral conscience and do not recognize unlawful behavior. Teachers want students to be good citizens. They want students who are patriotic, have a desire to learn English, are willing to obey the behavioral code and have moral values that are in agreement with the responsibilities of good citizenship. Without the desire to learn and will to obey, students often do not meet academic goals, which are required for citizenship and high school graduation. Some say that public schools are failing students; it might be that illiteracy, the lack of moral consciousness and the unwillingness to integrate into the American culture are causing students to fail.

Education That Matters addresses quality education that is imperative for all young children regardless of race, gender, religion or political preference. Free and public education is the right of every young person, under the age of 18, living in the United States. However, many students who exercise this right are literate and live in poverty. Illiteracy and poverty are of grave concern for teachers. Learning readiness is hampered when limited English is spoken in the home and forty percent of these students are considered living in poverty. Many adolescents and young adults drop out of school before graduation or graduate from high school and are still considered illiterate. They sometimes fail to take advantage of the basic education that is offered or might not understand the importance of good communication skills. Without the ability to read, speak and write in English, there is little chance for success in the work place, the military, or in college. In order to erase poverty, all citizens must realize the importance of learning the English language.

Morality and social skills are at the heart of a civilized nation and at the heart of *Education That Matters*. When the families fail to build good character in their children, teachers are often found on the front line. They often find it impossible to teach the academic curriculum without common moral principles in place. Defining and demanding virtues and principles will offer consistency to teachers when educating young students and for families when rearing their children. Negative social behaviors, such as, violence, bullying, substance abuse and media addiction hinder quality education. The social problems of gangs, illegal immigration, poverty, and illiteracy cause many young people to be on the wrong side of the law. All families, teachers, students, community and government personnel must accept moral responsibility.

Education That Matters identifies the role models that influence the behavior and moral principles of students. Role models can be families, teachers, community leaders, rock stars, sport heroes, TV personalities, businessmen and even politicians. They can be of any race or any nationality. Role models can be any gender and of any religious affiliation. However, in order to be the very best role model possible, they must share the common goal of being the very best citizen possible. Being the best citizen includes adopting the American culture, being patriotic, having high moral standards and knowing the English language. It is necessary for everyone to look into the mirror and decide if he/she is being the very best role model possible. Everyone must ask: "Am I worthy of being a United States citizen?

Far too many highly professional and well-educated teachers leave the profession within the first five years of employment. An unrealistic perception of teaching, the amount of time needed for documenting student progress, teaching to the many standardized tests and the demand and need to spend extra time in and out of the classroom are among the reasons given. Salary, insufficient parental involvement, the unwillingness of families to adapt to the American culture, student motivation, and behavior problems, are also mentioned as reasons for leaving the profession.

I sympathize with teachers, when their students have so many diverse physical, emotional and social needs that it is necessary to put academic learning on the "back burner". I sympathize with teachers when the demands of technology, documentation and testing take valuable time away from teaching students. Some active classroom teachers do not speak out for fear of loosing their job because of political correctness and social justice. Instead of criticizing and making more demands, teachers should be congratulated for their ability to erase the "isms" from the classrooms by promoting fairness and justice for all children.

Education that Matters is a voice for public school teachers in cities, suburbs and rural areas to demand quality education. These voices have many years of experience and understand the importance of learning the English language and building character in young students. They understand that literacy is fundamental to all learning. They understand the importance of tackling social and academic problems from the bottom up rather than from the top down. They understand the importance of positive role models. They know that when students integrate into the American culture, they have a much better chance for success.

Education That Matters gives teachers encouragement and guidance when they face that special class where the needs of the students far exceed the limited time and resources in the classroom. Many teachers are looking for ways of educating students who enter their classrooms with no knowledge of English and return to homes where English is not spoken. All too often, teachers are caught on the front line, needing to "put on the brakes" and address the negative behavior that is tolerated in the home and on the streets. Teachers can recognize negative behavior, and they can teach the academics and help eradicate literacy. They can even practice patriotism every day in the classroom. However, teachers cannot "go it alone". They do not go home with their students. They need the support of all responsible citizens to build character in the youth. Teachers want to have a classroom filled with eager students--- students who understand the American culture and practice patriotism. Teachers desire students who want to learn.

Every child living in America has the God given right to fulfill his/ her highest potential. A united voice of quality classroom teachers can demand quality education. A united voice of quality teachers will promote literacy that will produce successful students. A united voice of quality classroom teachers will demand social skills and moral values that will increase the safety and freedom of all students. A united voice of quality teachers will help students be patriotic and embrace the American culture. Teachers want and need all citizens, families and students to co-operate, respect and support their profession and quality education. Status quo in education is not acceptable.

Education That Matters is a voice for the majority of families who provide a caring environment, where patriotism is practiced, English is spoken and a moral code is well established. They understand that children learn far more from what they observe than what they are told. These adults understand the importance of outstanding role models and raise children that are respectful and eager to learn. These are the citizens who work behind the scenes to make the real difference in society and give freely of their time, talents and material possessions. *Education That Matters* will serve as reinforcement for those families and will encourage them to continue to give positive guidance to their children.

Far too many families are fleeing the public schools and seeking refuge in charter and private schools and home schooling their children. The flight from public schools leaves some public schools with the "left overs"---the children who have little or no knowledge of English, children who have little family support, children who are disruptive, and children who lack a moral conscience. Responsible families want a school that encourages academic learning; schools that encourage children to do what is right. They want schools that encourage responsibility. They want schools that promote the American culture and patriotism. They want public schools to be a place of refuge. Quality families want a quality school that offers a quality education.

My experience as a mother has encouraged me to congratulate the many adults who share my enthusiasm for quality education. I sympathize with families when their children are not making the progress that is mandated and when the curriculum in the public schools is not as strong as that in the charter and private schools. I sympathize with the families of public school children when they instill high moral values and teach social skills to their children and these are not evident or enforced in the lives of their peers and in the public schools. I sympathize with citizens who value the American culture and patriotism but do not see this loyalty in the streets. I sympathize with families who feel that their only alternative to quality education is to flee the public schools.

Education that Matters is a voice for law enforcement officers and other community workers who spend every hour of every day protecting liberty and freedom. Recently, law enforcement officers have been accused of "police brutality", when they have confronted those that display questionable behavior. I sympathize with them because, they, like teachers, understand that law and order must prevail in a free and democratic society. They, like teachers, know the harmful effects of bullying, violence and substance abuse. They, like teachers, look beyond the "isms", care about the welfare of all citizens and want everyone to feel safe in the streets and the home. They do their best to treat everyone fairly so justice may prevail. They know they need the support of the family and other role models. They know that when everyone is respectful, obeys the laws and has a moral conscience, their job will be a whole lot easier.

Education That Matters is written for the federal government that is always seeking ways to improve education. Perhaps, political involvement might be responsible for some of the decline in quality education. Some government leaders are poor role models for children when they bend the rules to meet their individual goals. Government policies often suggest that there are "winners and losers" or that "one size fits all". When policies fail, the government may initiate a "double standard". Some of the policies and mandates have used "isms" to pass judgment on teachers or they may claim social injustice for the students. These judgmental comments do nothing to enhance quality education and never reach the hearts and souls of children. *Education that Matters* illustrates how political correctness and social justice can interfere with teaching patriotism, literacy and positive principles.

Legislation and policies have cost billions of dollars for mandated achievement tests, better technology, improved textbooks, high speed Internet, and more highly educated teachers. Many of these programs emphasize changing the curriculum; adding new administrators, asking for more money or better technology. However, they often fail to focus on what individual students are learning---why they are not meeting the standards. The federal government often looks upon education as another federal political machine and in the process ignores the uniqueness and individuality of every student. When reforming public schools, it seems evident to me that we must look beyond the federal government solutions of money, technology and teachers. We must look into the hearts and souls of children. We must work from the bottom (the student) to the top (individual goals) and from the inside, out.

PART ONE

American Public Schools Will Be Great Again

Introduction

We might ask, "Why did our founding fathers place so much emphasis on education?" They wanted to create a united nation, free of division and chaos---a nation that is safe and prosperous. In order to have a truly unified country, everyone must appreciate American citizenship and practice patriotism. Everyone must share English as a common language and everyone must practice moral principles that are aligned with The Constitution. When citizens are united, patriotism, a common language and moral principles are universal and valued.

It has been said that we must look into the past before we can see the future. During the past 50 years, the federal government has become much more involved in dictating education policies and reforms---often prompted by social justice and political correctness. In 1983, President Reagan addressed public education by announcing "A Nation at Risk". During the Bush administration, the theme was "No Child Left Behind", for President Obama it has been "Race to the Top". Limited English Proficiency, Early Childhood Education, Third Grade Guarantee and The Common Core are some of the more recent innovative programs. In spite of many policies and reforms, public education does not adequately meet the needs of many students.

In some communities and schools, literacy and patriotism seem to be a thing of the past. Social skills and moral values are often overlooked. Some government policies fail to support the requirements of citizenship and downplay integrating into the American culture. These policies often pick winners and losers, create a double standard, and support a "watered down" curriculum. Without results, there is a continuous and constant advocacy for reform.

In December 2015, Congress passed the Every Student Succeeds Act. This federal legislation advocates four principles that will reform and improve education in the United States. These principles are more state and local control, parental choice of schools, accountability and transparency for teachers, and quality content. Certainly, the enactment of this program increases the need for more money to enhance education in the state and local communities. It places more responsibility on the schools and teachers. It will require new textbooks and software. However, this act does not seem to address the responsibility of the student and family. It does not address the heart and soul of the student and his willingness to learn. Therefore, I have added the Fifth Principles.

The Fifth Principle looks beyond local control, school choice, teacher accountability and quality content. The Fifth Principle looks into the heart and soul of the student and the family. This principle advocates that all high school graduates take advantage of quality content by becoming literate, patriotic and understanding the history and government of the United States. It promotes teaching the moral principles that are imperative when adapting to the American culture---the moral principles that every responsible citizen holds near and dear to his heart.

The Fifth principle suggests that education can be transformed into quality education when moral principles, literacy and patriotism are added to the first four principles. This principle places the responsibility of a quality education, not only on the schools and teachers but also on the family and the student. This principle solicits the assistance of the government by enforcing the laws and encouraging literacy and patriotism. The fifth principle asks: "What are the requirements for responsible citizenship?" "What can the student and his family do to transform education into quality education.

Citizenship requires high moral character, a basic knowledge of the English language, patriotism, and an understanding of American history and government. Quality education proposes that all high school students understand, appreciate and practice the requirements of citizenship before they graduate. These requirements will change education into quality education.

Chapter I

ESSA (Every Student Succeeds Act)

On December 10, 2015, Congress passed the ESSA (Every Student Succeeds Act). It replaced "No Child Left Behind" of the Bush Administration. It has received endorsement from *Conservative Leaders for Education* headed by former Secretary of Education, Wm. J. Bennett. The act advocates a return to local and state control of schools, giving parents school choice, asks for more accountability and transparency on the part of teachers and demands quality content.

Although all of these issues are important to the teachers and schools, from my point of view as a teacher and parent, state and local control is not enough; school choice is not enough; teacher accountability and transparency is not enough; and a quality curriculum is not enough. All of these proposals address how tax dollars will be used to improve education---the teachers, the curriculum, school choice and more local control. In order to have quality education, the hearts and souls of the families must be added and addressed. Therefore, I have advocated a fifth principle, the requirements for citizenship that will transform education into **quality education**.

State and Local Control

According to The Constitution, public education is the responsibility of the state and local governments. During the past 50 years, the federal bureaucracy has gradually inched (sometimes taken giant steps) into dictating policies and reforms---often prompted by social justice and political correctness. Many of these innovative programs have created additional social problems for the teachers but have failed to eliminate illiteracy and poverty. Illiteracy and poverty are of grave concern for teachers and seem to be systemic to public education. How many more ineffective policies will be passed in the name of political correctness and how many more times will teachers hear the word "reform" and we want the "brightest and best"? Getting to the root of the issue and finding out why these programs have not been effective might help understand the teacher's concern.

In spite of the many policies and reforms:

- international test scores have not improved and continue to spiral downward,
- an estimated 40% of children are living in poverty
- more money and technology have been given to schools
- illiterate young adults are graduating from high school
- lawless behavior is found in the schools and on the streets
- the moral conscience of many students seems to be non-existent
- family support for public education is deteriorating
- negative role models are everywhere---in politics, on social media and TV, etc.
- cost of educating one child ranges from $6,000 in Utah to over $19,000 in New York City
- teacher-student ratio has decreased from 1:17 in 1960 to 1:8 today (some say 1:3)
- more poor and illiterate children are enrolled in public schools
- patriotism has been overlooked in some public schools

There should be no cost too high for quality education, but there should also be no waste. Much of the federal money goes to providing grants, initiating new textbooks and curriculum, and of course supporting the federal bureaucracy. Without the interference of the federal government, the local school can take control of balancing the education budget.

At the local level, only about half of the administrative and instructional employees are teachers. Among the non-teaching staff are:

- guidance counselors
- multimedia centers hired staff
- curricular experts needed to define and implement state standards
- professionals to design and administer the tests
- instructional aids, new administrators to oversee policies
- administrators for disciplinary action
- attendance planners that conform with judicial guidelines
- administrators for the breakfast and lunch programs, and medical services programs (Paul E. Peterson "Saving Schools" p. 132-133)
- and too many federal "watch dogs" overseeing all of the federal policies and programs

Quality education would certainly be more teacher-efficient and cost effective with local and state control. Just think of all of the money and time that could be saved if there was no longer a Federal Department of Education dictating policies and reforms. Just think of the money and time that could be saved if the federal government no longer demanded new textbooks, technology, testing and documentation. Just think of the money that could be saved if fewer illegal children would be enrolled in the public schools. Just think of the family units that would stay in tack if foreign federal assistance was monitored and given directly to the education and safety of the children in their native country. Just think how the elimination of waste, fraud and duplication of services would reduce the education budget. If some of the administrative positions were eliminated, state and local budgets could be reduced and teachers could spend their time teaching. By returning the control of education to the local and state governments, the local district could decide which policies specifically apply to their students and which reforms are working in their schools.

Outcomes prove that students are not getting a quality education. With state and local control, quality education would:

- begin with the individual student at the local level
- be more personal.
- work with young people at the local level
- provide students with the ammunition to fight some of the negative social influences
- allow more time for personal communication with students and families
- allow additional time for enrichment and remediation
- encourage the enforcement of the laws of immigration that affect the language barrier
- give teachers the freedom and time to teach patriotism
- monitor the education budget more efficiently
- give teachers the authority to instill appropriate behavior and a moral conscience

When running for the President of the United States, Ohio governor, John Kasich, suggested combining over one hundred federal education programs into just four. Concerned teachers certainly agree with more local control. They want an education system that is smaller (return to a focus on local schools and individual students), simpler (emphasis on reading, writing and speaking in English, basic government and math) and smarter (insist on literacy, social skills and moral values).

QUESTIONS FOR SOCIETY: What federal programs can be eliminated? What will the cost of educating a child be once ESSA (Every Student Succeeds Act) is in place?

AUTHOR COMMENTS: I have had many discussions with teachers, principals and administrators regarding the involvement of the government in education. It seems that the government gets on every train that passes through town. However, the government never seems to know when to get off or leave some of the cars behind. Hopefully, the local and state governments will have fewer cars and those cars will be loaded with quality content.

Parental Choice

Public education is offered to every child under the age of 18 living in the United States. The majority of families take advantage of the free public education that is offered. It is certainly a privilege that is not offered in all countries.

There are other families who feel that public schools are not safe and do not offer a challenging curriculum. Therefore, they are fleeing the public schools, not only for academic reasons, but also for social reasons like bullying, drug abuse, violence, gangs, illiteracy and even the lack of respect for the principles of The Constitution and the American culture. Many of these are lawless behaviors and parents want to keep their children out of harms way. When the government supports moral principles, patriotism and English literacy, there will be fewer parents fleeing the public schools.

Social concerns that encourage families to flee the public schools are:

- bullying,
- drug and substance abuse
- violence and gangs
- illiteracy of other students
- improper use of technology
- desensitizing of youth through the social media
- resisting the American culture
- lack of respect for the principles of The Constitution
- disrespectful and lawless behavior

Dissatisfied families are choosing and even demanding alternative choices to public education that are academically challenging and enforce the moral and social behavior codes. Many children living in poverty have no choice but to continue their education in a public school. To provide more choices, the state and local governments are offering alternatives such as charter schools, school vouchers to attend private schools and have even developed programs for home schooling.

During the past several decades, demographic and cultural changes have influenced the content of the curriculum and the behavior or students. The United States' open door policy continues to encourage children to enter the United States and attend the public schools without meeting the outlined requirements for citizenship---literacy, moral principles and patriotism. These children receive the entitlements but little personal accountability is demanded.

Political correctness and social justice, promoted by the federal government, has gradually crept into every community and also into the public schools. In order to meet academic standards and justify the political policies, many schools have:

- "watered down" the academic curriculum to meet the needs of under-performing students
- created a double standard, which chooses "winners and losers", in the name of social justice.
- integrated The Common Core, which promotes "one size fits all" and can conflict with challenging individual learning goals.
- increased testing and documentation
- increased the use of technology for teaching under achieving students

The practice of "dumping" underachieving students into the public school classroom has broadened the divide between public schools and alternative schools. Therefore, many families feel that school choice may be their only answer to quality education.

Social issues and political policies such as same legalized marijuana, abortion rights, women's rights, and illegal immigration directly or indirectly affect the moral values and social behavior of students. These policies often affect the family unit and the role models found in society, which in turn affects the behavior, patriotism and literacy of the student.

Because of social issues, demographic and cultural changes in society, many students:

- do not understand the laws of the country
- do not realize that the rules of the school must be obeyed
- are often truant and absent
- practice behavior that is out of control
- have no moral conscience
- are illiterate
- lack respect for our country
- challenge democracy and patriotism
- are disrespectful of teachers, administrators and school property
- come from dysfunctional homes

There is no question that moral principles, government policies and reforms have changed the learning environment of the public schools. What has not changed is that teachers:

- continue to welcome all children.
- want all students to have a basic understanding of reading and math.
- want all students to know and obey the rules of the school and the laws of the country.
- want all students to graduate with knowledge to make them responsible citizens.
- want all families to no longer depend on entitlements for keeping their bodies healthy
- want all families to have proper food, shelter and basic health care.
- want all families to be patriotic and understand the American culture

- want everyone to be treated with respect and kindness.
- want everyone to obey the rules of the school.
- want all students and families to understand that literacy, responsibility and morality are imperative for liberty and freedom and also for quality education.

QUESTION FOR SOCIETY: The major question is what kind of schools do we want and are we willing to work together to achieve quality education which includes acceptable behavior and the desire to learn.

AUTHOR COMMENTS: I would suggest that there are no failing schools, no failing teachers and no failing students. Students are in a transition; learning the English language, learning about patriotism, and adopting social and moral behavior that are in line with the moral conscience of the nation. The failure comes on the part of the government, which does not insist that language, appropriate behavior, a moral conscience, and pride in being a citizen of the United States of America are present in the heart and soul of every student. Does anyone remember a first lady, who in spite of her Ivy League education had no reason to be proud of her country until her husband was elected President? She has also lost hope because someone is replacing her husband as President. Really?

SOCIETY'S STORY: School choice is a wonderful thing but it will never be a "cure all" for education. In the September 25th, 2016, issue of the Columbus Dispatch, it was reported 96 percent of the eighth grade students in Ohio's public schools and 97 percent of the eighth grade students enrolled in Ohio's charter schools did not pass the 8th grade reading test. Two weeks later, there was an article linking poverty to the test scores. There are many non-English speaking children who may also live in poverty. School choice is not nearly as important as the quality of the students who are in attendance. Quality students need hearts and souls that embrace the English language, moral principles and practice patriotism.

Teacher Transparency and Accountability

Most teachers welcome accountability for the academic progress and moral behavior of their students. Quality teachers:

- are life-long learners
- are well-educated professionals
- have high moral standards
- are educated to recognize the individual qualities of every student
- address families with respect and kindness in an effective and efficient manner.
- are educated to assess student learning
- use testing results for remediation and enrichment
- are positive role models for students and the community in thought, word and deed
- have compassion and a love for all children
- want all students to excel

Nearly all teaching colleagues share these same principles and diligently work with students to achieve academic and personal goals.

Teachers realize that they cannot "go it alone" when working with students. Teachers know that keeping the lines of communication open are crucial. They continuously attempt to solicit the co-operation and support of the family. Therefore, good teachers:

- provide time for parent-teacher conferences,
- send report cards home on a regular basis,
- send a weekly newsletter home with the child
- encourage an open line of written and verbal communication
- assess the progress of students on a regular basis
- make substantive comments about student achievement on student work that is sent home
- may call the home to acknowledge marked improvement or misbehavior

Unfortunately, teachers also recognize they are often more interested in student behavior and academic achievements than the family. Teachers become frustrated when all attempts to keep an open line of communication are not appreciated nor are they acknowledged. Frustration also sets in when families never want to take the time to meet face to face to discuss behavior and academic progress.

A teacher's job is very difficult without government policies that encourage literacy, moral values, behavior skills, and patriotism. Teachers have every right to expect parents and students to communicate in English since that is our common language. Teachers have every right to expect students to practice appropriate behavior both in and out of school. Teachers also have the right to complain when testing and documentation limit academic instruction time. Teachers have every right to expect business, political and social role models to be honorable, honest and respectful.

Teachers also know that expecting patriotism, English, moral values and social skills to enter the heart and soul of the student via the computer or by osmosis, is not feasible. If a classroom has too many non-English speaking students, too many behavior problems, too many students whose physical and emotional needs are not met, teachers will not be as successful in helping every child reach his full potential. If the child is illiterate, he/she will need extra time and encouragement and reinforcement from the home. If a child practices anti-social behavior, the student will need correction from the home and community as well as the school. If the child is unpatriotic, he will need positive role models in the government and in the community.

In many cases, the responsibility of teaching English, patriotism, common moral values and social skills have all been solely placed on lap of the classroom teacher and teachers are blamed when progress is not made. Teachers have been accused of prejudice---political, race, religion, sex, etc. Teachers often feel their hands are tied when attempting to instill social skills and moral values because they might be considered politically incorrect or lack social justice. Teachers want students who are respectful and value the American culture. The government, the community and family should have confidence in the classroom teacher.

Yes, it is very important to have teacher accountability and transparency. It is important for the teacher to have frequent honest communication with the family---not through social media and technology but in one-on-one confidential conversations. Teachers have the responsibility to report student progress in a regular and timely manner. In addition, assessments and student work need to be evaluated daily and contain substantive comments about the student progress.

Conscientious families have the right to expect the teacher to be familiar with all of the students and their progress. Families also have the responsibility to personally meet with the teacher in person. It is also important to have family accountability---for learning the English language, for behavior, and for patriotism. The outcome of quality education does not rest only on teachers; it rests equally on the personal responsibility of all family members.

The government has the responsibility of supporting the schools and the teachers by enforcing the laws that discourage negative behavior and address the troubling influences found in society. The government has the responsibility of enforcing the laws of citizenship and to question those who come to America to destroy rather than unite. It also has the responsibility of providing positive role models for the students and families. When demanding quality education, it seems evident that we must look beyond the federal government solutions of money, technology and better teachers. Let's replace money with moral values, technology with literacy, and be certain that all community leaders, teachers, and families are the best role models possible.

Quality Content

Teachers, both liberal and conservative, have the right to know and the responsibility to teach the truth. Textbooks in social studies and science should are factual, contain only truthful information, and have no political agenda. Mathematics should be basic, easily understood and meaningful for future application. Language arts should stress the ability to communicate in English, with basic skills in reading, writing and speaking.

Quality content begins with literacy. Illiteracy is of grave concern for teachers. Teachers know that the ability to communicate in a common language is the primary building block for all future learning. Teachers know that if students are illiterate they will have difficulty reading; writing and speaking in English. The inability to communicate in a common language will stifle student understanding of math, social studies, science and all other academic learning. All of the quality content in the world will not matter to the illiterate student. Without the ability to read, speak and write in English, there is little chance for success in the work place, the military, or in college.

Teachers know that illiteracy is often the result of poverty, a lack of an English rich environment, or a home where English is not the language of choice. Often, illiterate students:

- come from homes where entitlement programs provide for their physical existence
- come from homes that do not encourage or supervise homework
- come from homes where the social media and technology take precedence over reading
- do not obey the rules of the school and the laws of the community
- do not fit into the "one size fits all" of The Common Core
- may need remediation
- may need a "watered down" curriculum
- may need Head Start
- may need LEP (limited English proficient) classes
- may not meet the standards and benchmarks of any quality content
- may not meet the requirements of "The Third Grade Guarantee"

- may require a "double standard" to meet any benchmarks and standards
- may need to be "socially promoted" from one grade to the next

Therefore, teachers need to rely on other community helpers to help eradicate illiteracy, whether by eliminating poverty, by restricting the number of non-English speaking students in the classroom, by enforcing the requirements of citizenship or any other viable suggestion.

The federal government is always seeking ways to improve education and then they "blow the budget" by revising the curriculum with new textbooks, new software, new testing, new documentation etc. as well as additional administrators to implement these new programs. Textbook and testing companies gain financially. However, students and teachers may become victims of a slanted and liberal point of view, irrelevant information, and the promotion of one culture above the other.

The "watered down" curriculum can be a result of political correctness, illiteracy, the lack of disciplined behavior and the belief that "one size fits all." Double standards promote a culture of "winners and losers". Using social justice excuses such as race, nationality, gender and religion, divides rather than unites the students in the public schools.

The government mandates of more technology and a stronger curriculum involves new computer programs, different textbooks, more testing and documentation. Most textbooks and computer programs are the ideas of government bureaucrats who wish to dictate curriculum and testing. Other ideas come from the pens of publishers who want to push a political ideal. Others come from the theories of "inventive ideas" of professors that need to be explored and published. Some outside resources want to put everything into "fast forward" and disregard putting the building blocks in place.

Quality content requires:

- a rich curriculum with standards and benchmarks for each grade
- the ability to communicate in English, with basic skills in reading, writing and speaking.
- Mathematics that is basic, easily understood and meaningful for future application.
- textbooks in social studies and science that are factual, contain only truthful information without leftist slant and a political agenda.
- makes no excuses because of race, religion, gender or nationality

Please do not say that quality education and a quality curriculum cannot happen in the public schools or in any school of choice. While parents in large cities and inside "the beltway" feel the need to seek private schools, well-educated students can be found in many "fly-over" public schools all across the United States. Quality education is happening in schools where literacy and the desire to learn abound. Quality education is happening where families, teachers and students share the same moral values, value patriotism, and appreciate the American culture. The answer to quality education and content is dedicated teachers, devoted families and determined students and a government that supports literacy, moral values, behavior skills and patriotism for all.

SOCIETY'S STORY: Regardless of immigration status, a common language is needed in the schools. Recently, it was reported that one school's population of undocumented children rose from 8 at the beginning of the year to more than 100. The ages varied from 13 to 17. It was recently reported that in another community, 331 different languages could be found in the schools. It has also been reported that currently 20% of the people living in the United States live in homes where English is not spoken. When every student becomes literate, quality content will result in quality education.

Chapter II

Replacing Education With Quality Education

All four of the proposed principles of the Every Student Succeeds Act, (state and local control, parental choice, transparency and accountability and quality content) involve what the government and schools can do to promote education for everyone. The fifth principle addresses additional components that are essential for quality education. Literacy, moral principles and patriotism are all principles that demand the will of the inner heart and soul. When these principles are combined with the previous four, quality education will become a reality. **America's public schools will be great again!**

The fifth principle looks beyond what the governments, schools and teachers can do when educating students. The fifth principle looks into the heart and soul of the student and his family. The fifth principle asks what the student and his family can do to transform some of the failed policies and reforms into quality education. Without the heart and soul of every student and family, education will fall short of quality education.

Principle number five emphasizes the crucial role that families play in quality education. The families of concern are those who take no initiative to learn English, refuse to obey the behavior code, lack a moral conscience; and do not understand patriotism and the American culture. Citizens of concern are those who live in poverty and continue to rely on government entitlements for their existence. Students of concern are those who are illiterate, have no moral conscience, and lack loyalty and respect for their country.

I have chosen the universal requirements for United States citizenship as the foundation for my fifth principle.

The requirements for citizenship follow:
Must be 18 years of age
Must be a permanent resident for at least five years
Continuous residence and presence
Must be of high moral character
Must have a basic knowledge of the English language
Must have a basic knowledge of United States Government and American History
Must take an oath of allegiance to the United States of America

You might ask why I chose the requirements for citizenship as my fifth principle? The federal government has initiated these requirements for immigrants who wish to become citizens of the United States. These citizenship requirements certainly are not beyond the realm of expectation for most young people who have had the opportunity for thirteen (sometimes more than thirteen) years of free public education. The requirements for citizenship are universal and apply to all regardless of religion, race, nationality or gender.

Quality families find that the responsibilities of citizenship allow them to lead productive lives. They insist that their children are literate, follow the behavior code of the school, develop a moral conscience, and practice patriotism. Should not all American families; all young people and all citizens share this same sense of responsibility? Should not all Americans take personal responsibility for their knowledge and behavior?

The first three requirements for citizenship address the importance of maturity, continuous presence and residency as being fundamental for citizenship. Maturity, attendance and physical presence are also essentials when obtaining a quality education in American schools. Teachers are exhausted in trying to educate students who are sporadic in school attendance and lack social maturity.

The fourth citizen requirement is "must be of high moral character". Teachers are exhausted from teaching students who lack a moral conscience. Teachers want students who are well behaved and have high moral principles. When everyone possesses high moral principles there are no winners and losers. High moral principles provide unity in behavior, language and loyalty to the United States.

Requirement number five: Must have a basic knowledge of the English language. Certainly literacy is fundamental for citizenship, obeying the laws and being a contributing member of society. Some students may need more time to become literate, but no one should be given a free pass.

Finally, must have a basic knowledge of United States government and history and pledge allegiance to the United States of America. This knowledge and loyalty are imperative for understanding The Constitution and developing an appreciation of the American culture. The American culture will only be preserved when everyone has a personal commitment to The Constitution of the United States.

Literacy, moral behavior and patriotism are essential for quality learning in all schools throughout the United States. Meeting these citizenship requirements might be used when obtaining a drivers license and the privilege of voting. These same citizenship principles might be a requirement for graduation from high school and a requirement when applying for welfare.

The main goal of public education is to assure that all young people are given and equal opportunity to learn the English language, understand the behavior code of society, develop a moral conscience and accept the American culture and the responsibilities of citizenship.

America needs young adults who are dependable and willing to work. America needs informed voters. America needs students who are literate and appreciate a common language. American needs students who have a moral conscience and are mature in their behavior. American needs young people who are loyal to their country. America needs every young person to be responsible and respectful.

Why Moral Principles Are Essential for a Quality Education

William J. Bennett, former Secretary of Education and author of *The Educated Child (p. 526)*, often speaks of the importance of instilling virtues in young children. "Schools should teach youngsters to recognize traits such as honesty and compassion (and vices such as deceit and cruelty), both in themselves and in others. Students should learn the different forms that virtues take, what they are like in practice, and why they deserve admiration and allegiance. Children who leave elementary school with fuzzy notions about these moral fundamentals are headed for trouble."

Thank you, Wm. J. Bennett, for your wisdom.

Among the list of requirements for citizenship is: "must be of high moral character". Character has been defined as: "the act of developing the intellectual and moral facilities by education." A classroom that provides quality education includes positive behavior and students with a moral conscience. Being of high moral character is also necessary for integrating into the American culture.

Since moral principles are to be received through education, scrutinizing the moral values of the American culture will assist parents and teachers when teaching moral behavior. Years ago, the education of the heart and soul of a young child was primarily the responsibility of the family. Today, in some cases, the parental responsibilities of instilling moral values and behavior skills is left up to the schools. Without the support of the school, children may grow up without a moral conscience. Without good principles, innocent children may be harmed.

The United States is a nation of laws and these laws have social expectations. Laws help citizens make choices that support the American culture and The Constitution. Laws help determine what is right and what is wrong; what is good and what is evil, what is honest and what is fair. Laws keep children safe and determine what is right for society as a whole. Laws do not promote a double standard of behavior, nor do they choose winners and losers. Laws are for the safety for all---regardless of race, religion, gender or nationality.

A civilized and law abiding society demands respect, manners, discipline, responsibility, honesty, fairness, communication skills, a strong work ethic, knowledge, compassion, generosity, love, spirituality and many other virtues. When applying these virtues in daily living, a moral conscience can be formed in the heart and soul of every human being.

In a civilized society, strong moral principles must take precedence over negative influences. Most frustrating and damaging to the American culture is that not all cultures present in the United States share these same moral principles. Bullying, violence, illiteracy, and the abuse of drugs and other substances are negative influences that are often found lurking in the American Culture. Pop-culture, social media, TV, violent video games are so common that many youth have become desensitized to anti-social behavior. Some people, from a variety of ethnic and religious groups, have difficulty accepting the common virtues that the majority of American citizens hold dear. In the United States, all men are created equally and must meet the same social expectations.

Schools should not and cannot be solely responsible for instilling acceptable social behavior and moral values. Teachers need the support of families who understand the American culture; the support of families who are patriotic and appreciate liberty and freedom; the support of families where English is valued and spoken; the support of families who obey all rules and laws; and families where acceptable social and moral behavior are practiced. Teachers especially need the support of the government in monitoring immigration, poverty, violence, drug abuse, and the social media.

CALL TO ACTION: Every community and every school can join in selecting moral values that will perpetuate a positive learning environment. The selection may vary from community to community, from school to school and from home to home. The most important ingredient is a commitment to educate the hearts and souls of children. By providing consistent and constant guidance, teachers and parents encourage personal responsibility, social civility and principled living. The ultimate outcome will be a community and a country that eradicates illiteracy, possesses positive social behavior and outstanding moral values, and practices patriotism.

QUESTION FOR SOCIETY: Without moral principles and behavior skills, will children ever adopt the American culture?

Why Literacy is Essential for a Quality Education

Having a basic knowledge of the English Language is one of the essentials for citizenship and should be essential for high school graduation, for obtaining a driver's license, and perhaps the privilege of voting. The Constitution is written in English and all public schools in the United States teach classes in English. English is the national language of the United States of America. Knowledge of the English language assures an understanding of the laws and moral values, and the ability to communicate.

Statistics vary regarding the number of illiterate children in the United States. However, Wikipedia has reported that there are over five million (about 1/10th of children in all schools and 1/8th of children in public schools) children in the United States who are illiterate. Poverty and immigration are often cited as reasons for illiteracy. Many immigrants come to the United States with no knowledge of English. Some homes do not provide an English language rich environment. Some families encourage their children to "hang on" to their native language. These are the families that need Head Start, Limited English Proficient (LEP) instruction, and numerous language interventions in the public schools.

The Federal Department of Health and Human Services and the Department of Homeland Security make many decisions regarding immigration, poverty, and the health and safety of the children. Head Start and LEP goals of literacy are determined by the federal government and passed on to the states. The complex and challenging task of implementing these goals eventually ends up on the desk of the classroom teacher. The teacher has no control of the poverty that exists. Teachers have no control over who is allowed to immigrate into the United States. Teachers also have no control over the home environment. Successful education often depends on families who support the learning of English and integrate into the American culture.

The federal government is very generous in providing money, technology and high speed Internet to all students. The federal government often forgets that teaching literacy does not depend upon technology. Technology does not teach children to read. Reading is integrated into every subject in every school and for six hours each day five days a week, illiterate children are exposed, encouraged to read, write and speak in English. Teachers know that when students return to homes and communities where English is not spoken, their job will be more challenging. The public school teacher knows that non-English speaking students will take extra time, which often results in having less time for achieving students.

Each evening, many of these non-English speaking children watch their favorite TV programs in their native language, hear their native language in the streets, and, in some cases, even written on the very boxes of merchandise the family has purchased. President Obama even boasted that The Affordable Care Act could be accessed in over one hundred different languages. Providing interpreters for doctor appointments, school conferences and even for taking citizenship tests, creates dependency and apathy on the part of the illiterate.

The bureaucrats in Washington DC do not want illiteracy and negative behaviors influencing their children and therefore, they send their children to private schools or have them attend public schools in their home districts. These government employees have the financial resources to escape these negative influences. However, there are many parents who do not work for the government and have no alternative to public school education.

Many times the curriculum is "watered down" and unruly behavior is overlooked because of the language barrier. Although teachers believe in inclusion and integration, every teacher knows that children who are already proficient in English may not benefit academically, socially and morally when there are too many non-English speaking students in the classroom. It is my opinion that immigrants should be welcomed but not at the expense of tax-paying citizens and the hard working, green card immigrants who are literate, have adapted to the American culture and have worked for many years to gain citizenship. Perhaps undocumented children, "birth babies", and "anchor babies" should not be given citizenship until they are old enough to pass the citizenship test.

It is not a wonder some parents choose to home school, send their children to private schools or charter schools. It is not a wonder that teachers "burn out" without the support of the government and home. It is not a wonder that nearly all politicians in Washington DC send their children to private schools.

AUTHOR COMMENTS: I am not suggesting throwing illiterate young children into the streets. I am suggesting that they meet the same citizenship requirements as everyone else. Amnesty without meeting the citizenship requirements creates a nation of illiterate people. Graduation from high school without having a basic knowledge of English creates a nation of unemployable and illiterate people.

QUESTION FOR SOCIETY: Without knowledge of the English language, will it be possible for these children and adults adopt the American culture?

Why Patriotism is essential for Quality Education

The final requirement of citizenship and a quality education is patriotism. This includes knowledge and awareness of civics, history and pledging allegiance to the United States of America. Patriotism is respecting the flag and all of the liberty and freedom for which it stands. Patriotism is reciting the "Pledge of Allegiance" with the right hand over the heart and standing to sing the National Anthem with pride and dignity. Patriotism understands the uniqueness of democracy and the American culture. Patriotism promotes unity rather than diversity.

Patriotism is having pride in being a United States citizen and being proud of ones heritage and government. So proud that the laws are respected and obeyed. So proud that all citizens care about each other; so proud that citizens are loyal and respectful; so proud that freedom and liberty are valued; so proud to be an American---not just because of the many rights but also the responsibility of being a good citizen. Patriotism and loyalty unite the citizens as they work together to protect life, liberty and the pursuit of happiness.

Being a responsible citizen is:

- understanding The Constitution
- knowing factual events in American history
- understanding civics, without any "right wing" or "left wing" slant
- showing allegiance and loyalty to the United States of America

- being a responsible citizen is being of high moral character
- understanding and speaking the English language
- accepting the American culture

American citizenship is valued throughout the world. Immigrants and refugees come into the United States every day looking for freedom and liberty. In the rush to grant amnesty and citizenship, the meaning of patriotism and the requirements for citizenship are often forgotten. Many immigrants cannot read and understand the laws and even their entry into the United States may have been an act of lawlessness. High moral character, knowledge of the English language and American government and history are overlooked. Rights are given but responsibilities are forgotten. Before granting citizenship, it would benefit the schools if the government made certain that those coming to the United States do so because they want to embrace patriotism and the American culture. Everyone must be vetted, no matter how long it takes.

During the past five decades there has been a decline in patriotism and loyalty and the American culture has taken a big "hit". Hate crimes are being committed and flag burning is far too common. In some schools, patriotism is not taught and loyalty is overlooked in the name of political correctness and social justice. Veterans are disrespected and some have been denied medical assistance because of fraud and greed.

One myth about public education is that patriotism, loyalty and respect for the American culture do not need to be taught in the public schools. If loyalty and respect for the United States are not taught in the public schools, where will they be taught?

DENNIS PRAGER'S STORY: Dennis Prager, American conservative, national syndicated radio talk show host, columnist, author and public speaker sums up the importance of American culture and values in this manner: "This is an American public school, and American public schools were created to make better Americans. If you wish to affirm an ethnic, racial or religious identity through school, you will have to go elsewhere. We will end all ethnicity, race and non-American nationality-based celebrations. They undermine the motto of America, one of its three central values---pluribus Unum, "from many one." And this school will be guided by America's values. This includes all after-school clubs. I will not authorize clubs that divide students based on any identities. This includes race, language, religion, sexual orientation or whatever else may become in vogue in a society divided by political correctness.

OUR INTERNATIONAL STORY: My husband's business took us to Japan for three years. It was understood that every member of our family, including our two pre-teen children, was to abide by all of the laws of Japan. If any of our family members participated in using drugs or any other illegal activity, our entire family would be deported immediately. Our family respected the Japanese customs and laws. It was a fabulous experience and we enjoyed the diverse culture and extensive travel; however, each time we heard OUR National Anthem, it brought tears to our eyes and a longing to return to the greatest country in the world.

QUESTIONS FOR SOCIETY: Without patriotism, loyalty and knowledge of civics and history can children integrate into the American culture? Can our country survive without an understanding the American culture?

With literacy, moral principles and patriotism added to the other four principles, the *Every Child Succeeds Act* can proudly become not just education reform but "quality education". The *Conservative Leaders for Education* can be proudly renamed: *Conservative Leaders for **Quality** Education.*

CHAPTER III

What is Quality Education?

Quality education is imperative for all children regardless of race, gender, religion or political preference. The recent passage of the Every Student Succeeds Act will not significantly reform public education without addressing the hearts and souls of the families and children. While state and local control, parental choice, teacher accountability and transparency, and quality content are highly valued by the classroom teacher, they are not enough. The addition of literacy, moral principles and patriotism assure a quality education and success for every child.

Through research and life experiences, I have determined that the government solutions of money, better-educated teachers and technology are not the key ingredients in a quality education. The key ingredients to quality education are patriotism, literacy, and moral principles. It is my suggestion that money be replaced with manners, technology with literacy, better teachers with patriotism and loyalty. These are the commonalities that will unite all citizens and provide a quality education for all children. These are the qualities that bring back "world class" education to the United States.

Please do not say that quality education cannot occur in the public schools. Quality education IS happening in many public schools across the United States. While parents in large cities and inside "the beltway" feel the need to seek private schools, quality education and well-educated students can be found in many public schools all across the United States. Quality education is happening in public schools where literacy and the desire to learn abound. Quality education is happening where parents, teachers and students share the same moral principles and appreciate the American culture. The answer to quality education is dedicated teachers, devoted parents, determined students and a government that supports literacy, moral principles and patriotism for all.

In conclusion, we might ask: "What is quality education?" Quality education is teacher transparency and accountability. Quality education is quality content. Quality education is local and state guidance. Quality education is allowing families to choose an alternative school when public schools are failing. Quality education requires all students to read and write in the English language. Quality education supports the moral principles and social behavior of a civilized society. Quality education creates an understanding and appreciation of patriotism, the uniqueness of democracy and the American culture. Quality education develops character in all students. Quality education requires quality role models. Quality education requires the support of the government to place confidence in classroom teachers to provide an education that helps children realize "The American Dream". Yes, quality education gives hope to everyone.

It is my hope that every citizen will join me in demanding patriotism, good communication skills, outstanding social behavior, and a strong moral conscience for all children. Their support, determination and ability to be proactive will influence the future of all children and encourage success. When everyone appreciates patriotism, understanding the American culture and practices the requirements for citizenship, the public schools will be united. Then every one will understand that *Quality Education Matters* and American Public Schools Will Be Great Again.

PART TWO

Sitting Behind The Teacher's Desk

Introduction

During the past five decades, education reform has added more money, better technology and has placed more demands on the desk of the classroom teachers. Police are accused of brutality and teachers are accused of prejudice---gender, race, religion, or political. Families are fleeing the public schools for academic and social reasons. Politicians, both liberal and conservative, are becoming frustrated with the lack of student progress and feel they are not getting a "bang for their buck". They question the cost of education, which ranges from just over $6,000 per student per year in Utah to over $19,000 in New York City. They question why test scores in the United States have not risen in the past 50 years. When *Sitting Behind the Teacher's Desk*, the question is: "Could it be that the over reach of the federal government, through polices and social changes, has caused many public schools to fail?"

Sitting Behind The Teacher's Desk addresses the negative influences such as bullying, violence, gangs and substance abuse. Pop culture, violence on TV, violent video games and the continual use of social media has in many situations desensitized the youth. Many students roam the streets disobeying the laws and rely on the social media for communicating and acquiring knowledge. These are a minority of students; but they do exist. They are the students who do not appreciate the opportunity for public education. They are the students who do not respect the American culture. They are the students who often lack a moral conscience and appropriate social skills. They are the students who concern parents and teachers. They are the students who need positive role models.

Without a disciplined learning environment, chaos will exist in the classroom and learning will not take place. When *Sitting Behind the Teacher's Desk*, the question is: "Can public education survive without controlling negative behavior and helping students become law-abiding citizens?"

Perhaps the most fundamental requirement for a positive learning environment and responsible citizenship is literacy. The importance of a common language and the ability of parents, students and teachers to communicate are essential for a quality education. At one time, parents, teachers, and students shared a common language and communicated frequently. They shared a confidential relationship and received support from each other. Today, the advanced data collection and social media have replaced much of the individuality and confidentiality. Teachers may want to be transparent and accountable but often fail because the family does not share a common language or they may be unwilling to communicate. When *Sitting Behind the Teacher's Desk*, the question is: Can public education survive without a common language?

The social issues of literacy, immigration, and poverty are of grave concern for the classroom teacher. Many of these social issues are a result of an indecisive culture, a breakdown of the family unit and political decisions that create a double standard. They often diminish the individuality of the student. Social issues have created a culture of the "haves and the have-nots" and have divided the country. In some cases, the invasion of a "one size fits all" education has hampered the ability for teachers to work efficiently and effectively with individual parents and students. The unwillingness to integrate into the American culture has forced some schools to have a "watered down" curriculum. From *Behind the Teacher's Desk*, the question is: Can the United States survive without a willingness to integrate into the American culture?

With so many social issues affecting the quality of education, we must look at The Constitution, which is based on Judeo/Christian values and The Ten Commandments for guidance. In order to experience liberty and freedom, all citizens must practice responsible citizenship, which includes patriotism, behavior and moral principles and literacy. Defining and demanding virtues and principles will offer consistency to teachers when educating young students, for parents when rearing their children and for all citizens when interacting with others. When the guidelines of The Constitution are obeyed, there will be a united American culture. There will be learning in the schools and peace on the streets. When *Sitting Behind the Teacher's Desk*, the question is: "Can America survive without everyone accepting the responsibilities of citizenship?"

All families, government leaders, teachers and students are called to action to be outstanding role models and work together to erase illiteracy and promote patriotism, good social skills and moral responsibility. Everyone can look into the mirror and see if he/she can be a better role model. When this task is complete, quality education will occur in the public schools. When *Sitting Behind the Teacher's Desk*, the question is: "What kind of role models do we have and what kind of role models do we need?"

Some families, teachers, community leaders, and political figures fail to provide positive role models. Their values do not reflect the behavior of good citizenship. Although there is no such thing as a perfect parent, a perfect teacher, a perfect policeman, or a perfect politicians, students can overcome negative influences when they have quality role models---first in the home, in the schools, in the community and finally in the country. With the co-operation of the community, parents, teachers, and a few well thought-out changes, students will be encouraged to set academic, social and moral goals that are complimentary to the American culture, The Constitution and responsible citizenship. When *Sitting Behind the Teacher's Desk*, the big question is: "What kind of schools do we want and are we willing to work together to achieve quality education?"

Chapter I

A Teacher's Job Is Sometimes Tough

A TEACHER'S JOB IS SOMETIMES TOUGH By Myrna J. Sanner

States legalized marijuana---trying something new.
Drugs damage the brain and diminish the I.Q.
Adults are role models. Children want to know why
People can't find a job because they are "high".
The use and abuse of drugs makes the public school teachers' job
tough.

Children witness shootings, violent games, and much more.
The enforcement of laws, some seem to ignore.
Gangs roam the streets; parents don't seem to care
Their only concern: "I hope that policemen are not there."
Violence makes the public school teachers' job a little tougher.

There are bullies in the streets; they are sent to the schools
They run through the halls and forget all the rules.
Laws fail to punish wrong and ignore what is right
Social skills and moral principles are both out of sight.
Poor behavior makes the public school teachers' job a little tougher.

Poverty, illiteracy and entitlements abound.
Meaningful jobs just cannot be found.
Free lunches, free school supplies, and often much more,
Free health care, free housing are given to the poor.
Poverty makes the public school teachers' job a little tougher.

Illiteracy is common and English not spoken
Many wonder why all the school rules are broken.
Without English in the classroom and the lack of strict rules
Parents vie for a spot in the nearest charter schools.
Illiteracy makes the public school teachers' job a little bit tougher.

Yes, you brought teachers computers so they could all learn
How to document tests and report each little turn.
Smart boards soon followed and you attempted to explain
These boards are smarter than the dear teacher's brain.
Technology makes the public school teachers' job a little tougher.

Children twitter and tweet, play computer games galore
They prefer Facebook and Google to the new Common Core.
Computers and i-phones are both given free
And Teachers will monitor social media and pornographic TV.
Social media makes the public school teachers' job a little bit tougher.

Illegal children arrive and flood through the door
Fall asleep at their desks and gaze at the floor.
They cannot speak English. They don't understand the rule
Of behavior and conduct. They would like to be cool.
Integrating immigrant children makes the public school teachers'
job a little tougher.

You allow politicians to lie and businessmen too,
The American culture is in danger. What can we do?
We don't want double standards; we treat everyone fair
Please tell the Judicial System: "The Constitution is there."
Without understanding the American culture, the public school
teachers' job is tougher.

Yes, you say, "black lives matter". Do brown lives matter too?
Women chastise men and men chastise too.
Governments fail to punish wrong and ignore what is right
Social skills and moral principles are both out of sight.
Negative role models make the public school teacher's job a little
tougher.

We have a Constitution and declare it's for peace
When no one is watching our problems increase.
You've ignored our problems, our constant concern
You replaced them with mandates and government terms.
Cultural differences make the public school teacher's job a little
tougher.

Common Core brought teachers testing and documentation galore
The government keeps asking the teachers to do more.
"One Size Fits All", we know it's not true.
But you keep insisting this is something new.
Government control makes the public school teachers' job a little
tougher.

Sooner or later, the "brightest and best"
Will forget all your mandates and give up the desk.
Because the public school teacher's job is no longer possible.

Please trust us with children for we know what is best
Please support our decisions and allow us to test.
Put technology aside; speak English at home.
When sharing a common language, you are never alone.
A common language makes the public school teacher's job a lot easier.

Dear families remember, we are counting on you
To help your sweet children in all that they do.
We need you as role models for the students we teach
Please, don't tell us again that you cannot be reached.
Supportive parents make the public school teacher's a lot easier.

Teachers love diversity, they educate all
Politeness and kindness will help in the hall
When laws are enforced and moral codes are in place
Teachers don't look at religion, gender or race.
Quality students make the teachers' job a lot easier.

Sport heroes, rock stars, and businessmen, too
Is your behavior worthy for our children to do?
Do you show respect? Do you always speak truth?
Are you the role models we want for our youth?
The role models of quality citizens make a public school teachers'
job a lot easier

So, dear government remember the next time you reform
Teachers who care want children to conform.
Remember the American culture, The Constitution, too.
Stay faithful to these principles. We are counting on you.
And the public school teachers' job will once again be possible.

Chapter II

Negative (Troubling) Influences

Positive principles are America. Negative influences are un-American

The behavior and manners of children often define the life that is lead and the deeds that are done. Poverty, illiteracy, the social media, and a multi-cultural society often influence the behavior of children.

From birth, most responsible families are aware of what is watched on TV and what is read. They provide an atmosphere of learning and caring. They have meaningful conversations with their children. They teach heir children to be responsible for their actions. They teach moral principles and patriotism and help their children differentiate between right and wrong. They keep a watchful eye on the role models in their children's' lives. Responsible families monitor their own behavior and discourage the negative behavior that is found on the streets and in the hearts of some children and adults.

Teachers observe too many youth who are on the wrong side of morality. Children witness violence, bullying, substance abuse, poverty and illiteracy on a regular basis. Young people often mix drugs, alcohol and violence. They often misuse social media and the Internet. When used without discretion and improperly, negative influences may cause children to become insensitive to the welfare and feelings of others. The result may be illegitimate children, gang murders, drug addiction, violence and the lack of respect for others and their values.

Teachers do not define children by race, gender, income, religion or political affiliation. They do, however, define students by their behavior, moral values and willingness to learn. Teachers know that outward behavior reveals the moral principles that are lacking and must be taught. Teachers know that some children rely on the examples of dysfunctional adults for role models. Teachers know that some adolescents feel there is nothing to do and say they are bored and have little desire to learn. Teachers know that students have not yet accepted responsibility for their decisions because they have not developed a moral conscience.

Teachers know that until moral principles are taught and put into practice, children cannot self-monitor. A moral basis will help students differentiate between right and wrong; between what is acceptable in a civilized society and what is unacceptable. It is not excusable to think that "boys will be boys" and "girls will be girls". Middle school is often too late to change the ingrained negative behavior and put them on the right side of morality.

Through rules and laws, the government attempts to provide reasonable guidelines for teacher expectations. However, it does not always have the same expectations for the students. The government is often naïve and out of touch with teachers, who deal with bullying, violence, drug abuse, illiteracy, conflicting cultural values on a daily basis. It often forgets that moral principles dictate values, behavior, manners and patriotism. The government may be able to guarantee the equality of opportunity but only the students can guarantee the quality of behavior, moral principles, patriotism and literacy.

Some political leaders are more interested in political correctness and social justice and often look the other way. They may create a double standard that allows negative behavior. They may not recognize the influence that negative behavior has on the academic learning and safety in the public schools. They may take the attitude that if you don't see anything, don't hear anything then it never happened. Rather than taking on the negative influences, they are often willing to blame the teachers and pull one of the "isms" cards. These leaders want a quick fix by asking for additional money, more technology and better-educated teachers.

Cultures vary and moral codes are not consistent within all cultures. The public schools will be more effective when a universal moral code, that promotes unified behavior, is adopted and accepted by all participants. A common language, patriotism, acceptable social skills and outstanding moral values will unite, rather than divide, the citizens of the United States. When a teacher has a moral code to follow; the position is clear. When moral codes are uniformly reinforced in the community, negative influences can be deterred and possibly eliminated. There should be no such thing as a small misdemeanor. Misdemeanors left without correction often become big crimes and bigger problems. Disruptive infractions result in schools where chaos and disunity abide. Freedom without virtues is chaos.

During the 2008 Presidential campaign it was said that today's young people have lost hope for the future. We heard it again during the 2016 campaigns. The purpose of revealing some of the negative influences in society is not to present an outlook of doom and gloom. It is to instill hope---hope for the vast majority of Americans who embrace and practice the social skills and moral behavior of a civilized society. Hope to raise children out of poverty. Hope to recognize the real problems and work together to eradicate the negative influences. Hope to encourage political leaders to unite all citizens of the United States to work for the common goals of patriotism, literacy, and moral principles.

Let's work together to identify some of the negative influences and remove them from society. Let's get to work in our schools and replace the negative influences with positive principles so all students can learn and become contributing members of society.

MY STORY: Several years ago, I wrote to several political leaders regarding the moral decay in the public schools and the country. I suggested that a return to practicing moral values might enhance the quality of education in the public schools. I received responses from all parties; however, one political leader accused me of being a racist. Unfortunately, politicians often associate the lack of moral values with a particular race, religion or ethnic group. There is nothing racist about wanting to live in a country where law and order prevail. There is nothing wrong with wanting a classroom of well-behaved students. Patriotism, literacy, social behavior and moral principles have never been unique to any civilized culture.

Drug and Substance Abuse

States legalize marijuana---trying something new.
Drugs damage the brain and diminish the I.Q.
Adults are role models. Children want to know why
People can't find a job because they are "high".
The use and abuse of drugs makes the public school teachers' job tough.

Bullying, poverty, illiteracy and gangs are not a life sentence; however, heroin, cocaine and other forms of drug addiction may be. The increase of drug abuse and the prominence of the drug culture are frequently cited as the number one social problem in the United States. There are many social problems and negative behaviors that can also be attributed to substance abuse.

During the baby boomer generation, the most negative substance effecting the development of a healthy mind and body was alcohol. The next generation added illegal drugs to the mix. Today, violent video games, an emphasis on sex, more addictive and potent drugs, and violence have been added.

Harmful Effects of Drug Addiction

In the 1990s William Bennett, Secretary of Education, was very concerned about the effects of drugs on youth. He referred to the use of marijuana as the "gateway drug" to the addictive use of heroin and cocaine. In 1990, Mr. Bennett declared a "war on drugs". During his tenure the usage of drugs in the United States decreased from 23 million to 13 million. The usage of cocaine declined from 6 million to 1.6 million.

Anyone who has ever been addicted to a substance will tell you they started out with small doses of minor drugs. At first, they experimented with only minor drugs such as marijuana. They were "just being kids". They did not realize that marijuana might be a "gateway drug"; which once taken might lead to the use and addiction of more harmful drugs. Others begin using drugs to alleviate pain and some merely enjoyed the "high". Children may have watched their parents use drugs or may have been encouraged to participate by an adult. Some young adults "robbed" the medicine cabinet and became addicted to prescriptive medication. None of these young people certainly ever thought that they would become addicted.

Drugs and alcohol are addictive substances and detrimental to the physical health and emotional stability of young people. Much of the addiction is a result to youth experimentation and role models. Youth, by their very nature, are curious and look up to their peers as role models. When substances are available, teens will be certain to find a way to use them or abuse them. When one young person becomes involved in drugs, peers often follow. With the epidemic use of drugs becoming so widely spread, some public schools have become the equivalent of "drug emporiums".

Drug addiction is no longer a personal problem. Drug addition has become a problem for society. Mind altering drugs are quite prevalent in today's society. It is said that today's drugs are 10% more potent than the drugs in the 1960's. Statistics indicate that one in sixteen marijuana users will become addicted to more powerful drugs. Heroin and other opiate addictions are now claiming more lives that violent crimes and car crashes. In addition, many new synthetic drugs have been introduced into society. They contain substances that can cause instant death. Recently, it was reported that the life expectancy of US citizens is declining because so many young addicts die.

It has been researched and reported that the long-term use of marijuana (smoking pot) affects the brain and cause shrinkage, just as alcohol damages the liver. The O'Reilly Factor on Fox News reported during the week of June 7, 2015, that the excessive use of marijuana will eventually affect the I.Q., memory, and problem solving skills. {News Press, Tuesday November 15, 2016 p 13 A "Big victories for recreational marijuana use, USA Today}

AUTHOR COMMENTS: In July 2014, President Obama made a comment about putting "crack" into a cake at the White House. He has also told stories about his own childhood and how he used drugs and that drugs were no more harmful than alcohol. He may have thought the "cake" comment was cute, however, he could have used his childhood experiences as a teachable moment for young people either using drugs or thinking about using drugs. To teachers and parents who have lost children, the use of illicit drugs is not a laughing matter.

MY STORY: I know of several business owners who own trucking and manufacturing businesses. They pay very well and are constantly looking for responsible young people to hire. In all cases, they cannot find strong young people who are able to pass the drug test. When drugs are involved, people do not have the ability to focus to prevent accidents and are not dependable in attendance. Drug usage is also a reason that many young people are not accepted into the military.

QUESTION FOR SOCIETY: How is the legalization of marijuana affecting our youth? Could it be that: once an alcoholic, always an alcoholic; once a drug addict, always a drug addict?

Youth and Drug Abuse

Innocent babies are born with neonatal abstinence syndrome. Young children go home to families where substances are being abused. Everyday, teachers are called into action to discourage or help eliminate the harmful effects of drug addition. Teenagers know where to get drugs and how to use and abuse drugs. High school, middle school, and even some elementary schools face the use of illicit drugs, alcohol, and other substances on a daily basis. Some very highly qualified and intelligent citizens may be eliminated from the work force because of drug addiction and substance abuse. Some users will become addicted; other victims will die.

Many teachers and community helpers, working with youth, say that the students know when the "big black car" comes into the community, illegal drugs will be available. Young people use social media to set up appointments for obtaining drugs. When they run out of money, they express this and the drug dealers give them a free fix as their last fix. What the dealers know and the users do not know is that there never is a "final fix. The real culprits of drug addition are the drug cartels, "dope pushers" and any one who brings illegal drugs from foreign countries to prey on the young.

Monitoring and discouraging the use of drugs is a social problem that often finds its way onto the teacher's desk. Many feel that if drug use is stopped before children are of legal age, it might be possible that they will not abuse drugs when they become adults. If substance abuse is introduced during the pre-teen and teen years, it is much more likely to lead to addiction in the future. For years, teachers have been assisted by police officers to explain the harmful affects of drug abuse; sometimes with very little success.

Addiction and the use of drugs matter to teachers and educators because it affects brain function and can cause death. Addicted youth often practice erratic and inappropriate behavior. Substance abuse often effects the attitude of students which often results in poor attendance, the inability to concentrate, negative social skills and a depletion of moral values. The abuse of drugs impairs mental capabilities and decisions. Drugs and other substances may cause youth to become violent and join gangs. Once addiction sets in, productivity and moral responsibility decrease.

Instead of seeing the harm that drugs and alcohol present for society, several states, including Washington and Colorado, have made recreational marijuana legal. During the 2016 election other states followed in the footsteps of Washington and Colorado and made recreational marijuana legal.

MY STORY: May I share the story of one outstanding young man? He is very handsome, intelligent and has an outstanding personality. He played on a local high school varsity team and it was there that he was introduced to marijuana. He went on to college and graduated with outstanding grades. As he matured, several unfortunate incidents caused him to return to his previous drug habits. However, this time cocaine and heroine were in the mix. He soon became addicted and lost his job, his reputation, and his self-esteem. Today, he continues to struggle and will for the rest of his life. When anyone says that marijuana is not harmful, I insist that it is a "gateway" drug to more harmful substances. It will also, very possibly, ruin a life.

SOCIETY'S STORY: USA TODAY, Friday, November 18, 2016 1B Josh Hafner, The Surgeon General recently reported that 1 in 7 people in USA will suffer addition. He emphasized the need for compassion rather than incarceration for those who are addicted to drugs. "Every $1 invested in viable treatment for substance use disorder saves $4 in health care costs and $7 in criminal justice costs---it removes the stigma from addiction, creating more patients and fewer prisoners...

(drug addiction) is a chronic disease of the brain that deserves the same compassion that any other chronic illness does, like diabetes or heart disease." "That means parents talking to kids about addiction---early". The Surgeon General recommends that schools implement prevention programs and doctors receive training on how to screen, diagnose and treat substance disorders."

AUTHOR COMMENTS: With the legalization of marijuana, public schools and DARE programs will be given additional responsibility to discourage and control the use of drugs. Parents will constantly be asked to have a "conversation" with their children. Teachers and other community leaders will continue to be asked to help identify the sources of heroin and cocaine. Volunteers will continue to intervene. The responsibility of all citizens is to understand the realities of legalizing drugs. The responsibility of the government is to enforce the laws of legality---both in the selling and usage of all addictive substances.

QUESTIONS FOR SOCIETY: Can it really be that over 1,000 prisoners, who had been incarcerated for drug dealing and trafficking, were recently given pardon and released from prison? If teachers are attempting to develop critical thinking skills in their students, could it be that these skills might be impaired by the use of drugs?

Legalizing Marijuana

Addiction is becoming a multi-state and multi-generational issue. It seems that once the federal government, states, and cities, made marijuana legal, citizens began using more drugs more frequently. When the boarder patrol looks the other way, laws become ineffective. With more addicted residents, communities will need to rely on more medical teams to resuscitate and rehabilitate. When substance abuse is accepted in society, more abuse will soon follow. The message needs to get out that all drugs are addictive and detrimental.

Taking abusive drug habits back to the original source, prescription medial marijuana should be no problem. There are ill people who are in extreme pain and they should be given every medication that can control and eliminate the pain. The majority of substance abuse in the United Sates has nothing to do with illness or pain. When visiting clinics, many adults have reported that the health professionals often give prescriptions for pain medication when it is not needed nor requested. Prescription medication should be monitored and not given out freely.

The illegal side of the story looks very different. Most of the drugs and illegal substances are a result of "recreational use". Illegal drugs are brought into the United States at an unprecedented rate. Most of these drugs enter the United States by members of the drug cartel and drug pushers.

SOCIETY'S STORIES: News Press, Tuesday November 15, 2016 p 13 A "Big victories for recreational marijuana use, USA Today "Last Tuesday, voters in four states---California, Maine, Massachusetts and Nevada… approving ballot measures to legalize the drug (marijuana) for recreational use." "The big question is whether wide acceptance and easy availability will affect highway safety or entice more adolescents to experiment. Years of research show that marijuana affects learning, memory and attention and suggests that developing brains are most vulnerable."

Headlines in USA Today on Sunday August 28, 2016: (Section B, p. 1) "225+ heroin overdoes in 4 states in 1 week" by Terry Demio @tdemio The Cincinnati Enquirer). The article stated that during the past week, there have been two hundred and twenty-five cases of opioid, including heroin, in the states of Ohio, New Jersey, Indiana and Kentucky. Ohio alone had 174. The problem of substance and drug abuse has been a topic of discussion several times on CBS *Sixty Minutes*.

AUTHOR COMMENTS: I recently was engaged in a conversation with an undertaker's wife. She stated that roughly half of all the dead bodies that arrive at the mortuary are victims of drug abuse or overdose.

If someone wants to encourage the usage of drugs and other substances, they might also explain the consequences.

QUESTIONS FOR SOCIETY: Doesn't it seem self-defeating for some states to legalize marijuana, which has proven to be addictive and leads to the use of more harmful drugs like cocaine and heroin? Isn't it ironic that after passing laws to legalize marijuana, the government passes a law that assures that drug addicts will receive free intervention care?

Prevention, Treatment and Other Solutions

Statistics vary but some report that the number of prisoners who are incarcerated because of drug trafficking, drug addiction and drug abuse, may be as high as seventy percent. Many inmates are core addicts. Because of the over crowding of prisons, many communities have eased up on the number of young drug offenders that are placed in prison. President Obama recently released hundreds of inmates who have been imprisoned for trafficking and using drugs. If keeping drug offenders out of prison is the objective, then imprisonment will decrease. If the goal is to have more responsible and employable citizens, then perhaps the enforcement of the laws is more effective.

Mental health incarceration has also been suggested as an answer to address the drug dependency. The cost of mental health care for drug addition is becoming a burden on society. Rehabilitation is an intensive, extensive and expensive process and often does not last permanently. Although rehabilitation is available, it must be monitored and demanded. It is often not effective because heavy drug addiction is almost impossible to cure. Many times victims will die. Prevention is certainly a better alternative than incarceration or rehabilitation.

It seems that legalizing marijuana, inconsistent jail sentences, and the reduced cost have only increased drug usage. Instead of legalizing drugs and reducing prison sentences, the laws that prohibit the use and selling of drugs can be enforced and drug dealers can be prosecuted to the fullest extent of the law.

Whatever the reason, drug addiction is a social problem. Children and law-abiding adults are confused when drug dealers are allowed to come across the borders. Citizens question the release of prisoners who are drug addicts and "drug pushers". First responders and police officers are drained and exhausted because they are often called to revive drug users. Many victims of drug overdose receive shots of Naloxone to bring them back to consciousness and start breathing. The elimination of drug abuse must begin in the home and the community..

Teachers are concerned about the effects that legalizing marijuana will have on the minds of children. Teachers are also concerned about the illegal flow of more potent and harmful drugs into the communities. Their students are confused when drugs are present in their homes but not permitted in the schools. All of the DARE officers in the world will have little success in preventing drug abuse as long drugs flow freely in the community. The best cure for drug addiction is to never allow drug usage and never use drugs.

AUTHOR COMMENTS: Since marijuana has become legal, it has been reported that welfare assistance can now be used to purchase marijuana. Really? It is my perception that taxpayers are now paying for the use of harmful and addictive drugs. Taxpayers are also picking up the tab for mental health and rehabilitation. It seems unfair that citizens, who oppose the legalization of substances and do not participate, be forced to pay for rehabilitation and the purchase of addictive substances. Society can no longer afford to look the other way when the flow of drugs is harming our youngest citizens.

AUTHOR COMMENTS: It has been suggested that citizens on welfare be given a drug test before they are given public assistance. Not a bad idea! If people on welfare have money for marijuana, they are not using their assistance properly. When passed on to children, it is ruining another life. Perhaps another "war on drugs" is needed and William Bennett could be called back into action. Prevention and rehabilitation are great bandages; however, I would vote for abstinence.

SOCIETY'S STORY: Ohio is often plagued with drug trafficking. Three federal highways (Inner-state highways 71,75, and 70) intersect near Columbus, Ohio and allow for the swift movement of illegal drugs. Ohio has reported that one in every five residents knows someone who is fighting drug addiction. The state can no longer afford (neither emotionally or physically or financially) to place all of the drug offenders in prison. As a result, Ohio provides ninety-one Drug Courts in thirty-three counties, which allow drug offenders to be released into society. They must check in periodically and prove that they continue to be drug free. If they are not, they may end up in prisons. (Sunday, April 24, 2016, *Sixty Minutes*, CBS)

BOOK CONNECTION: One of the most compelling books I have read, regarding the harmful effects of drug addition and abuse, is *Breaking Night*, the life story of Liz Murray. Murray tells her story of being the child of addictive parents and how her young life was nearly destroyed. Murray overcame the influence of drug addiction, found refuge in a New York City school, turned her life into that of a responsible citizen and graduated from Harvard University. It was a tough road and not many children raised in these disadvantaged circumstances are fortunate enough to move on to a better life.

Violence and Gangs

Children witness shootings, violent games, and much more.
The enforcement of laws, some seem to ignore.
Gangs roam the streets; parents don't seem to care
Their only concern: "I hope policemen are not there?"
Violence makes the public school teachers' job a little tougher.

Gangs and violent behavior often surround youth who live in areas of crime, poverty, and un-employment. Many members have grown up feeling anger and defy obedience of the laws and rules. They sometimes participate in violent initiation events to show they are "tough enough" to warrant gang membership. Violent gang members not only belittle one another, they physically attack and kill each other to show their power. Gang members often claim race, religion, drugs and retaliation as excuses for their violent behavior.

Gang formation often begins in the streets of major cities. Members display social behavior that is unacceptable. This behavior filters into the halls and classrooms of the public schools. Many gang members are not conscientious students. Their infrequent attendance and inattentive behavior results in the lack of academic achievement.

Teachers become frustrated when learning is diminished and students do not achieve. They are frustrated when students are absent from school. The teachers also find the moral behavior of gang members unacceptable. Sad as it is and in spite of strict school security, violence will continue to creep into the hearts and souls of youth, unless a moral conscience is present.

Causes of violence

"When the bad get rewarded, the bad gets worse." (Netanyahu: when addressing the United Nations Assembly on October 1, 2015.)

Young gang members often display violent behavior because they are not capable of controlling their anger. They want to be "cool". They feel they can self-identify by joining a gang. Many have grown up feeling anger and defy obedience of laws and rules.

The causes for gang violence include:

- Many violent crimes are **drug related**. Although young adults cannot legally use substances before the age of 18, the presence of drugs in the United States is overwhelming the public schools and the law enforcement agencies.

- The **lack of communication** between law enforcement officers, teachers, students and families is also cited as a reason for lawlessness and violence. There is also a lack of communication between community leaders and those who do not speak English.

- The **lack of mutual respect** often creates a conflict between the police and gang members. Both the police and the perpetrators need to "walk in each others shoes".

- Violence is frequently observed when watching **movies.** Movies have very few restrictions regarding language and violent acts. The recent release of a violent movie broke all records during the opening weekend. Many young people were in attendance watching negative role models violently and disrespectfully attacking others and displaying actions of extreme hatred..

- Violent **video games** may desensitize youth. The frequent witnessing and active participation provided when playing video games often make young people unaware of the hurt and harm they may cause others.

- Adolescents often use **social media** to communicate with their friends. Social media has been used to incite rioting and violence. It has been used to communicate with drug traffickers. Social media is often used to say harmful and hurtful things about peers.

- Gang members may use violence to **retaliate** when they feel they have been treated unfairly. In retaliating, "An eye for an eye and a tooth for a tooth." is sometimes quoted.

- **Inaction and looking the other way** may be a reason that violence continues on the streets and in the schools. In order for justice to be served, all crimes must be investigated and prosecuted in a fair and unbiased manner.

- **Race** was mentioned as a reason that the gunman in Charleston, South Carolina killed nine people in a church. Race crimes are often referred to as "hate" crimes. There is no excuse for race crimes. As a united country, we all share the same freedom.

- **Religion** was given as a possible reason for the October 1, 2015, shooting at a community college in Oregon. It was reported that the gunman asked his victims if they were Christian. If they answered in the affirmative, he shot them in the head. If they did not reply or gave a negative reply he shot them in the leg.

There is no room for gangs or violence in a civilized society. Black citizens have suffered enough, black men have suffered enough, and the police have suffered enough. Students and teachers have suffered enough. In fact, everyone who cares about the well being of his fellow men has suffered enough. It is time to stop the blame game and start practicing love. It is time to replace violence and hatred with love and kindness.

AUTHOR COMMENTS: Students must understand the difference between looting and demonstrating. They must understand the difference between demonstrating and violence. They must understand that all people in authority must be respected---especially the police and teachers. It is important that the schools and community share information about the activities of the young people and families so they can better understand and eliminate problems that exist. It is also important to instill social skills and a moral code and conscience in the students so that they know right from wrong.

Violence in the Streets

Chicago is perhaps the city most noted for its street gangs and violence. Weekends and holidays seem especially dangerous for young people living in the major cities and youth are often the victims. During the weekend of April 19, 2014, Chicago reported the murders of 9 people and 45 shootings in the city. Over the three-day weekend during the Fourth of July, 2014, there were 11 people killed and 80 injured within 84 hours in the streets of Chicago. Memorial Day weekend, 2015, twelve people killed and 44 wounded. On July 4, 2015, it was reported on all news channels that in a 14-hour period, there were 21 shootings and 9 young people killed on the streets of Chicago. The youngest victim was a 7 year-old boy, whose father had just gotten out of jail. In 2016, Chicago realized over 762 deaths due to violent crimes.

These statistics are not unusual for Chicago and other major cities. Many of the shootings involved children and young teenagers. Many politicians suggest that the gun controls are not strict enough while others mention out of control "gangs" as the problem. Many say that the majority of the violence is black on black crime and others report that black males committed over 70 percent of all murders. It really does not matter what race or gender is committing violent crimes; every life is precious. What matters is that violence is taking too many young lives. Perhaps it is not guns that kill---it just might be angry people and hearts that are full of hatred, that kill. People who kill are people without a moral conscience.

Unfortunately, when allegations and decisions are made in defense of civilized society, demonstrations are sometimes held. They are often lead by radical leaders who did not get the outcome that they wanted or are unwilling to wait for justice to be served. These demonstrations often lead to rioting and looting, which may end in violent activity. Recently, violence erupted, police cars were demolished and people were injured at a political rally in California. Other examples of extreme rioting, looting and violence occurred in Ferguson, Missouri and Baltimore, Maryland. No one deserves to die a premature or violent death. All lives matter.

Violence is on the streets, in the stores and everywhere. During the holiday season, shoplifting and car jacking often occur. Often innocent people are hurt and even killed. News reported an intimidating and very hurtful game called "The Knock-Out Game". Gangs of violent young people attack some randomly selected innocent victim and knock him/

her to the ground. The gang members might even take a video and post the picture on Facebook.

CHICAGO'S STORY: On January 1, 2017, (USA TODAY, The Ness Press p. 3B) Aamer Madhani, "Chicago ends 2016 with many unsolved slayings". reported that in Chicago during 2016, more than 750 people were victims of homicide. Only about 30% of these murders have been solved.

AUTHOR COMMENTS: After yet another shooting, President Obama proposed that his administration make this a political issue---the necessity of addressing mental illness and the need for more gun control. President Obama has stated that violent shootings are very puzzling to him and he desires gun control legislation. For teachers who are involved in educating children in the public schools, this is not so puzzling---very concerning but not puzzling. Teachers know that guns do not kill---people kill. Teachers know that the moral conscience of students is decaying. Family values have diminished to the extent that students are not sufficiently corrected or reprimanded when they disobey the rules of society. Laws regarding social justice and political correctness often make excuses for negative behavior. When adults draw a clear line between what is right and wrong, gun control and additional regulations will be unnecessary.

Gang Violence and Youth

"Many argued that policies focusing on cold, statistical measures fail to take into account the messy, chaotic reality of teaching in communities where kids must contend with poverty and violence." (Time Magazine, *Rotten Apples*, October 23, 2014, p. 39)

Violence in schools, gang violence and gang membership are unbecoming to any teen-ager male or female---white or black, big or small, excuses or no excuses. Gang violence found in the community, is not unlike some of the behavior that many teachers face everyday. Many public school teachers fear for their students, the families of their students and themselves. Many families flee the public schools because they want to remove their children from a harmful situation. Without law enforcement and the support of the government and the community, there is little teachers can do to control violent behavior. If a safe and civilized environment is desired, people who educate and protect must be obeyed and respected.

Poor social behavior of gang members is often the result of drug abuse and the lack of a moral conscience. Social activists and the press often pass judgment and are eager to blame law enforcement officers or teachers when violence occurs. They rush to judge rather than wait for the whole story and justice. Mutual respect will minimize the existence of violence and gangs and will unite the lawless and the lawful.

Perhaps the most dangerous and violent of all gangs is the recent rise of ISIS. This terrorist organization is a group of bullies that raise their black flag, killing innocent civilians in every community they enter. In Syria, ISIS has crucified children, beheaded journalists, and conducted mass executions. This is not only violent; it is barbarian.

SOCIETY'S STORIES: The invasion of guns and violence in the schools has become far too common in recent years. The use and abuse of guns has affected the schools with mass murders. According to Morning Joe on Friday, October 2, 2015, there have 142 in school shootings since Sandy Hook and 45 to date in 2015. The previous day, 10 people were killed and seven injured at a community college in Oregon. A study out of Boston University found that there were 90,000 cases on in-school violence in the United States in 2014. Many of these required hospitalization.

AUTHOR COMMENTS: On New Years Eve, 2016, every newspaper and TV reported that four young people between the ages of 18 and 24 brutally abused and injured a 18 year old mentally challenged young man in Chicago. These four abusers videotaped their actions. Their behavior was cruel, offensive, abusive and despicable. They will probably be prosecuted; however, no punishment or time in prison will repair the damage that they did to the self-image of this young man. Many people are calling this a "hate" crime. It is sad that gang members are not remorseful but publicize their violent activities to their friends on social media.

It seems evident that many mass murders and violence are "hate" crimes (they certainly were not done out of love). Hate crimes are usually committed when there is a lack of principles and respect for human life. Perhaps many violent crimes are committed because the government, parents and teachers have not reached the hearts and souls of our youngest citizens. The cause may also be the abuse of drugs and other substances. Of course, the blame game, that has been raging for years, continues to go on---is violence the fault of the police, the mayor, the rich, or the poor. The list includes the lack of a family unit, built up resentment against the police and authority, drugs, gangs, etc. Perhaps everyone and all circumstances can be blamed. So may we ask, what each member of society can do to protect our children, our cities, and our country? Our teachers are trying; they need the support of the family and the community.

Violence at the borders

Violence is present daily on our Southwestern boarder where members of the drug cartel and child smugglers come across in alarming numbers. Mass immigration includes young children as well as young men and women. In recent years as many as 300,00 children, victims of organized human trafficking and exploited by their captors, have arrived from Mexico and Central America. Many of these vulnerable young girls are victims of sex trafficking and exploitation. Many of these young people have no documentation or proper papers for entry into the United States.

Another example of violence on the border happened during the first week of August 2014. An off duty border guard was killed in front of his wife and two young children. The two men responsible for this murder had been arrested previously---one two different times and the other four previous times. In both cases, these murderers had been released without a trial or punishment. This violent act could have been prevented if laws had been enforced, respected and obeyed. The law is really quite simple. Permission and documentation are needed before entering the United States.

In many other societies, there seems to be a lack of respect for human life. In Nigeria, young girls have been kidnapped and assumed either killed or sold as sex slaves. In Syria, people are fleeing to bordering countries to avoid persecution. ISIS is recruiting young people to commit acts of violence. Other young people are committed to practice violence in the United States, European countries and throughout the Middle East. Recently, it has been reported that ISIS sends 90,000 e-mails a day, recruiting vulnerable youth throughout the world. Once these young people fall for the propaganda, they are taught how to kill and persecute innocent victims.

AUTHORS COMMENTS: United States and nearly all civilized countries require a passport, permission and documentation before entering or re-entering the country. All law-abiding citizens and visitors respect this law and even appreciate it.

QUESTIONS FOR SOCIETY: Why would any political leader not respect this law and grant amnesty? Can ISIS exploiters actually call themselves civilized?

Stopping violence

- **Police Protection** is one way of ridding society of violence and gangs. One news commentator commented that the streets of Afghanistan are safer than the streets of Chicago. Mayor

Rohm Emmanuel has condemned this violence and has increase police patrols and protection. He has also claimed Chicago as a "sanctuary city". Yet, Chicago is considered the most violent city in the United States and violence continues. Every life matters! Communities just want the violence to stop.

- **"Stop and search"** has been quite affective in preventing street and gang violence in New York City. Fewer crimes were committed. Recently, stop and search has been eliminated and murders and gang violence have become more prevalent once again. When violent crimes become too frequent and are not prosecuted, it encourages more violence. When the press and activists rush to conclusions, without all of the facts, emotions and prejudice spill over into the community and rioting and looting break out in the streets.

- **Incarceration** is used to remove violent behavior from the streets. We cannot afford more prisons physically, academically, monetarily or emotionally. Perhaps federal or state schools might be needed to educate the minds, bodies, hearts and souls of young children until they are ready to assimilate into the American culture.

- A **lack of moral conscience** is also cited as a reason for violence. Blame may be placed on guns, video games and mental health; however, when a moral conscience is not in place, violence is more likely.

- The importance of **family unit** is of utmost importance when monitoring the behavior of young children. If parents do not monitor children's behavior, then teachers, law enforcement officers and government agencies will need to take on the responsibility and ensure the safety of all.

- Positive **role models** are essential when preventing violence. There are laws that provide police protection but few laws that require families to be positive role models for their children.

- Responsible **media and video games** are necessary to eradicate violence in the streets. In Baltimore, social media tipped off students to loot and riot. In Connecticut, loneliness and violent video games, were used by the perpetrator. When it comes to social media and violent video games freedom of speech is often given as a reason for continued use. Changing the heart and soul of violent youth will make the United States a much better and safer place.

AUTHOR COMMENTS: When rioting and looting take place, the perpetrators must suffer the consequences. Weapons and guns should be removed. It might be very beneficial to give each rioter and looter a hammer and nails and be asked to rebuild what has been destroyed. If money is not available to pay for the damage, these youth certainly have time. Young people must be forced to be responsible for their actions, repair the damage, and pay for the harm. It is time that peace and justice prevails in every corner of the United States.

A license might be needed before some one can use mobile devices--somewhat like a drivers license. Perhaps teenagers should undergo proper training before they are allowed to have their own media devices or use their family account for social media. They might need to be limited to a "flip" phone. Regulations regarding the use of certain words could set off an alarm. If there is misuse, the device might be removed and/or the license be revoked.

SOCIETY'S STORY: In Texas, a young man brought a device he had made into his middle school. He was so proud of this timing invention and shared it with his English teacher. Being conscientious, she feared it might possibly be a timing device for a bomb and reported it to the school office. (If you see something, say something.) The school office reported it to the police. The young boy was taken to the police station to determine the safety of the device. Although the student was proud of his accomplishment, he should have asked the teacher for permission before bringing it to school. I am certain that this English teacher would have been far more impressed if he had written an essay or described this object in writing before bringing it to school. English teachers love it when students go above and beyond in writing.

Bullying

There are bullies in the streets; they are sent to the schools
They run through the halls and forget all the rules.
You fail to punish wrong and ignore what is right
Social skills and moral principles are both out of sight.
Poor social behavior makes the public school teachers' job a little
tougher.

THE GOLDEN RULE: "Do unto others as you would have others do unto you".

Bullying is everywhere, Bullying is present on the Internet, in social media, in business, in schools, and in politics. Bullying is not unique to education, religion, race, gender or age. Children witness bullying every day through social media, violent video games and have even watched their adult role models bully. Bullying is a form of extreme manipulation and intimidation. It is often used to meet personal goals by defacing and degrading others and making fun of others.

Some psychologists feel that people who put others down do so to improve their self-mage and justify their behavior. In truth, individuals who bully often lack inner self-discipline and a moral conscience. Compassionate role models of teachers, families and other community leaders often use respectful communication in an attempt to curb bullying behavior. Building a moral conscience in the heart of all children will certainly help prevent all forms of bullying. Any bullying behavior cannot be tolerated in a civilized society and all bullies need to be confronted. When the behavior continues, punishment is warranted.

MY STORY: I recently attended a symposium lead by educators. The topics of discussion centered on the whole child and making certain that children are healthy, safe, engaged, supported and challenged. When discussing the issue of safety, bullying was mentioned. Some members felt bullying can be a result of peer pressure and the lack of discipline.

Some participants said that some children look upon law enforcement officers as an enemy rather than a friend. Some young people also perceive themselves as being victims. Throughout the entire session, social media, violent video games, poor role models, were all mentioned as negative influences in the school culture.

QUESTION FOR SOCIETY: If we cannot eliminate adult bullying, how can we expect children to develop a moral conscience of kindness and respect?

Mental bullying

There are parents who send their children to school and wonder how their child will be treated that day. Will their child be distracted by fellow students who make fun of the way he/she looks, dresses, learns, etc.? Some young people who are mentally challenged have said they have ALWAYS been made fun of because learning is more difficult for them. Bullying can diminish when differences are celebrated.

When bullying is permitted to exist at a young age, it often becomes more evident and severe when these young people reach adulthood. In some cases, children have learned that mental adult bullying is successful and does not have consequences. Children need positive role models to help them cope with the in-justice of bullying. Teachers and other adults attempt to curb this behavior through communication and punishment. With adult support, students should be guided to support those who experience difficulty and share their knowledge in a meaningful way.

MY STORY: Many young boys of elementary age have difficulty with their fine motor skills and learning to read. Writing is very labor intensive and reading vocabulary is often not as advanced as parents and teachers would hope. Many of these students work very hard, put a lot of effort into their work and often do not get the desired results. Many of the mothers of these children have approached me and shared that "my little boy" was being bullied going to and from school and also in the neighborhood. I do not only speak with the bullies; but, when opportunity comes along for a special favor or help, I choose these "bullied boys" to do special favors that will be noticed by their peers. Today, many of these bullied young men have matured, learned to read and write, and attend college with the brightest and best.

On an occasion, when I needed someone to accompany another student to the office for medication, I chose "my bullied boy" to be his partner. They could leave the classroom together when necessary. The outside bullying lessened; but more importantly, "the bullied boy" gained self-esteem and reassurance that someone valued his gentleness and kindness. I am not certain if I made the difference but at least, I tried. Hopefully, the ability to be a good role model for these students paid off.

Physical Bullying

Physical bullying has been present in communities for years and is all too prevalent in the public schools. Physical bullying often begins at a very young age and may have been witnessed in the home, in social media or in the community. Some children think their bullying actions will go unnoticed.

When responsible parents realize that their child is the bully, they should take time to teach compassion for the rights and feelings of others. If all children were taught and encouraged to follow the Golden Rule "Do unto others as you would have others do unto you", it is possible that physical bullying would be greatly diminished.

When families fail to stop the bullying, parents often confide and solicit the help of teachers. Teachers and community law enforcement officers must stand up to these bullies. Bullies must be taught to tell the truth, to respect others, to be kind and other positive moral principles. When bullying is allowed to go unnoticed, young people may resort to joining gangs and using drugs. Bullies must be reprimanded and should suffer the consequences.

Confidentiality is often necessary because the child and family might experience repercussions in the neighborhood. Some parents have addressed the problem of bullying by removing their children from public schools and sending them to private schools, charter schools or home schooling them.

Cyber bullying

Cyber bullying has recently received much national attention because of the excessive use of social media. It was recently stated on TV that as many as 160,000 students miss school everyday because of cyber bullying. All too frequently, we hear of a young teen-ager who has committed suicide because of some posting on the Internet or Facebook.

There seems to be a "false courage" that comes with cyber bullying. Many people who use cyber bullying feel they can operate behind closed doors and do not need to be accountable for their actions. Sometimes the message has been fabricated to harm someone they dislike or someone who sparks jealousy in the heart. Cyber bullies lack personal responsibility and accountability.

Young people should remember that whatever is posted on-line is public knowledge and can be traced back to the perpetrator and consequences may result. Monitoring and the removal of personal media devices might eliminate some cyber bullying.

SOCIETY'S STORY: On Monday, March 3, 2015. Kurt Shilling, famous baseball player, addressed the cyber bulling of his 17-year-old daughter. The comments posted about his daughter were words Shilling had never used and he was outraged that his daughter was degraded in such a manner. Within an hour he was able to identify all of the authors of these bullying e-mails. Hooray, for Kurt Schilling who has the name and resources to challenge the predators of his daughter! Schilling talked about his daughter's plight on "Meet the Press" (NBC), Sunday, March 8, 2015.

Political bullying

Political bullying often happens when two sides of the congressional aisle cannot reach a reasonable decision. Within the United States Congress, compromise seems to no longer be present and both sides are to blame. Sometimes when politicians cannot get the necessary votes, they use bullying and lobbying techniques. Recently both sides of the aisle seem to prefer "my way or the highway". When compromise cannot be reached, no laws are passed and nothing is accomplished. Everyone becomes frustrated and chaos results.

Journalists often enable political bullying when they do not present both sides of a story, when they slant the information so that people cannot make an intelligent decision between fact and fiction.

During the 2016 elections, we heard politicians calling other politicians by offensive names. Attacking political policies is one thing but personally attacking others shows disrespect. This is a bullying technique and sets a very poor example for our children.

SOCIETY'S STORY: The passage of Obama Care with no Republican votes on Christmas Eve might be regarded as political bullying---especially when the Obama administration knew that some of the information was deceptive. The recent power of the 'paper and pen' that President Obama used to implement amnesty is a form of political bullying. Political issues are often defended in the name of political correctness and social justice. It is important to remind all politicians that "truth and honesty should always rule".

Poverty

Illiteracy, entitlements, and poverty abound.
Meaningful jobs just cannot be found.
Free lunches, free school supplies, and often much more,
Free health care, free housing are given to the poor.
Poverty makes the public school teachers' job a little tougher.

Revisiting the War on Poverty

The "War on Poverty" has been raging for over fifty years. Initiated by President Lyndon Johnson on January 9, 1964, it has cost the United States government over eleven trillion dollars in the past fifty years. The purpose was to eradicate poverty and help the poor escape their poor neighborhoods and communities. However, many of the same families continue to experience poverty. Depending on the statistics, an estimated forty-five million people in the United States are considered living in poverty. (Trivia question) This number is the same since the 'War on Poverty" began over fifty years ago.

SOCIETY'S STORY: An article in USA Today highlighted the 50th anniversary of the "War on Poverty". It featured President Johnson's visit to eastern Kentucky fifty years ago to witness the economic pain of this region. Fifty years later, jobs are still scarce and many people still struggle. The unemployment rate in Martin County, Kentucky is close to 11 percent and the school district is still the county's largest employer.

The coal boom that brought many families out of poverty, no longer exists. After President Johnson, left, welfare checks came. People had very few options of making a living. People stopped raising chickens and hogs and relied on their monthly government checks. Poor people began using and selling drugs.

Today, many people in the community still live in the same housing they lived in many years ago. They use food stamps to buy soda; they sell the soda for cash and use the cash to purchase drugs. Today, "the War on Poverty" enables young people to live a lifestyle of dependency--dependency on food stamps, disability checks and prescription drugs.

It has been reported that there are at least ninety-two federal programs that have been designed to help eradicate poverty. In 2012, these programs cost taxpayers some $799 billion. With all of this assistance, it is said that the poverty rate is the highest it has been in twenty-one years. Without adjustments to the federal programs, it seems that young people will continue to come to school without hope of escaping poverty.

BOOK CONNECTION: All too often poverty is considered a problem for only minorities. There are also many non-minority citizens dealing with poverty in Appalachia. *Hillbilly Elegy* by J. D. Vance is a story of a young boy who overcame poverty and a dysfunctional family and went on to become a successful lawyer. This book is well worth reading when having the desire to gain understanding of the adversities that many young children living in poverty face. It also given insight into some of the social programs that are well intended.

AUTHOR COMMENTS: By removing jobs and providing an entitlement of food stamps and medical care, the government has created a population of entitlement. The self-esteem and dignity of hard work have been stripped away. The lack of opportunity for employment, has allowed too many people to have too much idle time on their hands. They resort to the use of drugs and dependency on the government. Many of these people would welcome the opportunity to return to the mines, the railroads and the sawmills without government intervention.

It seems that perhaps the only group of people that have benefited from the "War on Poverty" are the bureaucrats in Washington DC who now have desk jobs to pad their personal wallets. Many government employees are well paid to oversee the very poverty projects that are holding people hostage. When the government becomes involved, there seems to be a pattern of spending billions of dollars that never reach the people in need.

QUESTION FOR SOCIETY: Is giving welfare assistance the only answer to winning the war on poverty?

Poverty and education

Chinese Proverb: "It is better to teach a man to fish, than to give him fish."

Over eleven billion dollars are spent by the Federal Department of Education each year on literacy and education. In addition the federal government has spent trillions of dollars to eradicate poverty. Yet, there is still an over whelming amount of illiteracy and poverty in the United States. Could the use of government funds be monitored in the United States?

Some children who live in poverty will present a challenge for the public school classroom teacher. In the United States, every child under the age of 18 is welcomed to attend the nearest public school. Some may come from caring homes where poverty exists and they have lost hope for the future. They may have been evicted from their home. Their parent's may be incarcerated. They may come from a foreign country and have little or no knowledge of the English language or the American culture. They may be physically, emotionally or academically challenged. They may come from a community where social skills are not "cool". They may come from a home where there is no moral code. They may have left their previous school without any forwarding information. Poverty affects the education of students in many ways.

- The **instability of housing** sometimes presents a learning problem for the students and a teaching problem for teachers. In some schools only twenty-five percent of the students who begin the school year will continue for the entire year. This means that seventy-five percent of the students will move form that school community. Often families physically move when their lease expires or they are evicted from their home. In other cases, students might move to live with a relative in another community. They often do not withdraw from the school or let the school know where they are moving. This disrupts the continuity of their education and can result in school failure. In addition, the new student again needs to make new friends.

- Poverty is often directly related to **illiteracy** and literacy is often referred to as the key to erasing poverty. Just as the debate of "which came first, the chicken or the egg?" has been ongoing, it seems that this approach also relates to education. "Which comes first; poverty or illiteracy?" It really does not matter. When children are raised in an environment of illiteracy and poverty, they often have missed out on the readiness skills. They often come home to a family that does not speak and understand English. Thus, reading and writing become more difficult for them. They soon fall behind and give up. They are often passed from grade to grade and may even graduate from high school without the ability to communicate and are considered illiterate. They are then overlooked for employment opportunities. It takes work, co-operation, and high moral principles to erase illiteracy. When students become literate, they have the potential of rising out of poverty.

- The **English language** is fundamental to education. All other learning becomes very difficult without the ability to speak and understand English. Learning the English language is best achieved in early childhood. Head Start and the Elementary and Secondary Education Act are two of the programs than have been on going for the past fifty years. Yet, it has been reported that four out of five students living in poverty read below grade level. Some of the illiterate adults of today were the pre-school and elementary students of fifty years ago. Many have not found an escape route out of poverty.

- **Education** is most often cited as a method of eradicating poverty. One of the best ways to escape poverty begins in the classroom. Education provides the opportunity for upward mobility and employment opportunities. Economic mobility allows young people to live the American dream. Many young people living in poverty lack motivation or interest in learning. High quality education encourages young people to set personal goals and helps these young people achieve these goals. High quality education cannot be achieved without students committed to learning. The graduation rate in some high schools is less than 50 percent.
- Poverty may also be a result of the **deterioration of the family unit**. Many young children come from dysfunctional families. They may be involved in gangs and abuse drugs and other substances. They have not been able to reject the negative influences in their life. They may not have the privilege of positive role models.

In addition to the academic program, many full service public schools provide many additional programs to help eradicate poverty. Social workers, physicians, dentists, vision and hearing specialists, mental health and family counselors are some of the services provided. Some schools even provide childcare centers and resource centers to assist families in meeting every basic need. The ultimate goal of full service schools is offering assistance to families so they can become independent of welfare assistance and accept individual responsibility. (Parrett and Budge, p. 125-127)

Poverty seems to be perpetuated by many social issues. By eliminating gangs, illegal drugs, violence, and other negative influences, young people will be stable enough to stay in school, learn in school and ultimately get jobs and escape the plight of poverty. Encouraging literacy, and even demanding literacy before citizenship, would certainly be the beginning of helping young citizens find meaningful jobs and move up the economic ladder.

AUTHOR COMMENTS: Since poverty still exists, it seems that so many social issue have not been resolved. It has been reported that ninety percent of the people in poverty are illiterate and ninety percent of the illiterate public is in poverty. Since there is little chance for upward mobility when illiteracy and poverty are present, it might be time to examine all government programs to determine why significant progress has not been made. It seems that education, as we know it today, is failing to give our kids an escape route out of poverty.

SOCIETY'S STORY: Some people have suggested that children living in poverty are not given a fair chance at a quality education because they are placed in mediocre schools. I question that we have mediocre schools. We may have mediocre families, teachers, and students and these can produce mediocre schools. More often a mediocre curriculum is needed for families and students who are not ready to accept a quality education. The inability to speak English and lack social skills and moral values can cause mediocrity. The integration of children who do not understand English may also cause mediocrity.

OUR STORY: I was raised in a rural community in northwest Ohio and my husband was raised on a farm in central Illinois. We were both taught the difference between right and wrong and encouraged to attend school every day. We both had goals and our families also had goals for us. None of our parents attended college. Both of our mothers were high school graduates but our fathers had left school after the eighth or ninth grades and began to work on their respective home farms. Both sets of parents shared the goals of attending college with us and sacrificed many of their personal wants to help us achieve our goals. I wanted to be a teacher and my husband knew he was good in science and math. He applied to the University of Illinois, was admitted to their engineering school and received a scholarship. I chose elementary education as my major and proved my ability to teach by completing my student teaching with a top grade. We both worked hard while in undergraduate school. Neither of us had a problem getting a job. We both went on to get our Masters Degrees. We chose the "high road" and it has made a great deal of difference in our lives. Our advice to our children and to all young people is--- set your goals; rise above any adversity and work hard with good behavior, moral principles and communication skills---and don't forget how privileged you are to be an American.

ADVICE FROM CAL THOMAS: "Stay in school, don't have babies out of wedlock, get married and stay married, be a father to your children, adopt a religious life and don't take drugs. Those are on-ramps to the road to achievement." (The News-Press, Saturday, March 14, 2015. "Selma march important, but what about real issues?" by Cal Thomas.) I would add: be patriotic, learn to speak English, polish-up your social skills and prove to the world that you have a moral conscience. Those are on-ramps to the road of achievement.

BOOK CONNECTION: Rising above poverty requires determination and hard work. There are many stories out of the 60s where young people in poverty have risen to success. One might be Jon Huntsman who wrote *"Barefoot to Billionaire"*. In fact many people can write their own stories to success. Many of these people are not billionaires but are people who have worked hard and achieved their goals. They are the ancestors who have spent years of hard labor to achieve the family goals.

QUESTION FOR SOCIETY: Will our future generation ever be employable without social skills and literacy?

Poverty and Unemployment

Parrett and Budge found that poverty often stands in the way of language development. "Poverty effects health and well being, language and literacy development, material resources and mobility". (Parrett and Budge p. 119).

Although statistics show that the economy is improving, it is not a good economy for the middle class and the unemployed. Many large corporations have moved their headquarters to foreign countries where taxes are lower and people work for lower wages. Every time a robot is installed in a factory humans are replaced. Every time a human call center is moved to a foreign country, jobs are taken from our economy. When an illegal immigrant is hired to do a job for less pay and without paying taxes, a job is taken from a citizen and money from the government. If jobs are continually given to immigrants, robots and technology, poverty will not be eradicated. If jobs continue to be sent abroad, poverty will not be eradicated. Without a job, many families will continue to live in poverty.

The lack of a quality education is one reason for unemployment. Businesses that are people oriented, find that illiteracy, the lack of proper grammar or writing skills prevent them from hiring prospective employees. Many citizens have experienced the inability of a cashier to make change. A college professor recently stated that she continues to teach grammar and writing skills to her senior students. Employers in the trucking industry have difficulty-finding drivers who are "drug free". If the jobs offered require academic and social skills that are not present, a good look in the mirror might be very revealing.

It is unfortunate that some well-educated adults feel that they are entitled to a "free ride" up the economic ladder without proving themselves to be responsible and knowledgeable. Many college graduates feel they are over qualified and have unrealistic expectations of their worth. These unemployed may lack loyalty and integrity and may have been dismissed from a previous job. They may not realize that employment is not always about minimum wage or a college education; it is about literacy, a strong work ethic, high moral principles and providing knowledge or a service that is of value. No employer wants an employee who does not show up for work, lacks a moral conscience or who is dependent on drugs and other substances.

Literacy is a requirement for citizenship and citizenship or a green card should be a requirement for having a job. All jobs are important.

There should never be jobs that "nobody wants". When literacy, moral values and behavior skills are in place, there should be no one who is unemployable. Some say that they need luck in finding jobs. Luck may come to visit but it doesn't come to stay unless the employee is literate and possess the necessary social skills.

AUTHOR COMMENTS: So it seems, we can't alleviate poverty without a job. You can't get a job if you are unwilling to accept a job that does not meet perfect expectations. You can't get a job if you are addicted to drugs or are in and out of prison. And you certainly cannot get a job if you drop out of school or graduate without the ability to read, write and do math. It is up to the unemployed to determine if adjustments in attitude and expectations need to be made. It is common sense that anyone who is unemployable, will remain in poverty.

QUESTIONS FOR SOCIETY: Our country must also look within. Are the schools producing students who have a strong work ethic, high moral principles, are literate and loyal to our country?

BOOK CONNECTION: Amanda Ripley reported in "The Smartest Kids in the World" p. 5, she was puzzled when speaking with the CEO of a company that makes McDonald's apple pies (the CEO) was having trouble "finding enough Americans to handle modern factory jobs---during a recession. The days of rolling dough and packing pies in boxes were over. She needed people who could read, solve problems, and communicate what had happened on their shift, and there weren't enough of them coming out of Oklahoma's high schools and community colleges. Note: this CEO was looking for people who could read, solve problems and communicate. Is this not the very skills that teachers are teaching everyday in the schools?

Poverty and Available Jobs

Maya Angelou: "I've learned that making a living is not the same as "making a life".

It is interesting that when youth reach the age of eighteen, they are old enough to vote, drink alcohol, get married, and even collect public assistance; but they cannot find a job to support their future goals. The lack of education, imprisonment, abuse of substances, lack of moral conscience and rude and inappropriate behavior have all been mentioned as reasons for being unemployable.

Many of the unemployed have failed to acquire basic reading and math skills in the public schools. Without these basic academic skills, low skill and low paying jobs will be their only choice. The lack of being able to find employment might also depend on poor choices such as substance abuse, a poor attitude, lack of a moral conscience, a lack of social skills, and a lack of ambition.

Many people living in poverty depend on entitlements for their very existence. Some families have depended on entitlements for several generations. Welfare was never intended to go on forever nor was it intended to raise someone out of poverty. It was created as a safety net for those who are unable to find work. Common sense tells us that to fight poverty, you must empower and not enable or entitle.

Granted, everyone would like to make more money and become rich. However, this often requires proving oneself and starting at the bottom and working up the economic ladder. When young people continue to feel that they are above manual labor and have negative attitudes, the government will continue to issue work visas for manual labor and for the "jobs that nobody wants".

The good news is that jobs are available and poverty is not a life sentence. A recent report stated that there are 4.7 million jobs that have not been filled. In order to rise out of poverty, a steady and adequate income is necessary.

Manual labor jobs are often referred to as the "jobs nobody wants". These jobs require strong and able-bodied employees and often go to the immigrants who have work visas and a strong work ethic. These jobs provide a livable income and many offer an opportunity for upward mobility once the work requirements are met. A choice between minimum wage and staying unemployed may need to be made. When a worker proves his ability to do the job, pay raises and an opportunity to 'move up the ladder' will be available.

Unskilled or low skill jobs do not require a college or technical education. Unskilled jobs do require social skills and a strong work ethic. The ability to understand and communicate in English, possess good social skills and moral values are necessary requirements that promote a productive and positive working environment. A thirst for knowledge, willingness to learn and integrity to do what is right are qualities that will enhance the possibilities of a raise in pay and chance of being promoted. For those who truly wish to change their destiny, there are high schools in every community that offer a GED. Further education can be received at a college or technical school.

Some available jobs are in the area of **skilled labor**. These jobs often pay more and are more desirable. They often require retraining or additional education. When skilled labor is required, many employers prefer to train their own workers and educate them in the skills they will need. These jobs also require a strong work ethic, the ability to communicate in English, an outstanding moral conscience and behavior skills. There are also technical schools in nearly every community where skills can be learned.

College graduates, who cannot find employment, might consider the options of joining the Peace Corp, the military or offer their services to those less fortunate. These services provide a livable income and may offer training for future private sector employment. There is also the philosophy that perhaps a year or two after leaving high school, every student gives back at least twelve months of community service to his country. This could be helping others, building roads, etc. Minimum wage would be offered and the opportunity for advancement would be available.

Several decades ago, any able-bodied person who received food stamps and welfare assistance was required to report for some community service. These projects improve the living conditions throughout the country and help eradicate poverty. Community service also improves the self-esteem and prepares for participation in the workforce. When people are employed, they are busy during the day and tired in the evenings. When people are adequately rewarded for hard work, they no longer need entitlement programs that keep them locked into poverty.

SOCIETY'S STORY: During the recent recession, Toledo, Ohio has suffered with a high unemployment rate. Many people need jobs and stability. They need quality education---not entitlements. People must be empowered to move out of poverty and attain a quality education. "Too many anti-poverty programs simply build upon themselves, perpetuating both the culture of poverty and the poverty bureaucracy---the so called "poverty pumps" who come to do good and stayed to do well. Under the ultimate version of this patrimonial approach to fighting poverty, every poor family would get a case worker, a life coach, a course in living skills, a rebuilt home, and a rent subsidy. But not a job! To escape poverty, a person needs a job." (Toledo Blade, Sunday, August 31, 2014, p. B1 Commentary by Keith C. Burris.)

QUESTION FOR SOCIET: There are many children in poverty who are considered illiterate, will education be the answer or must these people also be taught to value education and the ability to read and write?

Help Is On Its Way…AGAIN!

Paul Ryan has a proposal for escaping the cycle of poverty. "Rather than running around to a series of different offices to qualify for and collect benefits, individuals will get a dedicated case manager or counselor who will help them put together a plan for getting back on their feet with measurable goals, including ultimately graduating from the program into self-sufficiency. Every recipient, except the disabled and the elderly, must be employed or looking for work. The counselor will help the clients budget their money and find a job. In order to provide a measure of responsibility and accountability, the client must show up for class and continually look for a job. If the client fails in this responsibility, the counselor will be allowed to dock their assistance---just like a boss would in the workplace. Similarly, if the client exceeds expectations, the case manager may also have the ability to provide achievement bonuses." (Paul Ryan, *The Way Forward*, p. 237)

Bill Gates appeared on MSNBC "Morning Joe" the morning of Jan. 21, 2014. The topic of discussion was the myths about poverty in underdeveloped countries. One of the myths is that poor countries stay poor. Many of the developing countries that have received financial aid are no longer poor. Well-monitored social programs reveal that almost ninety-nine percent of the money spent on foreign aid goes directly to the community. In order to accomplish this, he stated that the system must be monitored so that fraud does not take place. This ensures that the assistance is given to the places of most need.

The Koch brothers recently formed a group, *Stand Together*. This group is asking for donations to help eradicate poverty.

Illiteracy and English Proficiency

Illiteracy is common and English not spoken
Many wonder why all school rules are broken.
Without English in the classroom and the lack of strict rules
Parents vie for a spot in the nearest charter schools.
Illiteracy makes the public school teachers' job a little bit tougher.

NO WORDS ARE STRONG ENOUGH TO EXPRESS THE IMPORTANCE OF LANGUGE PROFICIENCY FOR EVERY

ADULT AND CHILD LIVING IN THE UNITED STATES. BY OFFERING FREE EDUCATION TO ALL, THE UNITED STATES GOVERNMENT EMPHISIZES AGAIN AND AGAIN THAT ENGLISH IS OUR NATIONAL LANGUGE AND THE ABILITY TO SPEAK AND READ ENGLISH IS A REQUIREMENT FOR CITIZENSHIP.

Dennis Prager, American conservative, national syndicated radio talk show host, columnist, author and public speaker, addressed the importance of learning English: "I am uninterested in whether English is your native language. My only interest in terms of language is that you leave this school speaking and writing English as fluently as possible. The English language has united America's citizens for over 200 years, and it will unite us at this school. It is one of the indispensable reasons this country of immigrants has always come to be one country. And if you leave this school without excellent English language skills, I would be remiss in my duty to ensure that you will be prepared to successfully compete in the American job market...but if you want classes taught in your native language rather than English, this is not your school."

Research on literacy paints a very dim picture for illiterate citizens of the United States. The web site www.statistic brain.com referred to a study that was done by the National Institute of Literacy, which is a division of the U.S. Department of Education. The study was completed on April 28th, 2013. This study reported that fourteen percent or approximately thirty-two million adults in the United States are illiterate. Twenty one percent of all adults read below the 5th grade reading level. Prison inmates had an illiteracy rate of sixty-three percent and nineteen percent of all high school graduates cannot read.

Reynolds writes about the importance of liberal art skills. "Though discussions of rigor often seem to devolve into commercials for science and engineering majors, there's plenty of room for rigor in liberal arts, I think the reasons people often hold out engineering, etc., as examples of rigor is that the liberal arts, in general, have lost much more of their former rigor. But traditional liberal arts skills---reading closely, analyzing, writing clearly---are not at all obsolete. They're just harder to find nowadays. I have a friend whose company hired two recent college grads, with degrees in marketing and journalism, basically to write product descriptions for catalogs, Amazon, and the like. She found that she had to go over their work repeatedly because even though they were recent college grads, they were incapable of writing clearly and within length limits. As I say, room for improvement." (Reynolds, (p. 42)

The ability to read has played a primary role in the success of nearly every person. Ben Carson's mother noted that the difference between her self and the families for whom she worked was that her employers read and studied constantly. This is what she wished for and demanded of her children. Not everyone is as fortunate as Dr. Carson.

It is extremely easy to integrate into the American culture without being literate in the English language. Products are labeled in multiple languages. TV channels are available in foreign languages. Many different languages are spoken in the streets and in the homes. Interpreters are available for those who need assistance when attending school and when visiting a health care facility. Language options are available when calling credit card companies and many businesses. In some states, even voting ballots are issued in a variety of languages. It has been reported that Obama Care is available on the Internet in over 120 different languages. All of these practices diminish the incentive to learn English. Too many languages may even confuse some immigrants.

MY STORY: In speaking with businessmen who work in the human resource area, the ability to read, write and communicate in English are primary requirements for employment. Good communication skills are necessary for almost every job. Dress, attitude, integrity, and a strong work ethic are also important. All too often the best jobs are not filled because of the lack of good candidates. As for computer training, each job is unique and those skills can be learned on the job if good reading and writing skills are already in place.

SOCIETY'S STORY: The United States government is suing Wisconsin Plastics, because they require all employees to speak English while on the job. This also applies to all foreign employees regardless of nationality. (Fox News, Wednesday, July 2, 2014) The federal government should certainly understand the importance of being able to communicate in English. It seems logical that if these employees have jobs legally (either a green card or United States citizenship) they have taken the citizenship exam or proven their knowledge of English. If they are citizens and cannot speak English, they are shirking their duties as United States citizens. Therefore, why not require English spoken on every job in the United States?

Excuses for illiteracy

People often make excuses for illiteracy or the lack of English proficiency. **Schools and teachers** are frequently blamed. In truth, the inability to speak English might be due to poverty, cultural differences, individual maturity, personal motivation, the lack of self-discipline and the lack of family support. Without the ability to speak English, it is very difficult to rise out of poverty or assimilate into the American culture.

Poverty and cultural differences seem to be the primary causes for illiteracy or the lack of English proficiency. Students living in poverty or immigrating generally have problems learning the English language and are often delayed in developing language skills. These children often lack an English rich environment, or return to homes where English is not spoken. Some immigrants have been granted citizenship without meeting the language requirement for citizenship. Others are indifferent to learning the English language. The indifference to learning English can result in the lack of understanding and obeying the laws. Unfortunately, too many people living in the United States are not fluent in English.

Individual maturation also plays a key role in the ability to read and write. Boys may mature later than girls and may not have the same aptitude for the language arts. Some students are visual learners and others are auditory learners. Some possess readiness skills at a young age and others need longer for readiness maturity. Some students come from homes where they have been exposed to literature since birth while others may have been allowed to exclusively access video games and TV programs. Teachers understand the individual differences of all students and continue to encourage all children to read and write. The lack of phonics, poor teacher education, lack of reading instruction in the upper grades, lack of boy books, and pushing literacy on boys too soon are also reasons for the literacy gap. (Whitmire, *Why Boys Fail* p. 59)

Many students lack **personal motivation and self-discipline** when learning to read. They do not understand that all other academic material rests on the ability to read English. Sometimes students look for instant gratification and are not willing to put great effort into learning to read. Learning, for many children, is hard work. For some students, it takes many years to progress from being an emergent reader to a fluent reader. It is hoped that upon completion of the fifth grade, all students (notice students, not children) will be ready to read almost all reading material with understanding and have success in middle school.

The time that is required to become a fluent reader often depends on the involvement and **determination of the family**. Families who do not read or understand English must rely upon the teachers and intervention specialists to give special help. Learning to read is a three way process---there must to be a teacher, a learner and a supportive family. If any of these is missing, failure may result. It is by learning English that citizens can intelligently participate in the election process, read and understand the laws, and communicate with doctors, teachers and other professionals.

Every quality teacher believes that nearly every student can learn the English language with the **support of the home and community**. The child's ability to become a successful student often depends on the extent to which English is reinforced in the home. When young children do not have the literary support of the family, there is often a gap between early childhood education and ongoing learning. If children enter kindergarten without readiness skills, they are not school ready and they may never catch up. Unfortunately, they will probably always lag behind which will be discouraging and will possibly prevent them from being college or job ready.

The **online world** has not lessened the demand for literacy skills according to Whitmire. "The online world inhabited by our children does little to lessen the demand for literacy skills while doing much to diminish those skills. The abilities to read challenging texts quickly and write incisive papers based on reading are the essence of college. And that makes writing a roadblock to either getting into college of graduating with a degree." (Whitmire, p. 76))

A united effort must be made to eliminate illiteracy. With international test scores diminishing, too many illiterate citizens, unemployment increasing because of unqualified applicants, the United States can no longer afford to pamper anyone or discourage anyone from using English and proper grammar in their homes and in everyday life. Language helps us understand the values and feelings of others. It promotes empathy and understanding. And most importantly, English is the official language of the United States. Language is a factor that will unite a country and its citizens.

Whatever the excuse for not being proficient in the English language, the ability to speak fluent English will enhance responsible citizenship and contribute to the quality of life. When society makes excuses, they are not doing the illiterate any favors. Literacy is perhaps the most important skill that any one can achieve because reading; writing and understanding weave their way into everyday lives---every student, employee, employer, and citizen.

MY STORY: Although we lived in Japan for three years and I never became fluent in Japanese. Feeling like an outsider in foreign city or country is not easy. Without knowledge of the language, ones self-esteem and self-confidence soon deteriorate. In Japan, I was considered illiterate. During the 1980's, English was considered the universal language. The Japanese people were very engaged in speaking and learning English; hence I was able to communicate in most situations---especially in Tokyo. During this same time, we visited China where every hotel, restaurant, and point of interest had an English speaking TV. When visiting and living in foreign countries, I realized that anyone not proficient in the language of that country are illiterate. I also realized that perhaps three years is not sufficient time to become fluent in any language unless outstanding effort is made.

Learning to Read

The language arts program in public schools has been evolving for many years. In the 1970's whole language became the password in the elementary classroom. Reading was taught as a part of social studies, science and other academics. In the 1980s, phonics was considered obsolete. In the 1990s, cursive writing was no longer in vogue. Spelling went out the classroom door somewhere around the turn of the century. Spelling has been replaced with "spell check" and teaching children to read often begins on the "smart board". In some schools, technology has replaced the innovative teacher.

Speaking English to newborns on a regular basis can be the beginning of literacy. Listening to others speak encourages children to speak and read. Hearing a language over a period of time increases the vocabulary and prepares young children for the reading readiness activities that are taught in preschool and kindergarten. Putting the building blocks of literacy in place is fundamental to all areas of learning.

During the past fifty years, the federal government has made many mandates and has directly or indirectly influenced programs and policies. The government, realizing that illiteracy may be the major stumbling block for success, has implemented pre-school Head Start education for three and four year olds. The children who qualify generally come from homes that do not provide an English rich environment. By laying a firm readiness foundation for future learning, teachers equip students with the necessary literacy skills to become well-educated and successful adults.

Learning to read often requires the use of many different strategies. Children learn in a variety of ways; therefore, it is necessary to approach learning to read with a variety of strategies. Teachers understand that different strategies work for different students. Teachers may use a combination of strategies and present these strategies as young students pass through the elementary grades. The goal is for a child to permanently retain skills necessary for fluent reading.

Success in reading often rests on individual evaluation and instruction. The teacher understands the individual differences of the students and sets realistic goals for each student. This is precisely the reason that small class sizes are preferred in the elementary schools. It is the reason that local governments are requesting funding for pre-school education. It is also the reason that universities teach student teachers how to evaluate and instruct with an eye on the individual student. There is not just one-way, or any perfect way to become literate: however, there is a way. Individual instruction and evaluation dispels the philosophy that "one size fits all".

Struggling readers are sometimes confused with illiterate students. Struggling readers have had all of the necessary readiness education, can speak intelligently; but read with difficulty. For these students, additional reading instruction will be needed. Repetition may be necessary. With literacy skills in place and focused learning most middle school students should be ready for high school. Hence, we might say, "Everything I needed to know, I learned by the age of twelve."

The Common Core, guidelines for teaching in language arts and math, has brought with it computer and smart board instruction. Teachers do not always have the time and energy to support constant change. They practice strategies that are successful for them and want the freedom to use their acquired knowledge to remediate and enrich students. Teachers are in the classroom to give encouragement to ALL students and help ALL students set life long goals. All children can be winners when the government works with the local communities and teachers to set individual goals and provide quality education for all.

There are many conscientious teachers who stand up to the new trends and realize that their knowledge and personal intervention far exceeds rote learning found in the technical world. They want to be creative in their teaching. They continue to teach using strategies that have proven to be successful and focus on individual learning. They strive to motivate their students to use critical thinking skills rather than relying on computers for their information. They assess their students with teacher observation and an occasional formal assessment. Conscientious teachers collaborate with their peers and use the documented information to guide their decisions of enrichment and remediation.

Quality teachers realize that memorization also plays a key role in learning the basic sight words and basic math facts. The more frequently information is recalled, the more automatic it becomes. A certain amount of memorization is good for the mind and instant recall of important information can save many hours using the calculator, computer, I-phone and other electronic devices.

It is the wish of teachers to "Let us teach!" Teachers have been educated to be responsible for student learning in an efficient and effective manner. Educators know that small group instruction and individual interaction are far superior to quality education than the "one size fits all" approach.

AUTHOR'S COMMENT: It is not that schools and the government are not diligently working on finding solutions to the problem of illiteracy. There are as many suggestions and programs as there are educators and politicians. The problem of illiteracy does not seem to rest solely on the teachers. English proficiency also rests is on the shoulders of the community and the government when making demands and dictating policies. Each literacy program should be carefully scrutinized---keep the good, eliminate what is unsuccessful and communicate with one another.

SCHOOL STORIES: During a recent school visit, a mother speaking broken English walked into the school office and said she wanted to enroll her young toddler in speech classes. The secretary did her very best to politely explain that speech classes were for children who had speech impairments and were already enrolled in the school. The purpose was not to teach toddlers to speak English.

Upon visiting a second grade class of many different cultures, the students had individual spelling words and were asked to work in pairs to give the list of spelling words. Chaos erupted when several students could not understand the poor enunciation of their partner. Others did not have the necessary skills for reading the words.

MY SCHOOL STORY: As a third grade teacher, I often looked at my students and felt that if I completed their basic education and filled in the gaps, these ten year old students would be able to understand any subject, acquire more knowledge in any area, and continue to build on their interests and goals. If the basic knowledge of math, reading, writing, and spelling are acquired before the end of elementary school and are applied on a daily basis, there should be very few illiterate children.

English is Our Common Language

Please trust us with children for we know what is best
Please support our decisions and allow us to test.
Put technology aside; speak English at home.
When sharing a common language, you are never alone.
A common language makes the public school teacher's job a lot easier.

Jacqueline Kennedy: "There are many little ways to enlarge your child's world. Love of books is the best of all."

The English language accompanied the colonists when they first arrived on the Eastern shores. The Constitution is written in English, as are the laws. In most states, ballots are written in English. English is a requirement for citizenship and citizenship is a requirement for voting. Nearly all political and most business transactions within the United States are conducted in English. Everyone must remember that English is our common and national language. In order to be a contributing and productive citizen, all citizens must share a common language.

Since there is a strong connection between literacy, education and jobs, learning the English language is imperative. Every working person in the United States needs to speak English. Every responsible United States citizen is responsible for learning the English language. If the goal of education is to eventually contribute to the well being of the country with either a job or service, then it seems evident that speaking English and knowing and obeying the laws should be a priority.

Illiteracy becomes a problem when the youth of all nationalities and races want a meaningful and well-paying job and yet have apathy for learning the English language. Some students are more than willing to allow computers and technology to do their thinking for them. They are very willing to post anything and everything on social media. What they are not willing to do is learn the English language.

AUTHOR COMMENTS: The overflow of non-English speaking children into the United States has caused a great deal of concern for the teachers who understand the importance of literacy and a common language. Perhaps, the buses that move undocumented children for processing throughout the country should deposit them at the door of the Department of Health and Human Services in Washington DC. There they could be processed, find responsible sponsors and be taught

English and responsible citizenship. At the same time, these students could be documented and appropriately placed.

A teacher's plea: Government, please help the classroom teachers develop English proficient students---not just in the classroom but also in the community.

MY INTERNATIONAL STORY: Recently, I was cleaning out the garage and ran across a sign written in Japanese. This sign had been posted in the underground garage of our apartment building about 6 months after we rented the apartment. We could not read the six newly posted items on the sign and assumed it had to do with parking directions and safety. My husband asked someone from his office to interpret the sign. We found that the sign posted six garage rules for our children---like no ball playing in the garage, no skateboarding in the garage, no loud noises, etc. Our children were very active and accustomed to having a suburban yard for playing baseball, riding skateboards, etc. and often migrated to the garage for out-door play. They had no idea that their play was annoying to others. If we had, however, not had the services of an interpreter available, we would not have been able to instruct our children on the proper use of the garage. We all realized that our life style and play areas needed to adjust to the physical features and the culture of the Japanese.

Moral of the story: If you can't read the law, it is difficult to obey the law.

QUESTION FOR SOCIETY: Why is English considered the common language for all Americans?

Help is on the way

Recently the mayors of New Orleans, Louisiana; Denver, Colorado; and San Antonio, Texas met to discuss what could be done to improve the literacy of the students in their cities. They emphasized the importance of parental involvement, teacher dedication and participation, and supportive policy makers. They also advocated for a longer school day, co-teaching with a master teacher in every classroom and technology reform.

In July 2016, *Conservative Leaders for Education* was founded in response to the Every Student Succeeds Act. This act promotes more local control, parental choice, teacher transparency and accountability and quality content. Former Secretary of Education, William J. Bennett, heads the coalition. To date, state leaders from Alabama, Arizona, Colorado, Kentucky, Michigan, Nevada, Ohio, Utah and Wisconsin are all members of the group. As an educator, I agree that all four of these external factors will improve quality education. However, I would add the fifth principle---the basic requirements for United States citizenship---being of high moral character, basic knowledge of the English language, knowledge of United States Government and American History, and taking an oath of allegiance to the United States of America. (Conservative Leaders for Education, website)

Other suggestions for assisting low income children to become literate are after school tutoring, eliminate lost time during the school day, Saturday schools for refugees (and their parents), and find out why students are tardy and absent, (Parrett and Budge p. 90) In some cases, summer school may be recommended.

AUTHORS COMMENTS: There are so many groups of concerned citizens who recognize the importance of literacy. They have developed many programs that identify the problem and make suggestions for improvement. Many of them feel they need more money to provide better services, technology and better curricula. Could it be that concentrating on the moral principles would be even more effective?

MY SCHOOL STORY: As a student teacher supervisor, I have visited a wide variety of schools. Some are urban and others are rural or suburban. I visit charter, private and public schools. I recently walked out of a suburban school and chills ran up my spine. The nurturing and learning that had taken place in the first grade classroom that I had just visited was overwhelming. It was thrilling to see how the two teachers (student teacher and co-operating teacher) were working in tandem, communicating about the needs of the students, and providing lessons that met the needs of all of the students in a very diverse classroom. In another inner city Montessori school, there was a great deal of independent learning in a less structured atmosphere. Both examples provide documentation that any school can be successful if the teachers are dedicated and children and families are co-operate and supportive.

Technology

**Yes, you brought teachers computers so they could all learn
How to document tests and report each little turn.
Smart boards soon followed and you attempted to explain
These boards are smarter than the dear teacher's brain.
Technology makes the public school teachers' job a little tougher.**

Albert Einstein: "I fear the day technology will surpass our human interaction. The world will have a generation of idiots."

Ben Carson MD speaks: "I've heard it argued that a broad base of knowledge is not nearly as important as it used to be, because most people have smart phones and can instantly access the Internet...there is no substitute for an ingrained broad base of knowledge...what we already know influences the way we process new information." (Carson, *One Nation*, p. 129)

"The online world inhabited by our children does little to lessen the demand for literacy skills while doing much to diminish those skills. The abilities to read challenging texts quickly and write incisive papers based on reading are the essence of college. And that makes writing a roadblock to either getting into college of graduating with a degree." (Whitmire. p 76)

The government and businesses have allowed technology to invade the classrooms of the elementary school often without being invited by all teachers. With new policies and reforms, teachers are encouraged (sometimes demanded) to adjust to high speed Internet, on-line lesson plans, smart boards and software. Administrators often insist on computer generated professional development forcing teachers into the technical world. In fact many highly effective veteran teachers have left the profession because they feel computers interfere with, student literacy, one-on-one communication, meaningful instruction and individual enrichment and remediation.

When computers were first introduced into the schools, they were considered an extra tool for recording grades and accessing information. In some cases, computers replaced encyclopedias and nearly all information could be available with the move of the "mouse" and the push of a key. As personal computers found their way into many homes, they also found their way into every classroom---even elementary classrooms. Soon all students were given computer instruction and tech personnel were hired to maintain and service the computers. Technology progressed quickly and soon many schools had as many computers as they had students. Within a few years many computers were considered obsolete and the school systems began replacing all computers about every three years. The integration of computers soon became very costly---in some school system the cost has been millions of dollars.

Computers have drastically changed the way teachers teach and the way they plan. Technology has brought on a barrage of testing, dictated curriculums, data collection, deadlines, statistics, power point, smart boards, outcomes, etc. The overabundance of data collection takes a great deal of time and, in some classrooms, has taken the place of student readiness, student goals, literacy, social skills, and positive moral principles. Individual computers, i-pads and i-phones, often hamper the ability of teachers to communicate and evaluate students on an individual basis. In other situations, all communication is done on the computer and personal one-on-one contact no longer exists. In some classrooms computers rule!

Teachers acknowledge that technology is developed by people with creative and brilliant minds and needs intelligent minds to use it properly. Teachers need to be pro-active in deciding what technology is useful in teaching and what needs to be eliminated. Teachers know that computers and data collection can be adversaries of quality education when they interfere with serious learning.

We may live in a technical world but teachers and children are not robots. A quality teacher not only knows the subject matter, a quality teacher has a compassionate and understanding heart. Children live, breath and have feelings. They live in a real world and return home to real people. They need to be educated to think, make decisions and communicate with real people. They need to be literate, possess good social behavior and have moral principles that will last a lifetime. With quality teachers, these skills improve each year as students put the building blocks into place. Literacy, social skills and moral principles are basic skills that assure society that high school graduates are ready for the working world or college.

AUTHOR COMMENTS: The removal of computers and smart boards might allow elementary students more time to focus and concentrate on the language arts. The money used to purchase technology could be used for additional teachers and aids. This would provide more "hands on deck" for intervention and remediation. Learning should be fun but it should also be meaningful. With the sole use of technology many children may be left behind.

MY SCHOOL STORY: About ten years ago, I attended a summer workshop. Teachers were invited to visit various businesses in the community. The question, regarding which computer skills teachers should teach to prepare students for the new world of technology, was often asked. The reply sounded something like this "Please teach the students to read, write, spell, communicate and have a basic knowledge of math. Every business is different and we would prefer to teach the specific computer skills necessary for the jobs that we have. We cannot turn back the hands of time and teach employees all of the fundamental literacy skills that are so necessary in all jobs." They further stated that a strong work ethic, good social skills and high moral standards also played a key role in determining whom they might hire. These companies were very well prepared to provide these young people with the technical skills that they will need to perform on the job.

Technology in the Elementary Classroom

Recent studies done in Texas, Chicago and New York found that there was no significant difference in test scores after years of using selected reading and math software. Schools in the state of New York recently dropped their laptop program. The school board president announced why: "After seven years, there was literally no evidence that it had any impact on student achievement-none." (Whitmire, p. 74)

Mark Bauerlein, author of the *Dumbest Generation*, reported that seven studies were conducted regarding the effectiveness of technology in the classroom. The backing of political and business leaders and the enormous sums of money poured into schools for technology, found that "students to earn good grades and test scores in history, English, civics, and other liberal arts, they need the vocabulary to handle them." (Bauerlein, p. 126-127)

Amanda Ripley has addressed the excessive use of computers in the schools. "...anecdotal evidence suggests that Americans waste an extraordinary amount of tax money on high-tech toys for teachers and students, most of which have no proven learning value whatsoever... Conversely, giving kids expensive, individual wireless clickers so that they can vote in class would be unthinkable in most countries worldwide. (In most of the world, kids just raise their hands and that works out fine.)" (Ripley, p. 214)

In some schools, computers, and calculators have replaced textbooks for the teaching of reading, writing and math. Many instructors cannot "think on their feet" or speak articulately without the aid of a smart board or teleprompter. Technology generated lesson plans require very little preparation and thought regarding the individual student learning. Smart board instruction allows teachers to teach from behind the desk and never explain or question the material that is presented. Tests that accompany smart board instruction are often designed by non-teaching companies and are given and graded on computers; therefore, removing the teacher from personal evaluation.

Statistics indicate that the extensive use of computers in the elementary classroom does not create literacy. Computers do not teach children to read, spell check does not teach children to spell. Calculators do not teach children how to solve math problems. Computers do not teach respect or responsibility. Computers are not able to navigate the thought process of the human brain. In addition young students, with little fingers, have difficulty properly navigating a keyboard. Computers and calculators are not needed on a daily basis in a well-organized and effective classroom.

Teachers teach the skills of reading and writing at every grade level. Speaking and listening are skills that are also taught. Teachers have full plates and do not need the constant maintenance and interference of computers. When a computer has a glitch (which is all too often) learning stops or is disrupted. A conscientious teacher evaluates her students in an authentic way by listening to them read, encouraging them to proof read their written material and to speak with articulation and correct grammar. Reading, writing, speaking and listening are skills that computers cannot teach.

Technology cannot be the sole source of finding reliable information. It is evident in today's technological and social media world that some people cannot think intelligently without an i-phone or computer in front of them. The Internet and texting may even take precedence over the ability to put words together to form sentences and paragraphs. When consulting Google and accessing other information, it is often difficult to differentiate between fact and opinion. Facebook and twitter feature undocumented information and social connections. Many children have a mind-set of instant gratification and enjoy interacting with machines. Educational games often interfere with serious academic learning. While the intentions of these programs are well meaning, technology does very little to stimulate the brain and provide an opportunity to store knowledge.

Student verbal participation is often limited when using computers and may interfere with meaningful discussions and personal interaction. The world of technology requires little human interaction and often eliminates the possibility of eye contact. It often causes young people to think they are invisible and no one will notice their behavior. The new generation might be referred to as the "push button, talk back generation", with little time for communication and storing of knowledge, but a lot of time for meaningless social interaction.

Parents and teachers understand that children need time to learn and retain information. Children also need time to make mistakes. Providing lessons via a computer is not really teaching; it is giving knowledge and opinions without feedback. Real learning and understanding are achieved when competent, knowledgeable and understanding teachers are present in the classroom and communicate with their students.

Every teacher knows that special strategies are needed for many special needs children who are in inclusion programs. Recently, there was a small study done regarding autism in young children. It was determined that autism is best addressed by the age of six months. It also stressed the importance of eye contact and the elimination of technology in the lives of young children.

When teachers are called upon to help and assist the children with special needs, it is the human element that can make a world of difference. LEP

(Limited English Proficient) students need the assistance and help of understanding teachers. They need to read, speak and listen to the English language. Many ADD (Attention Deficit Disorder) children have behavior problems in school and are unable to focus. Students with personal problems need the listening ear of a thoughtful and caring adult to give them courage and understanding. Special needs students, who have academic and behavioral problems, need kind, caring, and loving adults and peers to help them navigate a world of bullying and unkind comments. Schools need knowledgeable, caring, kind and loving teachers behind the desk of every classroom. Technology cannot understand, think or feel. Technology is not always the answer.

SOCIETY'S STORY: PISA (Program for International Student Assessment) recently reported that there was a need to educate students in critical thinking and deeper learning skills. Students can be very computer savvy but often lack deeper learning skills that are needed for thinking critically. "They upload and download, surf and chat, post and design, but they haven't learned to analyze a complex test, store facts in their heads, comprehend a foreign policy decision, take lessons from history, or spell correctly." (Bauerlein, p. 201)

AUTHOR COMMENTS: Our government wants to place high speed Internet in all of the schools, they are encouraging and in some cases demanding that teachers teach via smart boards and the Internet. English proficiency and the ability to interact are far more important than technological literacy. Personal interaction is important for all children learning the basic skills of reading, writing and math. Human contact builds trust and confidence. Personally, I am tired to seeing a little duck dance when a correct answer is given. A warm and complimenting teacher far outweighs little "duckies" dancing. Let the little ducks dance their way out of the classroom and onto the Internet. It might be best to remove all computers from the elementary classroom so that teachers and students learn to read, write and communicate. Perhaps elementary technology classes should be moved to the list of after school activities.

The additional school time could be used for teaching communication skills, moral values and social skills.

MY SCHOOL STORY: A recent visit to a classroom revealed that all learning stopped when the teachers' computer failed. The teacher became frustrated, her students became restless, and the student teacher could not continue the lesson. The tech team was out of the building. Because this was a mandated part of the curriculum and contained one of the building blocks for further learning, all learning stopped for at least a half-hour. It took time for the teacher and student teacher to became creative and find supplemental material. Meanwhile, concentration and focus were lost.

MY STORY: I recently had an opportunity to have two fourth grade students write a letter on the computer to a young man their age in a foreign country. Both young students used the computer to compose and send the letter. I asked to proof read their letter before it was sent. To my surprise, there were no capital letters and no punctuation in two paragraphs. The wording made sense but spaces were also missing. Both of these young men are very bright, very polite, and have caring parents. They attend an outstanding school. They are only ten years old; however, they have been raised in the era of technology.

Today, Einstein might ask: "Are we becoming a nation of literate adults or technological savvy idiots?"

QUESTIONS FOR SOCIETY: Are we willing to give up genuine student learning for technology?

Technology and Social Skills and Moral Principles

Einstein: "It has become appalling obvious that our technology has exceeded our humanity."

Paul Ryan: "If we do not control technology, it will control us."

On Sunday, September 13, 2014, Fox News reported that eighty-nine percent of children from birth to eight years old are using mobile devices. The excessive amount of time spent on mobile devices limits the amount of time for personal interaction. The blame is placed on the parents who do not regulate these devices.

The extensive use of technology has affected the social skills of communicating with real people. Dan Warner, columnist in The Fort Myers News Press, on Sunday, April 12, 2015 wrote an editorial entitled "Technology may be our downfall. The topic centered on how technology is preventing real people from getting along. In the article Mr. Warner stated: "...the major problems we know are present on the internet---cyber bulling, luring of children by sex offenders, financial scams, porn addiction, sexting, and worst of all, a culture of people who are turning away from human contact and spending their lives viewing a screen. And typing like speed demons using only two fingers."

Most teachers are people oriented and prefer to work and communicate with people rather than machines. Many teachers could care less about the use of advanced technology because they are more concerned about English proficiency and the moral conscience of their students. Teachers realize that they are dealing with real children in a real world. These children return to real homes and real communities. Teachers want to make a difference in the lives of their students---emotionally, academically, and physically.

Social behavior and moral principles must take precedence over any technology. Teachers, along with quality parents, care about the social development of children. Teachers want to promote principled behavior and a strong moral conscience. They want to protect the innocent from the negative influences and assist the students in understanding the rules or the school and the laws of the community. Students need to understand the importance of respecting others and accepting responsibility for their behavior. Teachers want a positive learning environment and teachers want to teach.

When negative behaviors, promoted by the use of technology, interfere with the learning and moral behavior of students, it must be re-examined. Social media is harmful when it encourages bullying, drug trafficking, lying, and many other social problems. Social media has also promoted rioting, violent behavior and even the recruitment of young children to join violent organizations. When the use of social media diminishes virtues, it becomes a problem for society. Teachers and families must be willing to control the technology that is used in the home and school, lest it should control them. Youth must realize that there are often consequences for untruthful and harmful comments.

AUTHOR COMMENTS: So much of the media is inappropriate for all people---especially young children and teenagers. Valuable time is consumed engaging in the overuse of technology and social media. Some students use the Internet to receive instant gratification and forget that hard work is necessary to be intellectually educated. Others feel that they do not need to store any knowledge in their brain because it is available at their fingertip. With the ability to post anything on the Internet, there is sometimes a disconnection between fantasy and real life. The excessive use of TV and other technology can hamper academic achievement and the ability to focus.

QUESTIONS FOR SOCIETY: Do families want a teacher, a highly qualified baby-sitter or a teacher who is proficient in computers? Are children learning the necessary social skills and moral values to prevent them from hurting and harming others?

Technology and Privacy

On Sunday, November 1, 2014 columnist David Brooks addressed how computers may eventually rule our lives and decisions. The article "Smart Machines make me Nervous" was written in the Columbus Dispatch. (p. F8). In the article, David Brooks stated: "To put it more menacingly, engineers at a few gigantic companies will have vast thorough-hidden power to shape how data are collected and framed, to harvest huge amounts of information, to build the frameworks through which the rest of us make decisions and to steer our choices. If you think this power will be used for entirely benign ends, then you have not read enough history."

Government computers are being hacked and confidential information is being exposed on a regular basis. Anything placed on a computer, on the Internet, on an i-phone or any other device can easily become public knowledge. Within our government there is much discussion about information that should be kept private and information that should be public knowledge. While intentions are good and information can be valuable, the privacy of citizens is being violated. The lack of confidentiality can be very hurtful and destroy human dignity. It might be fair and safe to say that there is nothing in cyber space that is private and anything on the Internet can be made public.

Technology has also created a concern for security and confidentiality in the schools. Personal information regarding student learning has always been important to teachers. Parent-teacher-student relationships have always been confidential and individual differences have been recognized. Before the invasion of technology, all personal records were kept in the school office under lock and key. If a teacher wanted to check a student record, a signed request was made. Teachers were not allowed to copy the information and professionalism kept teachers from discussing the information. The private information of the student was respected and there was evidence of who and how this personal information was being used. If complete privacy is desired, information must bypass technology and be stored in the brain, in the heart or under lock and key.

Advanced data collection often compromises the privacy of students and is often a waste of a teacher's valuable time. Teachers are constantly being asked to document student behavior and progress on computers. This often takes as much time as the actual teaching. When computers are hacked and documents are exposed, students lose their privacy.

It is evident that there will never be complete security for any information stored in a computer. It is time to decide which is more important, convenience or privacy, facts or opinions, data collection or quality teaching. In order to protect privacy, perhaps less information should be stored on computers and more information sealed in locked files. Either people are failing to use technology properly or technology is failing to protect personal information.

SOCIETY'S STORY: Hacking into computers and cyber attacks happen every day. In May 2014, nearly 1 million Americans and their families registered with the IRS lost their personal identity. In the spring of 2015, it was estimated that over 4 million government employees had their social security numbers and the numbers of their children stolen off the Internet. Schools also have been hacked and confidentiality compromised. Much of the stored information on school computers is available to the state and local governments and is also subject to hacking. In July 2015, it was reported that some 21.5 million people might be involved in the recent "hack" of government files. These files contained personal information and background checks on present and potential government employees. This was a breach of national security and the privacy of the individuals involved. This presents a problem for national security.

MY STORY: I recently needed some tech support after purchasing a new computer. I sought tech support and left a half hour later--- all questions answered and all problems solved. I was amazed at the knowledge of this young student and wished that I had been able to complete the task so rapidly. As I reflected on the situation, I thought: each of us has our own stored knowledge and ability. I wonder how this young man would have functioned in a classroom of 24 third grade students. I am certain he would have been just as overwhelmed as I was. I further reflected on the professions of all people. I certainly could not make the professional judgments of police officers when they face disruptive behavior on the street.

Moral of the story: Everyone cannot be knowledgeable about everything. All need to rely on each other for professional information.

QUESTIONS FOR SOCIETY: If parents purchase media devices for their children, should they be held responsible for how they are used? Can there be such a thing as "cyber addiction recovery"? Is it similar to "drug addiction recovery"? Can we hold the technology companies responsible for paying for this recovery or will recovery programs rest in the hands of The Affordable Care Act?

Technology Advice to Parents

Wm. J. Bennett's advice to parents: "Many parents feel overwhelmed by the questionable and so often pernicious messages coming at their children from TVs, movies, computer screens, radios, stereos, magazines, and some books. Cultural sleaze does influence youngsters' attitudes, but so do loving, caring parents. Spend time with your child and teach her the difference between good and evil. Do not give in to the worst of the popular culture. Monitor what your child sees and hears. Take a stand when necessary. Exert your authority to say, "no, I don't want you watching that", or to explain why something she's heard is wrong. It takes guts to turn off a movie halfway through, but sometimes it must be done. You are the best and perhaps only line of defense. If you surrender, your child will be fully exposed to an army of crass and corrosive values." (Bennett, *The Educated Child*, p. 536)

Dr. Gail Saltz's advice to parents: Dr. Gail Saltz, child psychologist, spoke on MSNBC. Morning Joe, about the effect that social media has on today's young adults. She encouraged parents to become involved in the social media of their children and exercise the right of reading all text messages. She also advocated that there should be no media devices in their bedrooms. Independence needs to be earned and consequences for disobedience begin at an early age. She further feels that technology is gaining prominence at such a rapid rate that the brains of children cannot deal with it at the same rate. Further she feels that teens who watch reality TV feel that it is cool to act disgusting. When asked why parents allow teens to watch such programs, she stated that often parents want to be a friend to their child and they also want their child to be popular with other teens. To enforce good media behavior, parents should have policies and also consequences if these policies are not followed.

De-sensitization Through Social Media, Pop Culture and TV

Children twitter and tweet, play computer games galore
They prefer Facebook and Google to the new Common Core.
Computers and i-phones are both given free
Teachers are asked to monitor social media and pornographic TV.
Social media makes the public school teachers' job a little bit tougher.

"It's easy to forget how big a role…the entertainment industry plays in conditioning young people of every race and ethnicity into its immorality. Remember, if you want to change the world, you must begin with the children." (Bruce: p. 139)

Mark Bauerlein, professor of English at Emory University and author of *The Dumbest Generation*" did research on the over use of social media. He found that the bedroom of a ten-year-old has become a multi-media center. When adding the time watching TV, computer usage and video games, the average screen time is 295 minutes a day. "Youths who watched one or more hours of television per day at the mean age of 14 years were at elevated risk for poor homework completion, negative attitudes toward school, poor grades, and long-term academic failure. Youths who watched three or more hours of television per day were at elevated risk for subsequent attention problems and were the least likely to receive post secondary education" (Bauerlein, p. 77)

"While our medieval forebears had too little information at their disposal, the advent of the Internet and social media has given us too much. Certainly the printed word and radio and television give crackpots and conspiracy theorists some scope for disseminating their opinions, but the Internet and social media allow them to instantly reach vast audiences. But what is truly remarkable is the credence given to demonstrably false ideas and new reality in which it has become politically incorrect for the intellectually discerning to challenge nonsense." "Bad information is everywhere and though such information can be relatively harmless, when lots of people buy into bad information the effects can be devastating..." (The News-Press, Sunday, February 28, 2015. "Ignorance in information age" by Ray Clasen.)

It has been reported that teens spend more time on various forms of social media than they spend sleeping---this is about seven hours a day. This may reduce the time for personal interaction and being physically active. It often eliminates some of their study time. It may interfere with family time and the development of personal relationships. Without eye contact, there is no personal interaction and little chance for discussion. Technological advancements may be well meaning but misuse can be harmful and addictive. Social media can display negative role models that destroy rather than build.

Children often live in a very complex social and multi-media environment with very few restrictions and almost no censorship. They often use computers, Facebook, tweets and twitters, i-phones and other forms of social media as a means of communication. Many postings are harmful and false which cause a great deal of hurt and harm to the victims. Social media has destroyed the reputations and lives of far too many teenagers and in some cases have resulted in suicide. The victims have no way of fighting back.

Many young people are addicted to social media. Face book and twitter allow social connections at the tip of the fingers and teenagers often act before they think. When using social media, youth freely communicate their feeling and thoughts and often disregard the feelings of others.

Often words written are much harsher than when ideas and thoughts are verbally communicated.

What teens do not realize or completely ignore is that future employers and college admissions officers will probably check all forms of social media before they hire, interview or admit students to college. Teens must be advised that anything that is posted on social media may follow them into adulthood. Teens often overlook how these ridiculous pictures and comments will look in future years. The proper use of technology is a social skill that can be developed in today's children.

Social media, TV, pop culture all affect the culture of the school community. Pop Culture has invaded many homes through entertainment and is playing a major role in the deterioration of social skills and moral principles of young people. Many of the rap stars use foul language and inappropriate body gestures that are often mimicked by young children. Some lyrics and "dance" movements of pop music, hip-hop and rap are degrading, deviant and disgusting. Some of these same "stars" have even been invited to perform at the White House. (Remember the importance of role models.)

The entertainment world can desensitize our youth to the realities of life. TV and movies are often violent, sexually suggestive, and filled with dishonest characters. All too often TV and movies forget who is in the audience. Violent entertainment that is seen on TV and in the movie theatre sometimes pales in comparison to violent video games. Violence is so prevalent in today's culture that our conscience begins to think that violence may be normal. It seems fair to conclude that some of the negative behavior that is found in society is a direct result of the excessive use of television, video games and movies. These technology devices also hamper students' social skills and moral behavior.

Teachers are in the business of creating positive relationships and teaching academic discipline. When teachers observe violent behavior, profane language, disrespectful behavior, lack of responsibility for academic learning, etc.---red flags go up. They realize that many times the cause of this behavior is the lack of adult supervision and an excessive use of TV, the Internet and various forms of social media. Often teachers feel that they should "put on the breaks" and prevent students from being over exposed to negative technology. Teachers can't go it alone. They need the help and support of families and the community.

Although the adults are the most important role models, in the world of advanced technology, many children are raised under the "not so watchful eye" of the TV and other social media. Sexting, a form of child pornography, is one of the pitfalls of technology. Recent social media (app called "secret") allows people to post anything they would like and give a false name. "Snap Flash", another social media outlet, uses the camera to capture pictures of activities. Some times these activities are immoral and may even be pornographic.

Parents often do not have the desire to change the channels on their TVs nor monitor their children's use of social media. Further, the government does not seem interested in making a cultural change and encourage "old fashioned" values. Healthy alternatives to Internet, TV, and social media are the arts and physical activities. Although young people seldom show it, they are starved for adults who can give them time and help them navigate the real world, teach them to communicate, and provide positive role models.

AUTHOR COMMENTS: I sometimes wonder if perhaps a license to operate computers and social media might become necessary to keep some of the harmful media out of the hands of children. Just as learning to drive requires proper training and operation, it might also be true for those involved in cyber communication. When parents fail to monitor their children, when children are given free i-phones and i-pads, it would be helpful if all media devices would be programmed to provide only academic learning.

In order for children to learn to read, write and do math, it might be best to remove calculators, computers, and other social communication devices until they have completed elementary school and have the necessary skills and moral values firmly in place. They will also be able to verbally communicate, solve life math problems, and read and write effectively with the knowledge they have retained and stored. It might be best to leave the high tech work skills to the community colleges and universities.

SOCIETY'S STORY: When the Newtown, Conn. killer entered the school and killed 23 people (mostly young children) it was determined that he had been spending many hours each day in the basement of his home playing violent video games and watching violent TV. Young people in our nation are said to spend some 7 hours daily in front of the TV, participating in social media, etc. If these hours are spent with violent activities, is it not a wonder that so much violence is carried over into society. We do not have school shootings because of guns; guns don't kill. Perhaps the de-sensitization of youth has created a society without a moral conscience. Perhaps the best solution of all would be for all adults to be positive role models for young children---it might be parents, teachers, community leaders, and government leaders. Social media, TV and video games can also be role models.

QUESTIONS FOR SOCIETY: Is there any way to carefully evaluate and effectively enforce the abusive use of social media, so children are not exposed to violence, suggestive sexual activity, drugs, etc. at a very young age? Although, no further government regulations are preferred, far too much harm is being done to the moral values of young people through these devices.

BOOK CONNECTIONS: Jack Thompsons author of *Out of Harm's Way* addresses the violence that is found in video games, the lack of parental supervision, the effect these have on society. Jennifer Senior, author of *All Joy and No Fun*, encourages good parenting and the importance of spending more quality time with children. Randi

Zuckerberg, author of *Digital Parenting and Digital Detox*, emphasizes the important role that parents play in monitoring media. Parents are not only responsible for their own media choices, but also for the choices of their children.

Illegal Immigration

Illegal children arrive and flood through the door
They fall asleep at their desks and gaze at the floor.
They cannot speak English. They don't understand the rule
Of behavior and conduct. They would like to be cool.
Integrating immigrant children makes the public school teachers'
job a little tougher.

This chapter will focus on the difference between illegal and legal immigrants. How literacy, moral values and patriotism can influence the effectiveness of the teaching environment. Finally, the cost of educating illegal children and why it might be best to educate children in their native land will also be discussed.

The Difference Between Legal and Illegal Immigrants

Before passing judgment on the realities of illegal immigration, we need to understand the difference between a legal and illegal immigrant and the difference between a visitor and a citizen of the United States. Legal immigrants and visitors obtain a visa or a green card and register with the government. The government knows their purpose and where they will be living.

An estimated one million people are given United States citizenship every year. In spite of this, it has been reported that there are over 11 million (some say as many as 20 million) illegal (undocumented---without a visa or green card) people living in the United States. Illegal immigrants by-pass the visa and green card requirement and often do not register with the government. They generally have very little knowledge of the English language. They also may bypass other requirements for citizenship---being of high moral character and pledging support and loyalty to the United States.

According to the U S Government website, the following are requirements for United States Citizenship:
Must be 18 years old
Be a lawful permanent resident for five years
Continuous residence and physical presence
Must be of high moral character
Possess a basic knowledge of English
Possess a basic knowledge of US Government and History
Take an oath of allegiance
Citizens are then rewarded the privilege of voting.

Among the many reasons the United States and other civilized countries require people entering their country to have passports, visas and register is to know who is in the country and the purpose of their visit. Visas are usually issued for a specific period of time and permission is more restrictive for citizens of some countries. There are visas for working, visas for studying and visas for vacationing. A work visa generally has a language requirement. Physical examination and vaccinations are often required for a vacationing visa. There are no language requirements for visitation because it is anticipated that visitors will return to their native country. Visas are either surrendered when leaving the country or renewed for re-entry. Some legal immigrants will leave at a designated time and others may unlawfully overstay their visa. Some college students on education visas may also fail to return to their native country and seek employment in the United States.

Refugees come with the permission of the government and are usually properly vetted to assure that they mean no harm. During the past 20 years, the United States has accepted refugees from Viet Nam, Somalia and many other countries because of poverty and political oppression. Christians and Jews suffering religious persecution throughout the

Middle East seek asylum in the United States. Women and children in Syria are being persecution and fleeing. Many citizens of countries below the southern boarder want to escape poverty, drugs, and gang violence. In Africa, people are fleeing for political oppression. The lists go on. In fact, there are immigrants who come to the United States from every continent. Many are 'tired, poor and wanting to be free". Immigrating to the United States and the civilized Western World has brought new hope for many children who are often victims of these horrific situations.

Immediate citizenship is given to all babies born in the United States. These babies are called "anchor babies". Pregnant mothers from foreign countries may be encouraged to come to the United States, deliver their babies, receive citizenship for their newborns and return to their native country with duel citizenship for their child. At the age of 18, this child will decide if he/she would like to retain their US citizenship. In some cases, citizenship is retained so that the young adult can attend college in the United States and find employment. They then become 'naturalized citizens'.

Some immigrants are granted amnesty and given legal status without meeting citizenship requirements. They may not speak English and are unable to take the citizenship test. Some are excited to gain this new freedom and have accepted the responsibility of integrating into the American culture. Other immigrants may refuse to integrate into the American culture. Some may have values that conflict with the values of the American culture. Others will choose to retain the culture of their homeland, which includes their customs and language. There is also the possibility that some immigrants may wish to do harm. The inability or unwillingness to integrate into the American culture often results in illiteracy and poverty.

Recently the federal government has looked the other way when people enter the country illegally. It has not enforced the laws of immigration and the responsibilities of citizenship. Many of the illegal adults who come across the borders, plan to never return to their native land. Those that find employment are often without a visa and do not pay taxes. They frequently send their earnings back to their country. Others live freely with relatives or sponsors and depend upon the US government for food stamps, public education, free health care, and other entitlements. Innocent children, often unaccompanied, have also become the victims of illegal immigration.

The question of border control and patrol has been ongoing for many years. If all boarders were secure, there would be no temptation to enter the United States without going through the proper channels. If the laws were enforced no one could become a citizen without being properly vetted and no one would be allowed to overstay their visa. If citizenship requirements were met, all would speak and understand the English language, be patriotic, and obey the laws. All would pledge loyalty to the United States, pay taxes and contribute to the welfare of their family.

However, we do not live in a perfect world. When too many illegal immigrants enter the United States, it drains the economy and also threatens the values of the citizens. While most immigrants come to integrate into the American culture and enjoy freedom, unfortunately there are others who immigrate and do not want to accept the American culture. They often take advantage of the many social programs that are paid for by the taxpayers. Some have even come to destroy the American values. Others bring their culture, which does not always co-inside with the American culture. Some bring illegal weapons, use young girls for sex-slaves, bring Sharia Law that restricts the rights of women, etc. Americans are taught to tolerate these cultural differences but when these differences infringe upon the rights of citizens and The Constitution, laws must be enforced.

QUESTION FOR SOCIETY: Is there anything wrong with having a five year waiting period for citizenship for all immigrants regardless of how and when they came to the United States?

Myrna J. Sanner

Illegal immigrant children

In 2014, it was reported that as many as 80,000 unaccompanied illegal immigrant children came to the United States. Most of these children came from Central American countries of Honduras, El Salvador, and Guatemala. These children come tired and poor---often after a long journey across the deserts of Mexico lead by "coyotes" paid to smuggle them into the United States. Many of the girls were kidnapped and will be sold as sex slaves. Some of the young boys are not innocent children but teen-age members of a gang. (MS-13 has been mentioned and has been seen on tattoos on the youth.) Many of these children are products of the ghetto culture, have diseases and are ill nourished. They may also have experienced psychological trauma. These children have only the clothing on their backs. They are naive and vulnerable.

The number is overwhelming and the government cannot properly handle the documentation of all of these illegal children. Many come without parents or guardians. These young children are sent to military bases, and other holding facilities until they can be processed. If these young children cannot be processed within 60 days, the federal law allows them to stay. These children are then bussed and flown to all corners of the United States, often without sponsors. Returning these young children to their country of origin is often considered inhumane.

Many of these undocumented unaccompanied illegal children show evidence of poor nutrition, poverty, and even substance and drug abuse. Most of these children will need public assistance for health care, housing and schooling until they reach the age of 18. They will be at the mercy of the Health and Human Services Department and the kindness of the American people.

Social organizations, foster homes, institutions and in some cases relatives will care for these undocumented children or adopt them. Many of these children will be placed in distressed situations; without the nurturing environment and opportunities their parents had envisioned for them.

(It has been reported that some sponsors did not present certified copies of their birth certificate. The FBI even eliminated criminal history checks for many of the sponsors.) The government's only concern seems to be placing them in the schools and allowing the community to deal with the social problems.

For many years the federal government has played a key role in demanding public education for all children---illegal or legal immigrants, citizens and non-citizens, students who obey the laws and those that do not, children who are co-operative and those who are not. This is a generous offer on the part of the federal government; however, once these children are dispersed throughout the United States, the education of these youth becomes the responsibility of the hosting state and community.

Nearly all-illegal immigrant children will eventually find their way to the halls of the public schools. Most American citizens understand the huge moral and monetary responsibility that will be placed on the schools, cities and states where these illegal children are placed. The federal government assumes that these schools will provide all of the nurturing that is missing in the original family unit. The federal government also assumes that law enforcement officers will keep children out of harms way.

Once enrolled in various public schools, the Federal Government may soon forget these young children. States and local governments will be forced to accept the responsibility. Very little consideration will be given to the teachers who are required to teach these non-English speaking students. No one considers the language disadvantage that these children face when they have no home support. No one considers the impact that these children will have on the education, social skills and moral behavior of the other students in the classroom. As more illegal youth integrate into the education system, the more costly education becomes, not only in money, but also in human resources.

The illegal immigration of unaccompanied young children causes a great deal of concern and conflict in the conscience of compassionate teachers. Without the love and support of their family, the child may suffer physically, emotionally and academically. With little knowledge of the laws and the inability to speak and understanding English, these children may become confused and frightened. These children may cause disruption in the learning process of others because of their inability to communicate. Negative role models may also influence the attitude of the children.

It is ironic that the federal government is concerned about the food that children consume, the signs for safety in the schools and yet they do not care enough about these children to find out where they came from and where they will be going each evening. Schools need to know where these children come from. Unless they can be identified, total help cannot be given.

Who will take over when the sponsors loose interest? Who will be responsible when the children do not obey the laws and rules? Who will be responsible for these children when they resist learning English and integrating into the American culture? Unfortunately, all too often, it will be the public school and teachers or the law enforcement officers who will come to the rescue.

AUTHOR COMMENTS: The government shows great compassion when it attempts to include these illegal children in the public education system. However, there should be no rush to provide citizenship. A more humane approach might be to prevent human trafficking and enforce the laws of immigration. If that were not possible, perhaps returning these illegal children to their Embassy would be the most humane answer. Their embassy could provide education and health support. When educated, these young people could become leaders in their native country and improve the wellbeing of their family and fellow citizens.

SOCIETY'S STORY: It was recently reported that in one community, 331 different languages could be found in the schools. One school's population of undocumented children rose from 8 at the beginning of the year to more than 100. It has also been reported that currently 20% of the people living in the United States live in homes where English is not spoken.

QUESTIONS FOR SOCIETY: Has the United States become so complacent that it is willing to accept this ghetto and immoral culture as a norm? Has the United States become so complacent that it cannot hold embassies responsible for the welfare of the children in their country?

Immigrants and Laws

Many politicians agree that the immigration system is broken. They, along with other politicians feel that the immigration system is unaccountable, inefficient and ineffective. The boarders are insecure and the laws are not enforced. The government no longer knows who is coming and who is going. This leaves our country and citizens vulnerable. (Ryan, p. 202) (Carson. *America the Beautiful*, p. 39)

ILLEGAL says it all. First, dishonesty is exhibited when immigrants enter the United States illegally. Next, most illegal immigrants cannot speak English and cannot answer questions about the requirements for citizenship. Illegal immigrants have been known to lie about their age or do not know how old they are, or perhaps do not understand the question. Often, they do not have knowledge of the laws. If immigrants have not come legally, the United States government has the responsibility of finding out who these immigrants are and where they come from. The federal government also has the responsibility of knowing why they are in the United States and where they go. It would be helpful to the United States government if illegal immigrants, who do not understand or believe in democracy, would consult their conscience before coming to the United States.

America is a country of laws and all laws must be fair to all people. For centuries, families have immigrated to the United States for religious and political freedom. They respected the laws of immigration and worked hard to meet the requirements of citizenship. They understood that the laws of the United States are based on sound moral principles that promote a civilized society. Immigrants understood the laws before they set foot on American soil and obeyed the laws while in the United States.

The mass influx of illegal immigrants entering the United States has recently caused a great deal of concern for some politicians, law enforcement officers and educators. During the past several decades, the government has become relaxed in enforcing the laws of immigration. The government has looked the other way as millions of people have come into the country without a visa or "green card". Far too many of the illegal immigrants are members of the drug cartel and members of gangs. Far too many are terrorists who do not respect the laws. Many of these lawless people are already in trouble with the law. Many have been deported previously and have returned. Many seek "sanctuary cities" where they can escape arrest and prosecution. Far too many want to do evil and diminish The Constitution.

The laws that rule immigration have always been firmly in place but somewhere along the way, certain people, citizens, immigrants, and the government have decided that these laws apply to other people but not to them. These laws are often ignored for personal benefit, voting advantage and political correctness.

Some politicians seem more interested in social justice, affirmative action and political correctness than personal responsibility and respect for the laws. Law enforcement officers may be accused of prejudice, when they attempt to enforce the laws of immigration and the laws of the country. When there are different laws for different nationalities, different requirements for different cultures, the principles of fairness and consistency are tossed aside. This often results in crating a double standard and choosing winners and losers. When the laws are not enforced, undocumented immigrants and lawless youth may take advantage of the generous and compassionate society. When perpetrators are not reprimanded, chaos results.

Today, some decisions regarding immigration and citizenship are made for political and social reasons. Fairness is overlooked and some are suggesting amnesty and automatic citizenship as ways of making illegal immigrants legal. Automatic and immediate citizenship bypasses citizenship requirements. This may result in citizenship being granted without responsibility and respect. This makes the laws of immigration meaningless and may encourage more illegal people to enter the country.

While President Obama is sharpening his pen to grant amnesty, millions of legal immigrants are patiently waiting in line for citizenship. It is extremely unfair that some immigrants wait many years for citizenship while others are granted amnesty or immediate citizenship. The United States can no longer be lax in enforcing the laws of citizenship. The United States cannot afford to give citizenship to people who are in the country to destroy rather than build, divide rather than unite, and accept the rights but not the responsibilities of citizenship. If citizenship is to be respected and cherished, immigrants should gladly wait in line.

Humane decisions are never easy; however, if fairness and consistency are desired, standards must be in place. Whether a young child or a mature adult, whether suffering religious or political persecution, everyone entering the United States should be required and willing to register with the government and spend at least five years proving their eligibility before citizenship is granted. The United States needs citizens who appreciate the English language, who are willing to abide by the behavior code and moral values. The United States needs more citizens who appreciate the American culture and show patriotism.

AUTHOR COMMENTS: Many underdeveloped countries are given money for the education and safety of children and families by the United

States government through their embassies. Many of these governments are often corrupt and are run by ineffective leaders. Unfortunately, this money often never reaches the children and families. Many churches and other social organizations in the United States contribute money for the education and safety of children in underdeveloped countries. They carefully choose the countries and monitor the money given. Some organizations estimate that as little as $500 per year will educate a child in his native country.

It seems unfair to me that every airline passenger can be scanned, searched, and insulted and nothing can be done about the illegal immigrants who enter by land and by sea. It seems unfair that many legal immigrants with green cards have been waiting for years for citizenship and need to go to the back of the line. It seems unfair to pass out citizenship, through amnesty, at no emotional and intellectual cost.

It might be necessary to change the law to no longer give citizen status to all children born in the United States---the values of these children may change over the years while they are in their native land. We must be assured that they appreciate the American culture and practice patriotism. All children should display loyalty to the United States and share the values of American Culture (speak English, have moral values and behavior skills that are aligned with the rules and laws of the United States, and practice patriotism).

SOCIETY'S STORY: In 2014, Amy Taxin, of the Associated Press reported that the laws of immigration are contained in four thick books of nearly 1,200 pages. It can take as long as three years for the process to be completed and the government is loosing track of these children as they are being shipped throughout the United States. In the meantime, the President has requested approximately 4 billion dollars to hire extra processing agents and take care of these over 50,000 illegal children. This amounts to about $80,000 per child for processing alone. It is time the American people do their math and realize the tax burden that is being placed on the citizens. (Sunday, September 28, 2014 Columbus Dispatch Page A3.)

QUESTIONS FOR SOCIETY: Can it really be that the United States has "sanctuary cities" (340 reported) where immigrants can go and cannot be prosecuted or returned to their native country? REALLY?

Immigrant Children and the English Language

In the United States education and citizenship are highly valued---so is the English language. In the United States, this means having a written, reading and speaking knowledge of English. A common language is necessary for communication and understanding laws. The ability to communicate is of utmost importance for responsible citizenship.

The business and political worlds, through political correctness, often discourage learning the English language. Food labels and assembly directions are written in a variety of languages. Many answering services allow conversations in any number of languages. President Obama prided himself and the department of Health and Human Services when they offered the opportunity to register for the Affordable Care Act in as many as 120 different languages. Some ballots are written in foreign languages. Interpreters are provided in the schools for filling out entry papers and for assistance during parent/teacher conferences. Interpreters also accompany people to the doctor offices and also to the hospitals. With all of these language services being offered to citizens and immigrants, it is no wonder that illiteracy has become a problem in public schools. Americans are willing to welcome and accept the diverse culture of immigrants; however, immigrants should also be willing and expected to learn the English language.

When non-English speaking students enter a public classroom, they must first acquire a basic knowledge of the English language. This basic knowledge will be the foundation of all future learning. The inability to speak and read English is a cultural disadvantage and students may become inattentive and disruptive. The inability to speak and understand English often results in a "watered down" academic program, not enough time to teach other subject matter and not enough time to enrich those who are ready to learn. "Watering down" the curriculum may equal the playing field for immigrants; however, it does not promote quality education for those who are ready to learn.

Most teachers will attempt to educate and integrate these students; however, illiteracy does take a toll on the learning of the class as a whole. Children do not learn by osmosis or by mere attendance. It does very little good for an illiterate child to sit in a classroom when he does not understand nor appreciate what is being taught. In some cases, teenagers are being taught survival language so they can integrate into the American society. Illiteracy or survival language can create division and a double standard within the public schools---a division between those who are ready to learn and those who are not.

Remediation and enrichment are a part of a teacher's responsibility in every classroom. It is easy to enrich children who are ready to learn because these children are often self-motivated and have the support of responsible families. Students who already know English are ready to understand the sciences, math, history and government. Remediation takes more time and must often be completed on an individual basis. While the teacher is busy remediating these special needs children, she will find it necessary to assign other students to computers, give the students "busy work" or have a disruptive classroom. This often creates division within the classroom.

Teachers cannot be responsible for failed policies that encourage illegal immigrant children to flood the schools without the support, readiness and preparation that is necessary for academic success. First generation immigrants often struggle because they return to homes where English is not spoken. Requiring the adults in the home to have knowledge of English before granting citizenship would provide motivation for those seriously wanting to live and stay in America. Illiteracy certainly can be eliminated but not without the support of the community, family and student.

SOCIETY'S STORY: According to a report by Brett Murphy of the USA Today Network, "270 immigrant teens still barred for high schools". These teenagers will be redirected to language programs at two nearby technical colleges. The school district argues that these students need additional English instruction because they are "not academically qualified" to attend high school or have aged out. They further feel that these students should first learn English, which would prepare them for classroom learning and normal curricula. Many of these unaccompanied children began arriving in the United States in 2013 hoping to flee the violence and economic turmoil in Central and South America. (The Fort Myers Press, USA Today, Tuesday, January 3, 2017, p. 1A)

MY STORY: I am often torn between empathy for the students who illegally come through the borders and children who are legal citizens of the United States. As a classroom teacher, I love a class that is diverse because it challenges my ability to meet the needs of all students. I also appreciate the willingness of the United States government to allow people of all nationalities to visit and also work if they have a green card. However, when students enroll in a public school with no knowledge of the English language, it takes much time and effort to provide them with an equal and quality education.

MY INTERNATIONAL STORY: When my husband was "tapped on the shoulder" and our family was asked to move to Japan, I was very apprehensive because I did not know the language or the culture. However, it was exciting because we had always loved to travel and living in a different culture would be a very rewarding experience for our family of five. Since our two oldest children were in elementary school, we expressed to our Japanese mentor that we would like a living location near a good Japanese school where the children could attend and be immersed in the Japanese language and culture. We were soon informed that our children would not be allowed to attend a Japanese school because they had no Limited Japanese Proficient classes and did not accept "gaijin" (foreigners) in their public schools. As a result, our children attended the American School in Japan.

Even if our children had been fluent in Japanese, they would not have been allowed in the Japanese schools because it would have slowed the learning progress of the other students. The average Japanese elementary classroom has about 30 students. Much like the private schools in some cities in the United Sates, the Japanese parents apply for the best pre-school. This school choice puts their child in line for the best elementary school, the best middle school, the best high school and ultimately the best college. For many, the ultimate goal is to send their child to the United States for the VERY BEST college education. I am not certain that I believe in the Japanese philosophy, however, I respect their decision and understand how my non-Japanese speaking children might have a negative influence on the progress of the Japanese children in the classroom.

QUESTIONS FOR SOCIETY: As illegal children are bussed throughout the United States, they become the responsibility of the communities where they are placed. Many of these communities are asking: where will they go home in the evening? Who will support their learning of English? Who will teach them right from wrong? Who will make certain that they become responsible citizens?

Immigrant Children, Moral Principles and Social Skills

The United States is a culture of many races, religions and ethnic groups. The Constitution is based on Judeo/Christian values and the constitutions of other free nations. Americans are proud of this heritage and are also proud that the American culture embraces patriotism, moral principles and an ability to communicate in English. The United States is a civilized society where people are honest and fair, compassionate and caring, responsible and respectful, hard working and loyal, where people understand and obey the laws. Vetting of all immigrants is necessary to make certain they have only good intentions.

It is fair to assume that all young adolescents immigrating to the United States want to embrace the moral responsibilities of the American culture. Young children entering the United States are generally innocent and have no ill intentions. However, as they mature, they often become frustrated living in their new culture and may disobey the laws. They may not understand or do not wish to follow the behavior and moral codes of the American culture. They have not developed moral values and behavior skills that are aligned with the American culture. This often allows the moral values of the school and community to be compromised.

The United States cannot afford to allow undocumented students (or any students) to break the laws of the country. Many youth riot and loot in the streets, use inappropriate language, use illegal drugs and other substances, and show disrespect for people in authority. Even illegal children must learn that there is a right way and a wrong way to escape their plight. Undocumented youth must prove their willingness to obey the laws and must wait in line to become a citizen.

Responsible schools cannot allow negative influences to destroy the values and virtues that are so dear to the hearts and souls of conscientious students. Degrading the rules of the public schools makes schools havens for the lawless and illiterate; for drug abuse, bullying and violence. When schools do not demand respectful and responsible behavior, disruptive and inattentive behavior may result. Teachers are responsible for education but they cannot go home with their students.

Public education does not always address the negative behavior of all students. Instead, teachers may be accused of lacking compassion and understanding of other cultures. Teachers may be accused of being prejudice when they discourage or reprimand unlawful behavior.

131

Teachers are often blamed when children do not learn and understand the English language.

Enforcing citizenship requirements for the young may help stop some of the negative behavior that is found in the public schools. As long as "prejudice" and "racism" or any of the other "isms" are used as excuses for lawlessness and misbehavior, progress in education reform will continue to be difficult. Unless the hearts and souls of all students have a high moral conscience, a peaceful and civilized society will not exist. As long as disrespect and a "watered down" curriculum is found in a public school, responsible parents will continue to flee to the charter and private schools.

SOCIETY'S STORY: On September 11, 2015, The Columbus Dispatch reported that President Obama has requested permission to receive some 100,000 Syrian refugees into the United States. (More recently, it has been reported that this number may increase to 200,000) It was reported that up to 60 percent of these refugees are males between the ages of 18 and 25---the perfect age to bring terrorism to the United States. Many of these young men will not be attending the public schools and will not have an opportunity to integrate into the American culture.

QUESTION FOR SOCIETY: Do we have double standards---one for the lawful and one for the lawless? Is it fair to assume that all undocumented children learn the laws of the community and rules of the school before they are given citizenship?

Amnesty for Children

Paul Ryan, United States Senator from Wisconsin and Speaker of the House of Representatives, addresses amnesty by stating: "We can't allow amnesty; that is unfair, corrodes the rule of law, and just creates a magnet for more illegal immigration. Nor are mass deportations a realistic solution. We need to find a way to honor the immigrant who came here lawfully and did everything right, while giving those who are here undocumented a chance to get right with the law." (Ryan p. 201)

Amnesty is granting rights without expecting responsibility--- responsibility for personal welfare, responsibility for social behavior, responsibility to integrate into the American culture, responsibility for obeying the laws, responsibility for being patriotic and responsibility to speak the English language.

There are many illegal children, who through no fault of their own have already broken the laws of immigrations by entering the United States illegally. When they are granted amnesty they avoid going through the process of obtaining citizenship. These undocumented children do not need to be 18 years old, do not need to display high moral character, do not need to possess a basic knowledge of United States government and history, and do not need to take an oath of allegiance to the United States of America. They are also not required to speak English. These children are not old enough to be responsible for their personal welfare- -food, clothing, shelter and health care. Of course, they have not had the opportunity to be a lawful permanent resident for five years nor continuous residence and physical presence.

The federal government is doing the public schools no favors when it grants unaccompanied children amnesty. While the government might consider this a humanitarian effort, these children often bring with them no knowledge of the American culture, the English language and the laws that make a peaceful nation. They may have moral values that do not agree with The Constitution. Most of these children have left their parents in their native country and will possibly never see them again, thus destroying the family unit. Illegal children often miss their families and their culture and long to return to their native land. These, mostly illiterate and homeless, sometimes unhealthy young people will be dispersed throughout the 50 States and placed in schools where sponsors and teachers will be expected to provide stability, teach them English and responsible citizenship. They are at the mercy of the schools.

The United States government must address the immigration problem if it wants public schools students to be as knowledgeable as students in charter and private schools. Often private schools and charter schools do not have the resources to provide LEP (Limited English Proficient) classes for those who cannot speak English. Therefore, the immigrant children end up in the halls of the public schools where the teachers are given the responsibility of teaching English to all children within two or three years. These young children are expected to understand English regardless of their background and ability and desire to learn. Realistically, very few non-English speaking children will be able to keep pace with English speaking students. Meanwhile the needs and abilities of the other students in the classroom may be diminished.

The sad part of this story is that not all immigrant students appreciate the free education that is offered. They may want the very best of America but do not want to integrate into the American culture, resist learning English and may miss their parents and their culture. In my opinion, American citizens can treat all immigrants with respect but they do not have to grant them immediate citizenship nor give them entitlements without responsibility. At the age of 18, when young adolescents have met the requirements for citizenship, they can decide if they want to take the oath of citizenship and adopt the American culture.

Every country has its problems. It might be poverty, disease or war. America is a very generous country; however, we cannot solve all of the problems of the world by offering amnesty to those who wish to escape. We cannot continue to give money to countries when it is used to build weapons rather than support humanity. Perhaps our immigration laws are too complex and too lax. If our military has a required code of conduct, whether at home or abroad, there is no reason why the entire country and every community cannot live within a code of conduct. This would make the job of the teacher so much easier.

AUTHOR COMMENTS: I have a very compassionate heart and wish that all children throughout the world could receive the same education and freedom that my children and all students in the United States enjoy. However, there is another side to compassion. Children learn best when they come home to a secure environment where they are loved. If young children are unaccompanied, they are coming to the United States without family support; they are coming without the knowledge of English, patriotism and the American culture. If citizenship is desired and granted, young children will need to be taught to be responsible for their social behavior and moral values. They will need to attend school, learn the English language, practice patriotism and develop strong moral character before becoming citizens. When the government ignores the problems that immigration has placed on public education, they are not being fair to tax payers nor are they being fair to the teachers and students.

QUESTIONS FOR SOCIETY: Could restricting and monitoring federal foreign aid be possible? Would it not be more cost effective and humane to keep these children in their native country, monitor the foreign aid, defend freedom and protect the family?

Cost of Educating Immigrants

It is appropriate for citizens of the United States to understand the cost of educating illegal immigrant children. One recent report stated that an average of 171 children cross this border per day---in teacher's terms that would mean at least an addition of 8 new classrooms per day to educate these immigrant children. It also means 40 new classrooms per week and over 2,000 new classrooms each year to integrate these non-English speaking children into the schools.

On Saturday, November 8, 2014 Fox News reported that some 38,000 illegal unaccompanied (without parents or guardians) children entered the United States in 2013. In 2014, the estimate number of illegal unaccompanied children was around 68,000. If my math is correct, over 100,000 illegal children have entered the United States during these two years. If distributed evenly throughout the United States, then every state will have added 2,000 illegal children to its rolls during those two years or 1,000 students per year. Without the knowledge of English, these children will be placed in a regular classroom with about 19 other students. They will receive LEP (Limited English Proficiency) classes and probably also qualify for additional reading assistance. They will need healthcare, shelter, clothing and food.

The numbers are staggering. Let's do the math. If it takes an average of $10,000 per year per child for public school education and each state takes 1,000 new immigrants each year, then each state will need to add at least $10,000,000 dollars to its budget each year. All of the states together will need to come up with $500,000,000 or a half of a billion dollars per year just for educating these illegal children. Multiply this by 13 (the number of free years of education) and the figure becomes $6,500,000,000 to educate these 100,000 illegal children during their 13 school years. In addition, it was previous noted that the federal government has authorized $5,000,000,000 to process some 50,000 illegal children. This was for processing only. These figures do not include the requests for reduced tuition when attending college and also the welfare assistance they will need and receive.

If the government does not address the affect, both morally and monetarily, that illegal immigration has on the public schools, they are not being fair to tax payers nor are they being fair to the teachers. They are being unfair to the immigrants who have worked hard to learn the English language and legally gain citizenship. They are also being very unfair to these vulnerable small children.

When possible, encourage children to remain in their native land

When possible, the government should make concerted effort to help young immigrants remain in their native country. These children belong in their native land with their parents, their native language and customs. Safe havens could be provided for these children and their parents in counties such as Syria, Iraq, Iran, Nigeria, Honduras,

Guatemala, and even Mexico. In the United States, they will need to learn a new language, experience a culture that is foreign and be expected to learn and abide by new laws. They will also be deprived of family support. In addition, it is far less expensive to educate these children in their home countries.

Many underdeveloped countries that experience poverty and political oppression have embassies. They receive financial assistance for education, welfare, defining laws, and eradicating poverty. Many of these countries also have Peace Corp volunteers. Through monitoring, the money and services will reach the designated purpose. When the funds are monitored, these children could become educated and literate in their own language. When they become adults, they will help raise their country out of poverty or apply for a green card to work in America.

Sadly, much of the government money given to other governments never reaches the children. The money often lands in the hands of the drug cartel, corrupt politicians and governments. It may even be used to purchase weapons to hold their citizens hostage. Perhaps the government should realize---all welfare must be monitored in order to be effective.

The United States has many doctors and nurses who travel around the world giving free assistance to children in their native land. It is generally thought that this money goes to improve the living conditions of the people living in that country. If the poor and disadvantaged people are not receiving the education, health, shelter, food and other assistance that they need, it should be up to the United Nations to help monitor the spending..

SOCIETY'S STORY: Recently President Obama asked congress to triple the money being sent to the South American countries. Over a billion dollars in additional aid will help improve education and spur job creation. (Monday, February 16, 2015…USA Today---News-Press, "We can't lose sight of Central America" by Alan Gomez, P. 2B)

AUTHOR COMMENTS: If the U.S. government has approved an additional billion dollars, this money must be monitored. The initial money might be used to return these young people to their families. After their return, a welfare system might be in order. The money that the U.S. Department of Education would save would pay for the increase control at our boarders. The compassionate citizens of the United States would see the results of the kindness and care that is given to educate children throughout the world.

SOCIETY'S STORIES: Many churches and other community organizations sponsor education programs to thousands of foreign students in their homeland. The cost of one such program is $38 each month to educate a child in the Dominican Republic. This amounts to less than $500.00 per child per year. Local education gives security to these young people because they are being educated in their own language and remain with their families. This is a far cry from the billions of dollars that the United States government gives each year to poverty stricken countries, for processing undocumented children and educating them in the United States.

QUESTIONS FOR SOCIETY: What are the foreign countries doing with the aid they are receiving from the United States? Where are the ambassadors of these countries and what are they doing to keep families together and safe?

Indifference to the American Culture

You allow politicians to lie and businessmen, too.
The American Culture is in danger. What can we do?
We don't want double standards; we treat everyone fair
Please tell the Judicial System: "The Constitution is there."
Indifference to the American culture, makes the public school teacher's job is tougher.

Tammy Bruch: "In recent decades in all walks of life, it seems that our society has been hurtling down a slippery slope of selfishness, immorality, and cultural laziness." (Bruce, p. 12)

"The American culture embraces the Constitution of the United States. The Constitution of the United States is founded on Western values because most of the early settlers emigrated from Europe. Some Western values proved detrimental to a unified country; therefore, thorough the years, many rights were added to The Bill of Rights. These bills have been responsible for ending slavery, raising the status of women, abolishing torture, combating racism, promoting religious tolerance, defending freedom of inquiry and expression, and advancing personal liberty and human rights. Many of these rights are the result of respect and tolerance that the citizens have for other cultures. Thus, American has become a multi-cultural society. The United States is a refuge for "the tired, the poor and those wanting to be free". (Schlesinger, p. 132)

"Many laws have been passed to protect the "fringe elements" in the name of social justice and political correctness. Social issues and all of the "isms" sometimes alter the American culture. Some of these same issues are demeaning to patriotism and loyalty. With cultural changes, we must not loose sight of the original American culture that is based on The Constitution and the Bill of Rights." (Carson, *One Nation*, p. 186)

Peggy Noonan, author of *The Time of Our Lives* recently stated that there seems to be no common culture in the Untied States. Noonan refers to the American culture as "a little bit of this and a little bit of that".

The American culture includes people of every race, every religion, and every ethnic group. There are some who would like to believe that within the American culture there is an African- American culture, a Native-American culture, an Islamic Culture, and even a Christian culture. Indeed, there are many cultures within the United States; but when The Constitution is embraced, all cultures become one. When people

139

embrace the American culture, there is no longer an African-American culture, a Native-American culture, an Islamic culture or a Christian culture. There is only one culture---the culture of the United States.

Welcoming immigrates has always been important to the American culture. Some immigrants come to the United States thinking that it is "the land of opportunity." They may have heard stories about liberty and freedom. Some have heard that there are jobs and they will soon become wealthy. Others want their children to be educated. Some come because of religious persecution and political oppression.

Although America has often been referred to as the "melting pot" of the world, many immigrants have very little knowledge of the American culture and what it means to be an American. They may not realize that the American culture embraces the English language, social skills and moral values that are aligned with The Constitution. They may not be aware of the laws and the responsibility of citizenship. They may not realize that a basic knowledge and understanding of history and civics is a requirement of citizenship. They may not realize that citizenship requires patriotism. When the American culture is understood, lived and appreciated by all, everyone will be united, live peacefully and enjoy the freedom of "life, liberty and the pursuit of happiness".

The founding fathers valued unity. People immigrating from the Western cultures often share language and values. Sharing language and values makes it easy to assimilate into the American culture. With so many non-western and diverse cultures present in the United States, finding unity is often difficult. Unity can be found in obeying the rules and laws. Unity can be found when practicing patriotism and loyalty to the United States of America and The Constitution. Unity is a reason for the "Pledge of Alliance" and the National Anthem. Practicing principled behavior and moral values make for a united, peaceful and civilized country.

Very few countries enjoy the freedoms found in The Constitution and The Bill of Rights. If people want to enjoy these freedoms, they must also accept the responsibilities that parallel the rights. They must be loyal to The Constitution. They must learn and understand the English language. They must desire peace and unity.

Schools and the American culture

Education is key to integrating into the American culture. Free public education is available to anyone living in the United States regardless of immigration status. It is available to citizens, children whose parents possess a green card, immigrants and even illegal immigrants. Education in the American culture involves putting forth the effort to learn--- English, social skills and moral values and to practice patriotism.

Teachers are very concerned when their students do not assimilate into the American culture. Every day, teachers attempt to instill good social skills and moral values in the students. Every day, the teachers spend hours teaching reading, writing, and math in English. Teachers teach loyalty and patriotism. They are very concerned when their students are not making the desired progress. Teachers are concerned when students display unacceptable behavior. Teachers are very concerned when students refuse to accept the American customs and practice loyalty and patriotism.

Teachers know that student expectations come with every government and welfare policy (sometimes-impossible expectations). The bureaucrats in Washington DC do not seem to understand the discipline and behavior problems that face teachers on a daily basis. Many of these behaviors diminish the American culture and destroy rather than unite. Every year the government sends more immigrant children into the public school classrooms. Every year the government does not understand why these children are not fluent in English. Every day the government ignores the deterioration of the American culture. Every day some teacher is accused of being unfair or prejudice. Teachers do not want to be accused of prejudice when their students are not successful and misbehave. Teachers want fairness and support.

Teachers need the support of responsible and caring families who are willing to integrate into the American culture and are willing to accept the customs. Teachers want families to understand patriotism and the moral virtues of the American culture. Teachers want help in meeting the personal and physical needs of their students. Teachers want firm guidelines for acceptable behavior and language requirements.

MY STORY: Recently, while in New York City, we visited the 9/11 Memorial. The respect of the visitors was reverent and you could almost hear a pin drop. I came away with sadness and anger. I felt sadness for the many people who had lost their lives and also for their family members who moved on without the support of their father, mother, brother, sister, etc. I felt angry toward the terrorists who would plan such a horrific attack on innocent civilians and anger because they did not appreciate our culture and value human life. These terrorists were granted permission to come into our country and they turned on the very people that trusted them. Although every culture is welcome in the USA, we also need to know what is in their hearts.

The American School Culture Includes A Common Language

The first strong basic fundamental requirement of United States citizenship is speaking and understanding the English language. The rules of the schools and laws of the country are written in English. Government policies are written in English and most business is conducted in English. English unites the citizens of the United States. Every man, woman and child should be expected to read, write and speak in English because English is our common language.

It is easy to define English as our national language but it is more difficult to require all citizens to speak English with fluency and understanding. Many children come to school without an understanding of the English language. Illiteracy continues to exist in the American culture in spite of public education and thousands of welfare programs. With little or no knowledge of the English language, there will be a delay in the learning process. This delay often takes away the opportunity for academic advancement.

In the diverse American culture, a variety of languages can be heard on the streets of nearly every community. Cultural diversity can be found in many classrooms throughout the United States. Culture diversity creates a problem for teachers when families wish to hold on to their language and customs and children are not encouraged to use English. The inability or lack of desire to learn the English language and integrate into the American culture might help explain why the Common Core, Early Childhood Education and The Third Grade Guarantee are sometimes unsuccessful and that "one size" does not fit all. In fact, in some schools, "one size" almost fits no one.

Teachers know that language must be understood before children can integrate into the American culture. Policies often suggest that all students can learn English at the same rate and reach the same goal at the same time. These policies do not take into consideration that some children return to homes where English is not spoken, where welfare money is being spent on drugs, where child abuse is present and many of other social ills plague the children. Teachers are often expected to teach all students the English language, usually within three years. Teachers are sometimes expected to integrate these children into their classrooms often at the expense of the education of other students. Every year the federal government incorporates more mandates, tests and documentation into the curriculum. Teachers do not want a government that dictates more standards, technology and offers only money and criticism. They do not want to be punished because their group of young individuals is not making academic progress. Teachers want understanding and support.

The lack of English knowledge and the deterioration of the American culture are reasons that illegal immigrants should not be given amnesty, that teachers burn out and leave the profession, and that parents seek alternatives to public school education. The American culture requires a common language, moral values and social skills. The American culture embraces patriotism and The Constitution.

SOCIETY'S STORIES: Following are two examples of cultural diversity that can be found in many public schools throughout the United States.

Case Number One: A second grade class of twenty-seven students---17 boys, 10 girls. Two students have IEPs, 100% have free or reduced lunch fees. Two students need to be seated away from distractions. Only ten of the students speak fluent English. Numerous ethnic groups and many different languages are spoken in the home and on the streets. Interpreters are provided for the parents when they need to communicate with the school. Dress codes cannot be followed because of religious beliefs. Moral values and social skills vary with each child.

Case Number Two: Second Grade Class: There are twenty students (fourteen boys and six girls) in the class. Two students have additional support with a reading specialist. Five students are identified as LEP (Limited English Proficiency) with one of the five speaking very limited English. Two students are being observed to begin the SAIL (Student Assistance and Intervention Liaison) program. Two students have IEPs for speech and are receiving services. One student has an academic IEP for reading and math and is receiving services in a resource room for an hour and a half every day; one student has gaps in academic knowledge because he has not had previous formal education.

As for their cultural backgrounds, many of the students are part of many different ethnic minority groups, and several of them are the first generation of their family to be born in the United States. Some were born outside of the United States. Many (most) of the students come from homes where another language is spoken. Several of the students have religious dietary restrictions. One student arrived in the United States the first week of school and no one in the family speaks English. Another was home schooled for two years prior to entering the public school and is not able to read. I would say that only four or five of the students have the possibility of being well prepared for their grade level.

The American School Culture Includes Behavior and Moral Principles

Practicing acceptable behavior and adopting moral principles are the second basic fundamental requirements of integrating into the American culture. Most families pass positive principle from generation to generation and practice them in the home. Other families are indifferent to learning social skills and moral values and find refuge in social justice and political correctness. When family members shirk their responsibility of instilling character in their children, teachers are often expected to provide the positive guidance. When the behavior and moral codes are compromised, parents often leave the public school in favor of a more discipline atmosphere of a charter, parochial or may home school their children.

Teaching acceptable behaviors can present an even bigger challenge than teaching English. Although cognitive ability and aptitude many vary with each child, every child has an equal opportunity to develop positive social behavior and a moral conscience. Teachers are very aware that when diverse cultures are present in the classrooms, positive behavior will not just appear because children begin attending public schools at the age of three, four, or five. Teachers know that all children can understand that America is a culture of love rather than hate; a culture of peace rather than adversity; a culture of people who have a moral conscience and follow the laws. These behaviors will preserve the liberty and freedom of the citizens of the United States. Positive principles must be taught.

Too many social problems can overwhelm the public school systems. The public schools have many students who lack proper nourishment, live in poverty and are illiterate. They may come from homes where English is not spoken, where drugs are abused and where other troubling behavior is present. Because of the lack of supervision, some students dress as they please, go to school when they please, speak English if they please, obey the laws if they please, and use drugs when they please. Parents may even take care of their children if they please. The Department of Health and Human Services offers assistance by passing out food stamps, providing welfare checks and administering other social programs. However monitoring these programs with fairness and legality does not always happen. Sooner or later, many of the social problems will be placed on the teacher's desk.

If a child is not able to understand the rules and laws of the country, he may present a behavior problem while in school. When a student misbehaves, he/she is given a reasonable opportunity to obey these codes. If the child is attending a charter or private school, the only alternative is the public school. When there is disobedience in the public school, the only answer is dismissal. Dismissal only releases the student from the school into the streets.

In order for the teachers to be successful, the support of parents and the entire community must be solicited to mold social skills and moral values into the American multi-cultural society. There can be no excuses in the name of political correctness or social justice.

AUTHOR COMMENTS: It is easier for the government to ask teachers to solve the social problems of poverty, illiteracy, violence or other social ills than to look at the root of the problem and their failed policies. The government often wants the privilege of making the laws but does not always enforce the laws. The government wants poverty to be eradicated but fails to monitor entitlements. The government often looks the other way when families do not accept responsibility for their children's behavior. It wants to regulate every social issue to please the minority rather than the majority in the name of political correctness and social justice. A teacher's love for her students goes well beyond politics.

The American School Culture Includes Patriotism and Loyalty

The third basic fundamental principle of the American culture is practicing patriotism and loyalty. Race, religion, and nationality do not matter when it comes to integrating into the American Culture; however, loyalty and patriotism do. America is a melting pot that embraces every culture and tolerates the beliefs and customs of others. However, these differences cannot stand in the way of a unified and peaceful country. Cultural differences cannot infringe on the rights and freedoms that are guaranteed in The Constitution. Cultural differences cannot stand in the way of patriotism and loyalty to the United States.

Unfortunately, some cultures within the American culture have not gotten the message of responsible citizenship and do not share loyalty and patriotism. They may rebel by being disruptive, disrespectful, irresponsible, and practice negative behaviors. They may refuse to co-operate and show little or no interest in learning the English language. They may refuse to adopt appropriate social skills and moral values. They also may not show respect for themselves, others, property or their country. Their culture may exhibit barbarian behavior and their government may also be their religion. Some may even desire to destroy democracy. Some would like the United States to adjust the laws to meet the wants of their culture.

Schools must encourage students to understand the culture of America. Schools must teach democracy, civics, and American history. Schools must teach patriotism and loyalty. The culture of the United States is more than freedom and rights---it is also about responsibility.

Responsible citizenship is accepting responsibility for actions and doing what is beneficial for other members of society; the responsibility of being literate; the responsibility of adopting the social skills and moral standards of the United States culture; the responsibility of being patriotic and loyal---loyal not only in government but also to the principles that determine the laws. Respect for The Constitution and obeying laws will unite the country.

AUTHOR COMMENTS; The recent desire of young adults wanting to return to their Islamic roots and joining ISIS is an example of unwillingness to integrate into the culture of the United States. Immigrants who come to America with the expectation that every thing should be printed in their language or they demand an interpreter are also examples of not wanting to integrate. Some expect free medical care, education, and food stamps. Some even want the right to vote. Voting is not just a right; it is the privilege that is available to all citizens. Immigrants will enjoy the privilege of voting once they become legal citizens---speak the English language, demonstrate appropriate moral behavior and practice patriotism and loyalty to the United States.

The American culture is a culture of unity

The wide range of cultures and the conflicting moral values make a united culture very difficult. Children that are raised in a different culture often have difficulty identifying with their new culture. While it is important to respect the culture of others, the United States cannot become all cultures to all people. As Lincoln once stated we want a "more perfect Union." (Carson, *One Nation*, p. 186)

Sometimes the American Culture seems to be a culture of lawlessness (criminals and drug dealers), a culture of entitlements (receiving without contributing), a culture of the privilege (money and fame give special privileges), a culture of violence (treating others with disrespect), a culture of permissiveness (can behave and do as one pleases), etc. The majority of Americans would prefer to live in a culture of laws, a culture of hard work, a culture of equality, and a culture of peace and unity.

Agreeing on the principles of our founding fathers and speaking English will create a culture of unity rather than division.

- The American culture is a culture of **freedom of speech**. Freedom of speech gives everyone the right to speak what he or she believes. The American culture allows for criticism of government, religion and values. When angry words are spoken and foul language infiltrates society, freedom of speech is abused. Offensive, demeaning and inappropriate language is not a part of the American culture.

- The American culture is a culture of **religious freedom**. Religious freedom is the essence of the first amendment and one of the most fundamental liberties that United States citizens enjoy. Americans tolerate various religions; however, when a religion conflicts with the basic values of The Constitution, this religion cannot be a part of the American culture. When religions teach brutality and oppression, these religions cannot become a part of the American culture. The American culture demands tolerance but it also demands peace.

- The American culture is a culture of **laws.** The Judicial system provides fairness and justice for all. It does not benefit the American culture when the government creates a double standard---one for liberals and another for conservatives, one for the "right" and one for the "left", one for the Caucasian population and another for minorities, one for the hard working middle class and another for the very rich or the very poor, one that promotes patriotism and another that does not. Lawful behavior requires obedience.

- The American culture is a culture of **moral principles**. These principles include honesty, fairness, hard work, compassion, love and much more. Responsible citizens often put the welfare of others before their own. They show empathy and sympathy and have the ability to "walk in another's shoes". They reach out and share life's joys and disappointments. They find dignity in work and pride in contributing to the beautification of nature, home and communities.

- The American culture is a culture of **generosity**. The government welfare programs, through the Department of Health and Human Services assure all residents that they will not go hungry; they will have shelter; they will have clothing; and they will have health care. Many other countries also benefit from the generosity of the United States. Through our embassies, community and church organizations, the citizens of the United States step in and give hope to those that are oppressed. They give generously of their time, talents and monetary resources. Instead of complaining and expecting more, everyone should appreciate the generosity of the churches, government and other charity organizations.

- The American culture is a culture of **manners, gratitude and respect**---respect for others, self, property and country. Manners are a great way of showing respect and gratitude. Some people think only of themselves and forget about others. They go about their "merry old way" and do as they please without considering how their actions might infringe on the rights of others. Many have dropped "Yes, Sir" and "No, Sir", "Please" and "Thank you" from their vocabulary. Respect puts others before self.

- The American culture is a culture of **responsibility**. The Bill of Rights outlines the rights of citizenship. For every right, there is a responsibility to not abuse the privileges and rights of others. Every citizen and immigrant has the responsibility of obeying the laws. Every citizen and immigrant has the responsibility of adapting to the American culture. Every citizen and immigrant has the responsibility of displaying principled behavior. These are the founding principles of the United States and without these principles; the lawless are not welcome.

QUESTIONS FOR SOCIETY: A recently editorial suggested that we "begin teaching and modeling what is necessary for African-American success and then make those standards a top priority of government, church and most importantly culture". When I read this article, I could not understand how educators and citizens should "begin teaching and modeling what is necessary for African-American success". Does African-American success look different than American success? What standards does the African-American culture desire other than the standards that are outlined in The Constitution? Does success mean different things to different cultures? (The News-Press, Saturday, March 14, 2015. "Selma march important, but what about real issues?" By Cal Thomas)

SOCIETY'S STORY: We have many diverse cultures living in the United States. The goal is for all cultures to assimilate into the American culture. About 15 years ago, three United States communities welcomed thousands of refugees. They were given all of the privileges of citizenship: free education, a checkbook, free housing and in many cases a job. Some moved into homes built by Habitat for Humanity. Many integrated into the American culture; others did not. Some have made no attempt to learn English and have resisted education. Those that integrated into the culture are doing very well; while those that practice resistance have not fare as well. In other words, some did not have the desire to integrate into the American culture.

Summary

Substance abuse, violence, and bullying are some of the negative behaviors that prevent schools from being safe havens for the students. Poverty and illiteracy are negative influences that affect the literacy of students. Families that lack the desire to integrate into the American culture often fail to learn the English language, practice patriotism and lack moral principles. TV, social media and other forms of technology often desensitize the youth and provide poor role models. All of these negative influences must be addressed, dealt with and erased.

Teachers are often called upon to help students tackle and navigate the real world. Academic progress will be made when literacy, moral principles and patriotism are engrained in the hearts and souls of young children. School rules must be enforced so all students have an equal opportunity to learn.

The government must stop ignoring the anti-social behavior of youth and dumping children on the doorsteps of the public schools. The government must stop blaming the teachers for the lack of academic progress. There cannot be "winners and losers" in the schools and there cannot be a double standard. We are all created equally and deserve fairness. Laws are made to provide safety for all and must be enforced.

Society would like miracles; however, miracles will not happen without the total co-operation of the government, community, school and home. With the co-operation of all adults and quality role models all students can be successful.

MOVING FORWARD: Teachers understand the importance of educating each individual child and instilling a moral conscience that agrees with The Constitution. They develop an academic curriculum and a behavior program to fit the needs of each child. All of the building blocks for the academics, including the knowledge and understanding of English, must be in place for success. Decide on the social skills and moral principles that are imperative for student co-operation and behavior. Demand an understating of the American culture and patriotism because they are essential for citizenship and success in school. An exercise of defining principles might be a good idea and instill these positive principles through example and repetition. Once the principles are defined, GET TO WORK!

Chapter III

Quality Role Models Diminish Negative Influences

Yes, you say, "black lives matter". Do brown lives matter too?
Women chastise men and men chastise, too.
Governments fail to punish wrong and ignore what is right
Social skills and moral principles are both out of sight.
Negative role models make the public school teacher's job a little tougher.

Quality education requires quality role models--- in the home, in the school and in the community. Role models are everywhere. Quality role models display behavior that can be modeled and possess a moral conscience that inspires. Good role models put aside the negative influences and realize that children are always watching. They set good examples for children. Role models can be found:

- in the community,
- in the home,
- in the schools
- in the churches
- in the government
- on social media
- on TV
- in the sport world

- role models can be found everywhere

Children need role models in the home because:

- Children need academic, physical and emotional support
- Children are not born with an innate knowledge of right and wrong
- Children learn far more from what they observe than what they hear.
- Families begin to instill literacy, patriotism, moral values and the American culture at birth
- From birth, children watch their family role models
- Families teach children to distinguish between right and wrong

Children are watching their family role models. Will families answer the call?

Teachers often become the role models that students follow when parents fail. Teachers in the public schools often face children who are not principled and have values that may conflict with the moral values of the American culture. If the environment is one of disrespect, bullying, dishonesty, poor attitude, lack of responsibility, truancy, there will be chaos in the classroom and academic learning will not take place. The teacher then becomes responsible for setting standards and creating a positive learning environment. Many times teachers will need to teach students to become responsible for their personal behavior and to respect the rules and laws. When the community values the role model of its teachers, they empower them by encouraging decisions, not only regarding academic learning, but also principled behavior.

Teachers are not the only role models outside of the home. Role models can be found in the community, on TV and in the political and business worlds. When the adults in the children's lives have a moral conscience and practice what is good and right, children will have positive role models in every area of their life and a chance for a bright future.

Because of the diversity of cultures, families and even communities may differ in what they consider outstanding role models for their children When cultural differences exist, everyone must return to the laws and rules of the school, community and country, which are based on the Judeo/Christian values found in The Constitution of the United States.

When uncertain, families must look in their mirror and ask:

- Does my behavior reflect my moral conscience?
- Am I using my resources to provide for my children?
- Am I teaching what is right and what is wrong?
- Am I providing a safe haven free of drugs and abuse?
- Am I encouraging literacy, social skills and a moral conscience?
- Am I showing by my actions to love rather than hate?
- Do I practice generosity rather than greed?
- Do I show unity rather than diversity?
- Am I being patriotic and loyal to the United States of America

Many adults want an easy answer to becoming an outstanding role model. Actually, the answer is quite simple. Outstanding role models begin in the heart and soul of every parent, teacher, community professional and every prominent figure in society. In other words, every citizen and visitor in the United States of America is a role model. Everyone who comes into contact with a child becomes a role model. There is no limit to the number of positive role models that a child can have. The more positive role models a child has; the better his behavior. Perhaps all adults should share that same family mirror and ask the same questions. Am I being the best role model that I can be?

QUESTION FOR SOCIETY: Are you making the future brighter for the children in your life?

Quality Families are Positive Role Models.

Dear families remember, we are counting on you
To help your sweet children in all that they do.
We need you as role models for the students we teach
Please don't tell us again that you cannot be reached.
Supportive parents make the public school teacher's a lot easier.

Wm. J. Bennett, author and former US Secretary of Education, admonishes parents of their importance in shaping their children's moral values stated "The best way to encourage the virtues is to exhibit them in your everyday actions. Show your child courage, respect and compassion in practice. Often you will fall short, but try to be the kind of person you hope she will become. That is the most any of us can do." (Bennett, *The Educated Child*, p. 533)

The family unit has always been treasured in Western civilization and as a part of the American culture. After World War I and World War II many children were raised in orphanages and many compassionate adults throughout the United States adopted orphaned children. Regardless of their heritage, these children were taught the American culture and customs. They were taught the moral principles of society. They were taught the English language. They were taught to be proud Americans.

Those of us (educators) who work with children on a daily basis know that so many of the government mandates and proposals will fall short if we cannot influence the attitude of the students and families---reach their hearts and souls. It really does not matter what a coalition or what politicians suggest and desire. What really matters is what families desire and how willing they are to open their minds and hearts to quality education.

There is a consensus that a responsible family is a key ingredient in quality education. It is the family unit that:

- fosters a love of learning
- introduces good social skills and moral values into the hearts and souls of children
- gives strength to the individual,
- gives a sense of belonging and support
- gives security to children
- shares joys and sorrows
- teaches children right from wrong
- encourages literacy through hard work and perseverance
- shares common goals
- monitors the use of social media and all technology

An estimated forty percent of the children born in the United States are born out of wedlock and many of these children live in poverty. Many of these children are illiterate and will remain in poverty because of the weakened family unit. Families must realize that if they wish to escape poverty, they must become literate through hard work and perseverance---no one can do it for them.

Some political policies and decisions have contributed to the weakened family unit. These policies have allowed parents, who have conceived a child, to walk away from their responsibilities through divorce and abortion. Political decisions have allowed immigrating families to continue to practice their customs and language. Policies have given entitlements without demanding responsibility for personal welfare. Many of these practices have been passed on from generation to generation. The attitude of the family will prevent the children from receiving a quality education.

Quality education requires a quality family---parents, children, grandparents and anyone who might be considered a part of the family unit. Every quality family should:

- accept the responsibility of communicating in English

- know the laws, abide by these laws and teach their children to do the same
- discourage substance abuse and use
- display behavior of love rather than violence
- know the difference between right and wrong
- be built on positive principles rather than negative influences
- embrace the moral values of love, compassion, honesty, fairness and respect
- embrace quality education
- practice patriotism and appreciate the American culture

Families must adopt the American culture---what values and customs should be held dear and what behavior no longer agrees with The Constitution. Families must take responsibility and strive for a common language, high moral character, and knowledge of heritage and government.

QUESTIONS FOR SOCIETY: Is the family unit a principle that the American culture holds dear? If so, how can we preserve the family unit?

SOCIETY'S STORY: Recently, there has been an influx of unaccompanied illegal children. (It has been estimated that as many as 100,000 illegal immigrant children have entered the United States during the past two years.) It has become a problem of compassion because so many of these young children have been torn from their families. Some of these children have left their parents behind; others are coming to the United States in search of their parents. Many young girls have been kidnapped and sold as sex slaves and many young men have been members of gangs in their native country. When the government looks the other way, children without family support become a problem for the schools.

Quality Students are Essential Role Models

Teachers love diversity, they educate all
Politeness and kindness will help in the hall
When laws are enforced and moral codes are in place
Teachers don't look at religion, gender or race.
Quality students make the teachers' job easier.

How often has a teacher stood before his/her class and looked at a field of angry or defiant faces? No amount of knowledge or preparation can reach the minds of students if their attitude is tainted with anger and an unwillingness to learn. Some of these students may have missed some of the important "building blocks" and are, therefore, unprepared to move forward. Others may live in poverty and see no future. Still others may be victims of bullying, drug abuse or other negative influences found in society. Many students come to school with "heavy baggage" and less than desirable role models. A positive attitude toward learning gives students hope to achieve; hope to rise above their plight; hope for the future.

Quality students can be found in society regardless of race, gender, religion or political preference. The diverse backgrounds of students affect literacy, social skills and moral values and can either be an enhancement or detriment to holistic education When the minds, bodies, hearts and souls of young children are educated, classroom performance will improve and students will be ready to enter the adult working world. *The three essential requirements for being a quality student are literacy, patriotism, and outstanding moral principles.*

Quality education requires quality students. Quality students:

- understand the importance of a strong work ethic
- have perseverance to achieve their goals
- are willing to put aside the social media and focus on the academic learning

- have a behavior code firmly engrained into the very fabric of their personality
- communicate in a respectful and polite manner
- have a moral conscience in their very heart and soul
- have the ability to walk away from bullying, drugs and other negative influences
- value personal relationships
- are raised with social skills and moral values that contribute to a civilized society
- have a heart that loves, cares and gives generously
- are able to show compassion and walk in the shoes of someone else
- treat others as they want to be treated
- are leaders rather than followers
- do not rely on what others are thinking
- do not allow others to do their thinking for them
- are patriotic and loyal citizens

All individuals have different mental aptitudes, personalities, physical build and determination. For too long, the government has told young people that everyone should have a college education. For too long, society has suggested that anyone can become President of the United States, a beautiful actress or handsome actor or perhaps a highly paid NFL or NBA player.

Students often become frustrated when success does not happen immediately. Success depends on setting realistic goals and achieving those goals. Goals are reached with hard work, a lot of practice and some rejection; in some cases luck of being at the right place at the right time. Success is finding employment that is sufficient in providing for a family and using talents to produce goods or services. Success is in the eyes of the achiever.

On the other hand the government has failed to demand that literacy and a moral conscience be present before applying for college admission.

Instead, they suggest free college education for all. The government often forgets that success requires hard work and perseverance. They also forget that in order to be successful, knowledge of the English language, patriotism, outstanding behavior skills and moral principles are essential. A "watered down" college education will mean nothing to a future employer. The illiterate, ethically challenged and morally deficient are not wanted in the military, in college or in the work force.

AUTHOR COMMENTS: Perhaps a solution would be that everyone, at the age of 18, be required to give a year or two of service and time to help others. This would allow time for some individuals to mature and "catch up" and others an opportunity to "give back". When all young people are entitled to free health care, free education and other entitlements; certainly, some personal commitment should be required.

MY STORY: When I was in high school, I wanted to play basketball. I made the team but my height of only five feet made success very difficult. As I neared high school graduation, I thought of becoming an airline stewardess. This dream was also dampened with the realization that no one less than 5 feet 3 inches need apply. In addition, my high school advisor discouraged my decision to attend college and major in elementary education. I was determined. Consequently, I put on my high heels, headed off to college. I did not want to be just any teacher. I wanted to be the best teacher I could be. I wanted to be a positive role model for my students and I continued to learn from my mentors. Perhaps my first two goals and expectations were disappointing. They were also unrealistic because of my physical stature. I decided to face my physical limitations and move on. To date, I have not only completed my Bachelor's Degree in Elementary Education, but also, my Master's Degree in Education majoring in Counseling and Guidance and National Board for Professional Teachers Certification in middle childhood education. Today I continue to mentor teachers and am a life-long learner with a passion for quality education.

Quality Teachers are Essential Role Models:

Common Core brought testing and documentation galore
The government keeps asking the teachers to do more.
"One Size Fits All", we know it's not true.
But you keep insisting this is something new.
Government control makes the public school teachers' job a little
tougher.

We have a Constitution and declare it's for peace
When no one is watching our problems increase.
You've ignored our problems, our constant concern
You replaced them with mandates and government terms.
Social problems makes the public school teachers' job a little
tougher.

Sooner or later, the "brightest and best"
Will forget all your mandates and give up the desk,
Because the public school teacher's job is no longer possible.

BEN CARSON WRITES "We need professionals in the classroom… people who build learning and not people who merely talk about student learning." (Carson, *America the Beautiful*)

How many people can wake up every morning knowing they are doing something to make the lives of others more rewarding and enriched? When talking to teachers there is often a sparkle in the eye---immediately telling that they find their job meaningful and self-fulfilling. There is certainly nothing boring about teaching and there is much that is rewarding. Teaching is a labor of love; for students, for learning and for developing character.

Since teachers may be the most positive role models that many students will ever observe, all student teachers, entry year teachers, and veteran teachers should be role models worth emulating. The role model of the teacher often makes the difference between student success and failure. By example, teachers:

- model what is right
- display virtuous behavior with positive moral principles and social skills
- are trusted and trust worthy.
- demonstrate a positive attitude
- work diligently throughout the day and even stay after school when necessary
- dress appropriately
- refrain from using foul language
- praise students for their effort
- show their students how to live and love
- exhibit exemplary communication skills
- have compassion and love for all children
- are confidential in their relationships with parents and students
- use correct grammar, articulate speaking skills, accurate writing skills and good listening skills

These are the qualities that are worthy of student emulation.

Today, in some cases, the government has given teachers the resources and the responsibility of monitoring not only the academic learning but also the responsibility of:

- detecting child abuse,
- monitoring food before, during and sometimes after the school day
- reporting the medical needs of the students
- intervening in bullying, drug abuse, violence, and other negative behaviors
- teaching appropriate behavior
- instilling a moral conscience
- implanting patriotism and knowledge of the American culture

As teachers become more involved in educating the whole child, they are asked to fill many different roles in the classroom. They may become the parent, a counselor, a social worker, and even a nutritionist.

- **Quality teachers are transparent and accountable.** Quality teachers teach the benchmarks and standards in an effective and efficient manner. They evaluate the learning of their students and enrich and remediate as needed. They communicate with the families on a regular basis.

- **Quality teachers are professionals.** Quality teachers rely on their knowledge to put the building blocks of learning in place and educate each student holistically. Quality teachers are life long learners. They engage in professional development and know the curriculum requirements for the children they teach. Teachers are often blamed for the lack of student motivation and success. Teachers cannot be blamed when restrictive government mandates must be followed. Quality teachers do not rely totally on technology. The government and families must have confidence in the skills of the teacher. Teachers deserve to be treated as professionals.

- **Quality teachers are well educated.** Teachers receive licensure after at least four years of continuous study of theory and methods. They have the support and advice of university professors and mentors who have been teaching for many years. Teachers are very well educated and deserve the support and respect of parents when making decisions regarding the education of students.

- **Quality teachers are good communicators.** All teachers need good oral and written communication skills. They should have an embedded knowledge of grammar, spelling and be able to read with fluency and expression. When communication fails, there is a break down in understanding. It is important for all students and their families to share the same enthusiasm for a common language. Communication is a two way process.

- **Quality teachers are role models for behavior and moral principles.** More and more, teachers have been brought into the role of reaching beyond the academic realm. Teachers know that for the first time, some children are learning that there is appropriate behavior and a moral code. When clearly defined behavior and moral codes are in place, principals can support the teachers and students. When principals and administrators abide by the same social skills and moral principles; everyone, including custodians, secretaries, cafeteria workers, etc., will be encouraged to be positive role models for the students. The "welcome mat" can only be out for personnel who are good role models and have a positive influence on children. Teacher must set the standards to provide a positive learning environment.

- **Quality teachers are team leaders.** Leaders realize that race, religion, sexual preference, gender, social status, political affiliations play no role in who receives a quality education. These social 'isms' are sometimes overplayed, often for political reasons. Teachers who are good leaders can put the "isms" aside and look at the students as individuals. Teachers are leaders when they are willing to speak out when social justice and political correctness overshadow their ability to teach. Teachers are leaders when they practice what is right and are positive role models for their peers and students.

- **Teachers are honest and fair.** When teachers insist on literacy, moral values and patriotism from their students, they are often accused of prejudice. Teachers are fair and do not favor one child above another. Quality teachers only speak the truth and relay information to their students without a political slant and without deceit. If teachers are free of prejudice, parents, students and all members of the community must also be free of prejudice and not blame teachers when students do not perform to their ability.

- **Quality teachers are counselors.** Sometimes a teacher looks into the eyes of his/her students and sees no soul. These students seem hardened to the other youth around them, they seem determined to destroy everything that is good. They speak, dress and act in a manner that is detrimental to their well-being and show a lack of respect for other people. Quality teachers will intervene and re-direct these students.

- **Quality teachers are social workers.** Often, young children come to school thirsty and hungry. Students fall asleep at their desks for lack of much needed sleep. The school can be their safe haven from gangs, drugs and other negative influences. The teacher is often called upon to monitor school behavior and work with students and find the cause that keeps them from being attentive and in a learning mode.

Many of the teaching goals are also requirements of the Constitution and American citizenship. They should also be the requirement of every responsible student. Teaching goals embrace:

- the education of all children
- all students graduate with enough knowledge to make them responsible citizens
- all students have a basic understanding of reading and math
- all students know and obey the rules of their school
- all students know and obey the laws of their community and country
- all students have a basic knowledge of United States history and government
- all students understand how to care for our natural resources
- all students have some basic knowledge of earth science and biology
- all students know how to keep their bodies healthy with proper food, shelter and health care
- all students practice patriotism and loyalty and understand the American culture
- all students treat their fellow men with dignity and respect
- all students understand that responsibility and morality are imperative for liberty and freedom

The government wants to recruit the "brightest and the best" to enter the teaching profession. There is no lack of intelligent people who are already in the teaching profession. Teachers are intelligent and knowledgeable. Quality teachers are achievers, have outstanding oral and written communication skills, respectable social and moral behavior, patriotic and are open-minded. They are the "brightest and best". Is there any other profession where each day is the most important day in a young child's life?

Quality teachers ask:

- How does each child learn?
- What are the student's strengths and weaknesses?
- What are his/her interests?
- Does he/she have any physical or academic limitations?
- What might be happening in his home and community that is preventing learning?
- What are the social needs of each student?
- What are the academic needs of each student

MY STORY: When I moved from northern Ohio to central Ohio, I was hired as a third grade teacher. My new school system was heavily ingrained into the "whole language" philosophy at that time. The first conferences were held in October and a parent confronted me regarding my language arts program. I was asked if it included spelling and grammar. We discussed the current "whole language" philosophy of integrating spelling and grammar into the reading program and all other academic areas. I did, however, assure her that I felt that spelling and grammar were very important and would be part of my program. I then created a more formal language arts program that included spelling and grammar and worked diligently with all students to incorporate these skills in their reading and writing. I continued to use and upgrade these programs throughout my tenure in this district. One year, to my surprise, I was awarded the *Golden Shamrock Award*, nominated by parents and students, for academic excellence. Guess whose name was at the top of the list of supportive parents.

Moral of the story: If you believe in yourself and know what quality education practice looks like---go for it!

Quality Citizens are Essential Role Models

Sport heroes, rock stars and businessmen, too
Is your behavior worthy for your children to do?
Do you show respect? Do you always speak truth?
Are you the role models we want for our youth?
The role models of quality citizens make a public school teachers'
job a lot easier

So, dear government remember the next time you reform
Teachers who care want children to conform.
Remember the American culture, The Constitution, too.
Stay faithful to these principles. We are counting on you.
And the public school teachers' job will once again be possible.

"You...need people of generally good character who know that their actions speak volumes. In the business of teaching character, nothing is more important than the quiet power of moral example. (Bennett. *The Educated Child*, p. 527)

Influential role models grace our movies theaters and TVs. They are found in the business world, political world, media world, sport world and religious world. Role models can be found in all walks of life and youth should be encouraged to imitate only virtuous behavior. Virtuous principles build strong moral character. Please join with me as we look at the role models outside the home and school. Do theses role models practice behavior that is worthy of emulation?

- **Community helpers are moral role models.** It takes an entire village of parents, teachers, social workers, police, doctors, nurses and emergency workers to keep the children in the community healthy and safe. These community helpers may be the first to witness crimes, gang violence, substance abuse, and other lawless behavior. They work together to prevent unlawful behavior from spreading within and outside the community. Quality community workers display the highest moral standards and deserve awe and respect.

- **Politicians are moral role models.** From the President of the United States, to the state representatives, to other Government workers---everyone is watching. The majority of politicians are responsible, respectful and honest; however, questionable political policies and practices are sometimes defended in the name of political correctness and social justice. Some politicians use bully and lobbying techniques to pass laws they desire. Unfortunately, some politicians lie because they feel they are above the law. When politicians do not earn the respect of their citizens and think they are above the law, everyone becomes frustrated and chaos results.

- **Sports heroes are role models.** From the college hockey captain to the Super Bowl champions, children are watching. The vast majority are positive role models who possess good communication skills, use appropriate language, show compassion, are patriotic and act responsibly. Many responsible stars and heroes give countless hours to help instill high moral principles in the youth. However, there are also some stars and heroes who nurture their own ego and display behavior that is not worthy of imitation. There are never too many principled role models in a child's life.

- **TV and movies:** From the Red Carpet to the rap star---children are watching. Young people frequently emulate popular role models that grace the TV and the movie screen. The power of these role models can often out weigh the power of family. Media outlets can do harm when violence, poor behavior, off color language and sexual implications are shown. The dishonest and slanted news media often chooses "winners and losers" and prevents making intelligent decisions. Poor role models in the media set poor examples for children. Responsible parents must be constantly vigilant---discussing the virtues of popular role models.

- **Social media:** The Internet, U-tube, I-phone, Facebook and Snap Chat are forms of social media that, when used without supervision or discretion, can create a culture that makes evil stronger and more personal. Some suggest that the Internet and social media are promoting a culture of hatred and sarcasm. Some users love the game of hating and enjoy saying hateful things because they are seemingly invisible. The misuse and over use of social media can be violent and often degrades others, may ruin reputations and can even be detrimental to the well being of others. When technological communication is out of control, bullying, making fun of others, spreading false information, etc. become problems for society. Adults must constantly and consistently be vigilant when children begin looking for role models on social media.

- Today's **pop culture** operates in a world with few checks and balances and can provide negative role models for children. Their behavior, often acceptable in the world, does not exemplify the principles that are preferred in the schools and the working world. Their behavior often diminishes virtues and character building.

One of the goals of quality education is to educate children to become adults with outstanding moral character. On a whole, teachers are "owning up" to their share of the responsibility by exhibiting outstanding moral character and being positive role models. Teachers not only practice fairness, honesty, respect, and many other virtues; but, teach these virtues to their students when allowed. Teachers have very little control of the other role models in a child's life.

Any inappropriate, offensive and dishonest behavior sets a very poor example for children. Negative role models, that promote violence, brutality, drug abuse, etc., can be found in the government, in the sports world, on TV, in theaters, and video games. Children are exposed to unfairness and a double standard when the simple standards of right and wrong are taught with subjectivity, political correctness and moral relativism. Children, who are raised without high moral principles become conflicted, confused and unsettled when they receive mixed signals from negative role models. Negative role models cause children to live a double standard---one that they see every day, another that promotes respect and discipline.

The list of role models in every child's life is endless. Role models are the individuals who are watched by children every hour of every day and every day of every week. The responsibility of choosing positive moral role models can be placed on the laps of the family and others in the community. Parents and other adults must decide how each role model measures up to the principles they want in their children. Responsible families must be constantly vigilant---discussing the virtues of every role model in their child's life.

SOCIETY'S COMMUNITY STORY: Recently, some community organizers, politicians and news personalities have questioned the integrity of police officers. Demonstrations were incited in the name of social justice and created unrest and violence in the streets. By rioting, these disruptive people overlooked the need to respect those in authority and did not wait for justice to be served. Just as teachers need respect in the classroom, police officers, fire fighters and all community helpers need respect on the streets. Parents and other adults have a responsibility to teach children how to respect and co-operate with those in authority. The community has the responsibility of allowing the courts to provide justice.

SOCIETY'S POLITICAL STORY: An example of political bullying might be the passage of The Affordable Care Act on Christmas Eve. This might also be considered dishonest, when it was revealed that the Obama administration knew that some of the information was deceptive. It is important to remind all politicians that "truth and honesty must always rule". Note to politicians: You are not above the law and children are watching you.

QUESTION FOR SOCIETY: What is society doing to increase the chances that all students will become adults with outstanding moral character?

Children Learn What They Live by Dorothy Law Nolte

If a child lives with criticism, he learns to condemn.
If a child lives with hostility, he learns to fight.
If a child lives with encouragement, he learns confidence.
If a child lives with praise, he learns to appreciate.
If a child lives with fairness, he learns justice.
If a child lives with security, he learns to have faith.
If a child lives with approval, he learns to like himself.
If a child lives with acceptance and friendship, he learns to find love in the world.

PART THREE

Educating the Hearts and
Souls of Young Children

Introduction

In order to have quality education, we must look into *The Content of Character* of all children and adults. Fifty years ago, America's public schools were ranked at the top in every academic area. Every country revered and respected the American public schools. Fifty years ago, there was no technology; no social media---most family units were in tack and the majority of parents taught their children to be respectful and insisted on proper social behavior. Parents also instilled a moral conscience in their children. All families strived to speak English in their homes and on the streets. Citizenship and patriotism were sources of pride.

During the past five decades, the negative behavior and social ills have spilled over into the schools and *The Content of Character* has diminished. Patriotism and loyalty are often overlooked. The decay of moral principles and inappropriate social behavior of the students has placed added responsibilities for the teacher. Teachers often shy away from insisting on a moral conscience for fear of being socially incorrect or being accused of one of the 'isms". When teachers insist on positive behavior and following the rules, they are not being prejudice; they are protecting the rights of all students in the classroom.

Thirteen positive principles that exemplify positive character development have been selected. These principles address moral values such as respect, manners, honesty, and fairness. The inner core is evident when students accept responsibility, practice self-discipline, and show love, gratitude and compassion. Academic achievement is accomplished through a strong work ethic, a positive attitude, good communication skills and a thirst for further knowledge. Each of the defined virtues is accompanied with a line of dedication to groups of people who exemplify these characterizes. Among the identified role models are politicians, religious leaders, volunteers, police officers, military personnel, journalists, lawyers, coaches, family members, students and of course teachers.

There is a need for the government to listen to the voice of teachers and parents. It is the government that controls the purse strings of the schools and they must also be held accountable for student learning. The government can encourage every school to teach patriotism, civics and American history without a political agenda. The government can insist that every citizen speak and read English. And finally, the government can support the laws that instill positive social behavior and moral principles into the heart and soul of every student and every citizen. *The Content of Character* will become more universal in the American culture when all citizens unite in practicing literacy, moral principles and patriotism.

Can teachers build character? I certainly hope so. *The Content of Character* begins by defining character. The character of an individual is the inner core that is often dictated by the moral values and behavior that are present in the home and community. Character is reflected in how a child feels and acts.

The Content of Character embraces the concept that every child can become literate. When building character, teachers should stand their ground and insist that character development is necessary for a quality education. Every child can practice acceptable social behavior and develop a moral conscience. And every child can adapt to the American culture by being patriotic and loyal to The Constitution of the United States. However, these principles must be taught---in the home, school and community.

Chapter I

The Content of Character

The Content of Character by Myrna J. Sanner

Let's build character in our children,
There is so much leaders can do
They teach by example.
Character building begins in you.
Role Models build character in children.

Respect those in authority, respect property and country, too.
When you respect others, they will respect you.
Have self-respect, self-control and think about others.
Treat everyone kindly, like your mother and your brothers.
Mutual respect is necessary for developing character in children.

It's nice to have manners, say please and thank you.
Don't take advantage of others, who care about you.
Hold doors and shake hands, it's the right thing to do.
Show gratitude and appreciation for all that given to you.
Manners and gratitude are essentials for developing character in children.

Children need boundaries. They need discipline, too.
When practicing self-discipline, they know the right thing to do.
They treat all with respect. They obey all the rules
They do all their homework and listen in schools.
Self-discipline is needed for developing character in children.

Responsible children obey laws. They go to school every day.
They complete all their homework and do what authority figures say.
They never blame others for the decisions they make.
Responsibility for their actions; they must always take.
Responsibility is required when developing character in children.

Honesty is taught by example. We must all speak the truth.
By thinking through our decisions, we are role models for our youth.
When everyone is honest and does what is right,
There is peace in the country and the future is bright.
Honesty is indispensible when developing character in children.

When behavior is offensive, don't look the other way.
No double standards in the classroom. We demand only fair play.
We need coaches who are fair and Justices, too.
Schools need to be fair in all that they do.
Fairness is vital when building character in children.

A positive attitude sure matters. Always think that you can.
Set realistic goals and make only reasonable demands.
Be the best that you can be; put arrogance aside.
Be humble, have hope, let courage be your guide.
A positive attitude is critical for building character in children.

Communication is about English; using proper grammar, too.
It's about enunciating clearly and listening too.
It is putting away social media and speaking the truth.
It is sharing a common language, and educating our youth
Effective communication is fundamental for building character in children.

Complete your homework on time. Attend school every day.
Go above and beyond, learning the American way.
Show up at the job site, set goals just for you.
The oval or corner office will soon be waiting for you.
A strong work ethic is basic for building character in children.

When knowledge is stored and wisdom is gained
Common sense always rules when the mind is well trained.
Artificial intelligence gives us answers when knowledge is in vain.
But the wisest human knowledge is stored in the brain.
Knowledge is important for building character in children.

Give of yourself---time, talents, and treasure.
When showing compassion, give without measure.
Have empathy for others; show sympathy, too
Show kindness and caring; stand in another's shoe.
Compassion is critical for building character in children.

Put love in your friendships. Fairness is a must.
There is nothing more faithful than a friend you can trust.
Friendships are precious; friends cannot be replaced
Friendships go beyond, sex, religion or race.
Love and friendship are obligatory for building character in children.

A moral conscience is essential, put impulsiveness aside.
Think through your decisions; let your conscience be your guide.
Before you take action, ask for guidance from above.
May all of your actions be for peace and with love.
A moral conscience is compulsory for building character in children

The goal of education is to build character from within
Educating the hearts and the souls, make boys into men.
When moral principles are in place and we all speak the truth,
Women are ladies and children become responsible youth.
Quality education is essential for building character in all children.

William J. Bennett, former Secretary of Education, often speaks of the importance of instilling virtues in young children. "Students should learn the different forms that virtues take, what they are like in practice, and why they deserve admiration and allegiance. Children who leave elementary school with fuzzy notions about these moral fundamentals are headed for trouble." (Bennett, *The Educated Child*, p. 526)

Dr. Martin Luther King: "We should not judge others by the color of their skin but by the content of their character." (*I Have a Dream*: Speech)

"Principles" has been chosen to describe the moral values and social skills that build character in young children. The word 'Principle' is defined as "a rule or code of conduct". There are several additional words that relate to a character building. Ethics is the discipline of dealing with what is good and bad with moral duty and obligation. Ethics requires a set of moral principles and values. Moral principles relate to right and wrong behavior, expressing or teaching a conception of right behavior by acting on the mind, character and will. Virtues are commendable qualities and traits that encourage conformity to a standard of right. Therefore, ethics, morals, virtues and principles all relate to the development of a moral conscience that builds character in the heart and soul. When put into practice, these principles often become known as codes of conduct or rules of behavior. A code of conduct or a moral conscience is essential for teachers when monitoring the behavior of students and when self-monitoring. Once manageable behavior is in place, true learning can begin.

BOOK CONNECTION: C.S. Lewis, author of *A Mere Christianity*, *The Chronicles of Narnia*, and *The Abolition of Man: How Education Develops Man's Sense of Morality* and others, predicted the adverse consequences of children who are educated in a world without an objective code of morality and ethics. The results are cheating on campuses, bullying by children, and political leaders who lie and deceive the very people who vote them into office.

Principles (Virtues) Build Character

"You...need people of generally good character who know that their actions speak volumes. In the business of teaching character, nothing is more important than the quiet power of moral example. (Bennett. *The Educated Child*, p. 527)

What is character? Character has been defined as one of the attributes or features that make up and distinguish the individual. Therefore, the total character of an individual does not only include the physical appearance, mental attributes and achievements but also incorporates the content of the heart and soul. The heart and soul is the inner core of a person and can often determine moral principles. These principles are reflected in how a person feels and acts---in other words, his character.

Years ago, the education of the heart and soul of a young child was the primary responsibility of parents and guardians. Parents also provided for the physical needs of their children---food, clothing, shelter and health care. Teachers were given the sole responsibility of providing a quality academic education in the classrooms and solicited the help of parents when behavior became disrespectful or disruptive. However, today, in some cases, the parental responsibility of providing for the physical needs of children is left up to government entitlements. The development of moral character is left to those in society who care, often the classroom teacher.

With so much money being spent on collecting data, research, and developing a "one size fits all" curriculum, governments often overlook the social and moral issues that affect student learning. The federal government has constantly and consistently attempted to improve student performance with more government mandates, education reform, more money, higher taxes, more technology, new textbooks, better curriculum standards, etc. None of theses suggestions seem to be improving the learning that is taking place in the public schools and none address the character of the students.

The newly proposed ESSA (Every Student Succeeds Act) has identified more local control, school choice, teacher accountability and transparency, and quality content as their four principles for improved education. However, none of these reforms and mandates addresses the inner heart and soul of the students---their character. Good moral character will encourage children to be principled and have behavior that is complimentary to classroom learning and also to being an American citizen. Common moral values and social skills can provide guidelines for following the rules of the school and laws of the community. When inner discipline and moral character are in place, it is hoped that students will desire to integrate in the American culture and learn.

Fortunately, the vast majorities of citizens possess a moral conscience and are law-abiding. However, today, in some cases, the parental responsibilities of building character in their children are non-existent, half-hearted or left to the schools and government. Their children are the students who have fallen through the cracks and are of grave concern for teachers. They may be illiterate. They may live in poverty. They may come from families that are morally deficient and ethically challenged. They may refuse to obey the laws, and lack loyalty to their country.

Therefore, teachers must focus on the positive principles that unite and eliminate those negative influences that divide. The entire community must solicit the co-operation of the families to live by the moral standards of the American culture. Remember: "United we stand; divided we fall."

Chapter II

Thirteen Positive Principles

Mark Twain: "God has put something noble and good into every heart his hand created."

"As a nation, we need to spend more time understanding who we are and what those principles are that define us. Once we identify them, there should be no apology and no compromise in applying them." (Ben Carson MD, *America the Beautiful*, p. 191)

"...most Americans have forgotten or never learned what is distinctive about American values." (Prager, *Still the Best Hope*, p. 10)

In April of 1999, thirteen students and teachers were murdered in the halls of Columbine High School in Colorado. Shortly after The American Children's Fund was established in memory of these victims to assure that good came out of this tragedy. This charity was designed to promote character building in schools. The purpose was to create a new approach in character education and prevent further tragedies from happening.

The American Children's Fund encouraged high school seniors through out the United States to acknowledge principles that build character. Since thirteen is the number of people who were murdered during the Columbine massacre, the program encouraged American high school students to collectively unite in choosing thirteen character traits that defines each public high school community. These characteristics confronted violence, apathy and under achievement and were meant to inspire. Students who vied for this award and scholarship were to select one of the most desirable positive character traits and associate this trait with a historical figure--- such as Abe Lincoln and honesty. Each year, students who exemplified these character traits would be recognized and rewarded with scholarship money. It was hoped that positive principles would be imbibed in the hearts and souls of all young people so this tragic event would never be forgotten.

(Thirteen is also the number of the personnel killed at Fort Hood and also the number of the original colonies. For elementary school students, twenty-four positive character traits might be chosen in memory of the twenty-four teachers and students killed at Sandy Hook.)

Although, these scholarships are no longer provided at Columbine High School, the program continues in several high schools. Internet research revealed three different high schools in Baltimore, Maryland that have taken on the responsibility of building character. In Baltimore it is called Character Revolution 13 (CR13). Each school chooses thirteen characteristics as their unique hallmark. Although each school differs, several character traits were common in all three sites that posted this information. They were: respect, leadership, determination, confidence, teamwork, responsibility, golden rule, and loyalty. Integrity, vision, courage, diligence, justice, self-control, and compassion were also mentioned as important characteristics.

Building on this concept and in memory of the lives lost at Columbine High School, I have taken the challenge of The American Children's Fund and CR13. I have defined thirteen principles and behavior traits that I feel are essential for building character in young children. By clearly defining these virtues and positive behaviors, it is hoped that students will accept ownership of their behavior and responsibility for their rights and freedom.

SOCIETY'S STORY: In spite of CR-13 in three Baltimore High Schools, students recently rioted and looted in the streets of Baltimore. Unfortunately, this poor social behavior was more publicized than the students who were rewarded for their essays on respect, responsibility, the golden rule, justice and self-control as desirable social traits. These looters showed no respect for property, the law, or law enforcement officers. They showed no responsibility for their actions and did not practice self-control. Constant blaming others and demanding social justice only results in death and violence.

1. Respect

The Golden Rule: "Do to others as you would have them do to you."

This chapter was inspired by a visit to a rather large public school campus is an integrated community of many diverse culture and social backgrounds. Throughout the buildings, often in bold letters, were mottos of respect--for self, others and for property. These constant reminders stressed the importance of respect in their school and in their community. The polite and mannerly students moved orderly from class to class and were actively engaged in learning. In spite of their cultural differences, they were united in showing respect to everyone and everything.

Respect those in authority, respect property and country, too.
When you respect others, they will respect you.
Have self-respect, self-control and think about others.
Treat everyone kindly, like your mother and your brothers.
Mutual respect is necessary for developing character in children.

Respect for others builds character.

Respect influences behavior and leaves a permanent impression on others. Everyone needs and deserves to be treated with dignity and respect. Respect (self-respect, respect for others, mutual respect and respect for property) is a social skill that all children can learn. Many families teach their children at a very young age to respect adults and listen to them. When families fail to teach respect, teachers and law enforcement officers are often placed on the front line of solving another social problem.

Within the past decade, there has been a significant decline in the respect for authority. The recent events in Charlotte, Baltimore, New York City and in Ferguson, Missouri are all confrontations that could have been avoided if young citizens had shown respect for law enforcement officers. When drugs and other substances are involved, people can no longer rationally control their actions and deeds and they become disrespectful. When young people emotions rise and name-calling begins, violence, rioting and looting often take over. When reprimanded, citizens sometimes become belligerent and display behavior that is threatening to authority. They often forget that authority figures are trained to protect society, and not destroy.

Negative role models often show disrespect by using inappropriate language, bullying, condoning violent behavior and practicing dishonesty and can be harmful to the moral development of children. Many politicians, rap stars, and TV personalities use highly offensive language and are disrespectful of their audience and peers. Many youth use the social media to show disrespect. Disrespect for teachers is often observed in many public schools. It is important to teach respect during the elementary years rather than waiting until middle school and high school after disrespectful behavior has been accepted for many years.

Having a defiant attitude certainly shows disrespect for teachers, parents and other adults. When citizens disobey laws, no matter how minor, they should expect to be questioned. When students disobey the rules of the school, they must also expect to be questioned. When questioned, students should always respectfully answer. They must understand that they have the responsibility of doing what is right. Teachers also have the responsibility of listening to the student. Teachers must respect the students and reprimand in a caring and sympathetic way. Students must accept the consequences without being defiant.

Society often looks the other way in the name of social justice and political correctness. When disrespect is overlooked, children may think that dishonesty, rude behavior, inappropriate and profane language, and other disrespectful actions are acceptable. Looking the other way gives children mixed signals and will do little good when teaching respect and developing a moral conscience. If a law has been disobeyed and disrespectful behavior has been harmful to others, certainly punishment and disciplinary action are necessary in both the community and in the school. When children make poor choices, there cannot be two different codes of conduct---one for the responsible and another for the irresponsible. When everyone shares the same moral values, respect will abound.

SOCIETY'S STORY: Spring 2015 brought many college students to Panama City, Florida. Evidently, this location has been a haven for students who felt the need to "let off steam" after months of rigorous study. News stations reported that a fraternity party in Panama City, Florida resulted in young men spitting at disabled veterans, urinating on the American flag and displaying other disrespectful and disgusting behavior. There was substance abuse, students passed out on the beach, gang rapes performed and a lack of respect for authority. Perhaps the most disrespectful behavior was the lack of respect that the students showed to the disabled veterans who where sharing the same beach. The fraternity members have been punished; however the veterans will always be saddened when they remember this event. Whatever the cause, the lack of respect for others and property cannot be tolerated in a democratic society.

Self-respect

Many students show a lack of self-respect by their uncaring and irresponsible personal behavior. Students may show a lack of self-respect by the way they dress (or don't dress), the manner in which they speak, how they abuse different substances, and their participation in wanted and unwanted sex. When students have self-respect, they do not need to hide behind a "hoodie" but can hold their heads high and take pride in their accomplishments.

The lack of self-respect is shown when social media is used to degrade their own reputations and allow others to invade their personal privacy. When young people post inappropriate pictures of themselves on Twitter and/or Face Book, they show very little self-respect. Inappropriate "selfies" and "sexting" can be self-degrading and damage reputations. The 4th Amendment guarantees the right to privacy and this right should not be diminished by the inappropriate use of social media.

Students who have self-respect believe in themselves, can self-monitor their behavior and practice what is right. They care about their friends, what they do and how they act. They want friends who share their values and behavior. Students who have self-respect also have self-esteem. This results in self-confidence and the ability to think and speak with conviction.

Mutual Respect

The Golden Rule, "Do to others and you would have them do to you", is a motto for mutual respect. There must be mutual respect in the school---teacher-to-teacher, principal to teacher, teacher to student, parent to teacher, and student-to-student. Listening to the opinions of others shows an attitude of mutual respect and understanding. If young people want to be respected, they must display an attitude of mutual respect for everyone.

Mutual respect builds self-esteem in both the giver and the receiver. Mutual respect creates friendships and promotes a caring relationship. Mutual respect goes a long way in preventing frequent occurrences of violence and misbehavior. Mutual respect does not mean total agreement; however, being gracious to those with different points of view is necessary. When mutual respect becomes the norm in the school culture, relationships and behavior improve.

SOCIETY'S STORY: In September 2014, a community of teachers went on strike. Although they appreciated an offer for an increase in salary, one of their greatest concerns was for the lack of respect they were receiving in the school and in the community. Many teachers had previously left the system, not for higher pay but because positive student behavior and parental support were lacking.

Respect for Country and Property

Respect for the United States, its flag and National Anthem should head the list when showing respect for property. The Constitution and flag of the United States are symbols of freedom and should be revered and respected. America is the greatest country, and as of now, the citizens have more liberty and freedom than in any other country. All citizens should respectfully stand during the National Anthem and hold their hand over their heart or salute the flag when the American flag is in view. The lack of respect for the American flag and American values shows a lack of respect for our country. Out of respect, there should be no burning of the flag, graffiti on public property, destruction in cities, national parks, or any other place.

The destruction of property, defacing desks, walls, destroying computers and school property does not show respect for the very institution that is trying to educate. Many years ago, students might have been asked to undo the defacing with paint, erasers, etc. They might have been asked to write: "I will respect the property of MY school" many times. Others might have been asked to research the cost of replacing all of the items destroyed. If looting and rioting are involved, students might be given hammers and nails to help rebuild. Undoing the wrong might be returning all stolen goods. When possible, punishment and discipline should be related to the incident. Students need to take responsibility for their behavior and realize that there are consequences.

SOCIETY'S STORY: Recently, an NFL football player refused to stand for the playing of the National Anthem. He protested because he felt there was unfairness in the treatment of a certain race. When people are so dissatisfied with judicial decisions and show a lack of respect for symbols of freedom, perhaps they should search for a society that they can respect.

OUR INTERNATIONAL STORY: My husband's business took us to Japan for three years. He was required to obtain a work visa and we both needed green cards. Our children were enrolled in The American School in Japan. Before, we left the states, it was understood that our pre-teen children were to abide by all of the laws of Japan. If any of them participated in using drugs or other illegal substances, our entire family would be immediately deported. Thankfully, this was not a problem for us because we respected the Japanese customs and laws. It was a fabulous experience and we enjoyed the extensive travel; however, each time we heard OUR National Anthem, it brought tears to our eyes and a longing to return to the our country, the greatest country in the world.

QUESTIONS FOR SOCIETY: How do you show respect for others, yourself, and your country? Would respect be one of the principles that you would select to improve your school and community?

2. Manners and Gratitude

This chapter was inspired by the vast majority of students who practice good manners and social behavior in classrooms throughout the United States. Many of these students show their gratitude with kind words and thoughtful deeds. It is especially dedicated to the well-manned and polite students who passed through the doors of my classrooms. I am grateful for their manners of kindness and respect.

It's nice to have manners, say please and thank you.
Don't take advantage of others, who care about you.
Hold doors and shake hands, it's the right thing to do.
Show gratitude and appreciation for all that given to you.
Manners and gratitude are essentials for developing character in children.

Manners

Manners and politeness are the foundation for respect. Children are not born with good manners. Good manners and politeness are taught. In a responsible home, children, as soon as they begin to talk, are asked to say "please", "thank you", I'm sorry", etc.

Manners must be taught. Children are taught to hold the door for others and not interrupt with someone else is speaking. Children are taught not to talk back, speak when they are spoken to, and not to use profane language. It is certain that nearly every teacher and every parent has had to remind some child to use their polite words and manners. Politeness is a social skill that should never go out of style.

The opposite of good manners and politeness is rude behavior. Rude behavior is displayed when citizens refuse to stand for the National Anthem, show disrespect for the American flag or show disrespect for others. Rude manners are often publically displayed on TV when people talk over each other. Rude behavior is shown when people do not listen to the opinions of others. Some citizens practice rude and destructive behavior when they loudly demonstrate and have no regard for people in authority or property. They may make excuses for their inappropriate behavior by accusing others of being unfair and prejudice. If allowed to go unchecked, rudeness will replace manners and meanness will replace rudeness. There is no place for rudeness in a civilized society.

SOCIETY'S STORY: In a recent conversation with an educator, I discussed the lack of "thank you", "please", and the other polite words that are often taught in pre-school and kindergarten. The reply was that the use of these words of politeness and gratitude are no longer used or recommended because it might make the young children feel sub-servant or inferior.

Myrna J. Sanner

Gratitude

In today's world, many children feel that they are entitled to anything that is within reach regardless of their age or effort. They do not have to politely ask for food, clothing, health care, or personal possessions. They don't have to say "thank you" because the government never holds back on its promise that they will not go hungry. They are given i-phones and i-pads and are not asked to limit the usage only for appropriate behavior. They do not have to take care of their bodies because the government will pay for the repair through Medicaid or The Affordable Care Act.

Young adults show a lack of gratitude for free public education when they fail to put their best effort into their lessons. They often know that they will be promoted regardless of their effort. They do not need to learn English because an interpreter will be provided or they will receive citizenship without meeting the requirements. They express their lack of gratitude to the law enforcement officers and emergency workers when they are disrespectful. They show their lack of gratitude for their freedom and the laws when they riot and loot. Thanks to the relaxed laws and lack of accepting personal responsibility, these provisions are given to all children and are theirs for the taking. They do not have to say "thank you" or show their appreciation.

Entitlements are gifts of the government. Gratitude is showing appreciation. It would be wonderful if children would pause and realize that every benefit they receive from the government is due to the hard work of their family and other members of the community. Thinking about the many blessings of living in a democracy reinforces the need for expressing gratitude. Everyone should be grateful for the opportunity to live and visit America. Americans should be grateful for- --freedom, liberty, parental guidance, caring teachers, loving spouses, free education, medical service, law enforcement officers, the military, food and all of life's essentials. The list goes on. Being thankful for all of the blessings certainly overshadows the constant complaints that no one is ever doing enough for "me". Gratitude is a virtue that results from humility and showing appreciation. Fortunately, gratitude can be taught in the home and reinforced in the school.

GID POOL'S STORY: "At a recent gig, he noticed two young women in the front row texting on their phones. His confused-sounding voice, "Excuse me, is that one of those fancy phones that get the Internet?" "Yeah," she said, smirking. "Could you Google 'manners'? The audience roared. (Pauley, p. 58)

The following is a list of simple manners that everyone could easily practice:

1. If you can't say something nice; don't say anything
2. Show gratitude for every blessing
3. Wait your turn to talk
4. Respect your elders
5. Don't talk back to those in authority.
6. The use of profanity shows a weakness in vocabulary development
7. Always use polite words like "please", "I'm sorry", "yes sir" and "no sir", etc.
8. Gentlemen always hold the door for a lady
9. Let others go in front of you.
10. Above all, always be grateful and say "thank you"

MY SCHOOL STORY: Children love to write thank you letters. After each special event or room party, my students wrote letters of "thank you" to the room helpers for their participation and gratitude for the memorable occasion. The students never tired of proudly taking these notes home to their family. Just as adults show gratitude by writing "thank you" notes, so students should practice this social skill. Now, when I give a gift to a graduating senior, it is with great pride that I receive a gracious letter of thanks. These young people have manners and know how to show gratitude.

QUESTIONS FOR SOCIETY: How can gratitude and manners be instilled in the hearts and souls of our youth?

3. Discipline and Boundaries

This chapter is dedicated to our children and grandchildren, who had boundaries and were frequently reprimanded when they were young. As they grew and matured, they had the guidance of caring and loving parents and adult role models who taught them right from wrong.

Children need boundaries. They need discipline, too.
When practicing self-discipline, they know the right thing to do.
They treat all with respect. They obey all the rules
They do all their homework and listen in schools.
Self-discipline is needed for developing character in children.

"Professional educators---people who spend thousands of hours with children every year—should understand one fundamental truth about kids: they yearn for boundaries. Whether they care to admit it or not, they want to be told "no." They crave the security that comes with the knowledge that there are adults in their lives who care enough to set limits." (Beck p. 126)

Principled families determine behavior expectations for their children at birth. Behavior expectations may include good manners, respect, gratitude, honesty, fairness and many other valued principles. Responsible adults teach their children what is right and encourage good behavior at all times. If positive behavior is going to last, it must be maintained and nurtured.

Teachers need a disciplined environment in order to meet the moral obligation of instilling sound positive principles in the hearts and souls of students. When discipline is present and rules of behavior are enforced, students will act more responsibly, have better manners, work harder, practice honesty, show respect for adults and above all, will listen to the voices of adults. When discipline and boundaries are present in the community, home and school, the environment will be safer for everyone. The demand for moral principles should be universal.

Appropriate behavior in the schools is sometimes difficult to define because social behavior varies from culture to culture, home to home and community to community. Parents vary in their expectations of child behavior and do not wish for their children to be reprimanded or punished for infringements that are allowed in the home. Teachers in public schools sometimes overlook the social and moral issues because they do not want to be accused of one of the "isms". Inconsistent and inappropriate student behavior often occurs when a code of behavior is not defined, established, or enforced.

Borderline behaviors need a united agreement of acceptability between the community, home and the school. Common moral values and social skills will provide guidelines for students when following the rules of the school and laws of the community. This code of conduct prevents a double standard and provides structure, sets boundaries, and enforces the rules of discipline.

The lack of classroom discipline is most disruptive. The lack of respect for teachers, other students and property hinders the learning of those who wish to learn. Charter and private schools often insist that the family agrees with the code of conduct before admission. If students become disruptive and do not obey the discipline code, they can be dismissed. On the other hand, public schools often do not have the option of student dismissal. Disruptive students are often allowed to remain in school regardless of their behavior. These students may be given a pass in the name of social justice or political correctness. When maintaining good discipline, agreement between the community, home and school regarding appropriate behavior is extremely important.

Children, more often than not, will "try" parents and others in authority by pushing the envelope to test their boundaries. When children fail to observe the rules or behavior is inappropriate and too offensive, consequences are in order. When children ignore corrected behavior, those in authority must be pro-active rather than re-active because preventative discipline is preferred above punitive discipline. These adults must be persistent and lead by example. These adult role models will discipline by acting swiftly and decisively and setting boundaries. The punishment should be meaningful, not too harsh, and should be related to the infringement that has taken place---in school, it is often the third offense that requires outside action. When outside action is taken, there must be an agreement between the family and the school that this behavior must stop and mutual and consistent discipline must be carried out. When discipline is absent, chaos rules!

Self-discipline

Self-discipline is a virtue that is necessary for a principled democracy and is always preferred above imposed discipline. The purpose of instilling discipline in the public schools and the home is to set boundaries so students can self-discipline. Self-discipline is a principle that is expected of children after they have been taught what is right and what is wrong, what is good behavior and what is unacceptable behavior. Families, teachers and law enforcement officers hope that every child, every citizen, will become self-disciplined.

Children do not live in a vacuum and must learn what is expected of them. They can learn and practice self-discipline. They can learn how their behavior affects not only themselves, but also others. They can learn to show compassion for others and eliminate personal selfishness. By observing codes of self-discipline, young adults can decide if their behavior is appropriate and resist temptation to do wrong. As children grow into adulthood, they realize that they are "the captain of their soul and the master of their fate". When all citizens are self-disciplined everyone can live in a peaceful environment.

When someone practices self-discipline he is able to self-monitor. Children prefer to monitor the behavior of their peers. Self-monitoring is very difficult for young children and that is perhaps the reason that they "tattle" when they see someone doing wrong. Parents and teachers attempt to educate children to self-monitor when they tell them to "just say no" when someone is doing something wrong or when they feel they are in harm's way.

Self-control is a form of self-discipline when monitoring ones behavior and temper. Self-control determines eating habits, shopping, poor language choices, passions and impulses, and even the control over one's life and development. Self-control involves the heart of soul and must be nurtured on a daily basis.

My Ten Commandments for self-discipline in today's world:

1. Put your i-phone out of sight when in the physical presence of others
2. Listen to the adults in your life, they have far more experience
3. Be honest in everything you do; people are more forgiving than you might think
4. Read quality material at least one hour everyday and apply it to your life
5. Recognize that there will always be someone who is a smarter than you
6. Always walk in another person's shoes…you may need compassion some day
7. Do unto others as you would have them do unto you
8. Watch only one hour of TV each day and make sure it makes you laugh
9. Don't post anything on the Internet, face-book, etc. that might embarrass you or others
10. Reject violence, bullying, and all of the negative influences of society

Myrna J. Sanner

AUTHOR COMMENTS: Children learn most by the examples, experiences and conversations with adults. In the process of maturing and with the guidance of a caring and loving family, they can become self-disciplined and practice self-control. They will cultivate a moral conscience of knowing right and wrong. As adults they will be able to self-monitor their behavior. As my daughter would say, "You can't always get what you want."

MY SCHOOL STORY: On the first day of class, a high school teacher promised five extra points to everyone in the class if there was no evidence of i-phone or other electronic device being used during his class. For each infringement, a point would be taken away from every student in the class. Their final grade would include the extra points earned. Therefore, the class was "in it together". If one student failed to obey the rule, all students would be docked a point. At the end of the semester, all students received the additional five points because all students had obeyed the rule of no i-phones or other media in the classroom. These students practiced self-discipline by refraining from using their cell phones during class.

BOOK CHOICE FOR PARENTS: *Positive Discipline* by Jane Nelson has suggestions for teaching children self-discipline that includes respect and responsibility.

4 Responsibility

This chapter on responsibility is dedicated to all of the mature family members and politicians who are accountable for their actions and provide outstanding role models for all children. These responsible adults do not blame others for their mistakes but take full responsibility for guidance and governing. They realize that for every right there is a responsibility. They realize that they are role models for young children.

Responsible children obey laws. They go to school every day. They complete all their homework and do what authority figures say. They never blame others for the decisions they make. Responsibility for their actions; they must always take. Responsibility is required when developing character in children.

"Responsible persons are mature people who have taken charge of themselves and their conduct, who own their actions and own up to them---who answer for them." (Bennett, *Book of Virtues*, p. 186)

There is a tendency in human nature, when things do not go as planned, to blame others and pass the responsibility on to someone else. All adults should be accountable for their actions and the decisions they make. When someone is responsible for their actions, there is no finger pointing and there is no blaming others. Irresponsible behavior is immature. As President Truman once said, "The Buck Stops Here".

Responsibility in the Home and School

When parents conceive and bring a child into the world, there is an assumption that these parents will also accept the responsibility of raising the child. When one or both spouses reject this responsibility, a grandparent, a guardian or even the government may be asked to take over the responsibility of parenting. They will provide food, shelter, health care and education. The child may suffer the lost opportunity of being raised in a family with family values.

In some cases, the first breakdown in family responsibility may begin before or at birth since some forty percent of today's children are born out of wedlock. Statistics also reveal that over forty percent of all marriages end in divorce. Mature adults accept the responsibility of their commitment to marriage and raising children. Mature adults accept the responsibility of providing for themselves and their families, following the laws and being good citizens. Responsible adults accept the responsibility for the personal health, academic learning and moral behavior of their children.

Myrna J. Sanner

An elementary school child can display responsibility in a variety of ways. Responsibility for a young child may be helping with household chores, doing homework, practicing for athletic participation, and achieving in the classroom. If the child has not been taught responsibility for his behavior during his early years, it makes it difficult for teachers to instill the responsibility of personal hygiene, academic learning and social behavior. Poor social behavior and ;negative influences may override the teacher's ability to provide a quality education.

Total reliance on the community workers, the government, teachers, etc., is not responsible adult behavior. If sufficient role models are not present or motivation is not provided, history often repeats itself and the cycle of irresponsibility continues. This is perhaps one reason why four generations may not have been able to move out of poverty and why many families continue to live on welfare for decades. As the child matures and enters middle school and high school, the decision of accepting responsibility plays a key role in future college or work place success.

SOCIETY'S STORY: After the street riots and looting in Baltimore, the "mother in yellow" was praised for accepting parental responsibility for her teenage son. She boldly entered the streets and ordered her son to return home before he got into trouble. She said: "He is my boy". She feared for the safety of her first-born and wanted a better life for him. I would vote for her "mother of the year" because she seriously accepted the responsibility of being a good parent.

Responsibility in Government

"For malignant narcissists, however, everything does revolve around them. Everything awful that happens is someone else's fault" (Bruce, p. 155)

Practicing responsible behavior is important for everyone---all politicians, all police officers, all teachers, all parents and all role models.

Responsibility is to seek peace rather than diversity. Responsibility is to respect the rights of others. Responsibility is to be honest and fair. Responsibility requires decisions that are best for society as a whole and agree with the laws of the country. Responsibility is to contribute to the well being of all citizens and being generous to those who are less fortunate. Accepting the responsibility of good citizenship is important for everyone. People who do not take responsibility for their own actions and blame others often do not want to accept the consequences of their behavior.

For politicians, blaming others dodges the responsibility of the oath of office. Politicians sometime respond to mistakes or public criticism by blaming others. Politicians dodge their responsibility of fairness when they make exceptions for not following and enforcing the laws in the name of human rights, social justice and political correctness. When they enforce one set of rules for the responsible and another for the irresponsible, they create a double standard.

The Bill of Rights is a wonderful document and assures everyone the right to "life, liberty and the pursuit of happiness". Good citizens will accept the responsibilities that accompany the rights. Responsible citizens learn and appreciate the language and obey the laws. They accept the responsibility of learning about their country and practicing patriotism. They respect the American culture.

QUESTIONS FOR SOCIETY: Can government employees and politicians, who lie, be held accountable for their actions, or are we creating a society of double standards?

MY STORY: It seems appropriate to encourage and sometimes reward the personal responsibility that students accept when practicing good behavior and manners. In my classroom I had suckers available for good behavior, outstanding achievement and personal responsibility. Each day that all of the students performed exceedingly well in a particular subject, had outstanding manners and good behavior, we would put a sucker in the jar. When the jar was filled with enough suckers to share with the entire class, we would have a sucker party on a Friday afternoon. This would include an educational video and a sucker for each child. The sucker kept them from being noisy and disruptive and also served as a reward. We never had more than one party a month and we never put more than one sucker in the jar on any given day. This helped keep the system meaningful and under control.

5. Honesty

Honesty is dedicated to all journalists and politicians who put aside political preferences and prejudices; journalist, who practice objectivity and honesty when reporting; politicians, who pass laws and reforms that agree with The Constitution of the United States.

Honesty is taught by example. We must all speak the truth.
By thinking through our decisions, we are role models for our youth.
When everyone is honest and does what is right,
There is peace in the country and the future is bright.
Honesty is indispensible when developing character in children.

Einstein: "The ideals which have lighted my way, and time after time have given me new courage to face life cheerfully, have been kindness, beauty and TRUTH."

Words from my father: "Honesty is always the best policy."

Honesty is one of the principles of our founding fathers. Honesty is telling the truth in all situations. Honesty is the ability to own up to a decision and take responsibility for ones actions. When honesty is present, trust soon follows and trust creates friends. Being honest is a social skill that every elementary school child can learn. Honesty builds character in children.

Dishonesty and deceit are the opposite of being honest. Dishonest people often feel that it makes little or no difference if they tell the truth. Some people, often without a conscience, think that lying does not matter as long as they are not caught. Often half-truths, excuses or lies are used to avoid punishment and embarrassment. While dishonesty may protect the perpetrator, it can cause bodily and emotional harm to others.

Honesty in the Schools

Children need to be taught to tell the truth so they can be trusted. They need to recognize when a lie is told. They need to be educated and informed so they can discern the difference between a lie and false information. Children, who are honest, refrain from cheating, stealing, and being deceitful. Honesty founded in early childhood is most often carried forward into middle and high school and also into college and the work world. Truthfulness should be embedded in the heart and soul of every child.

Teachers want their students to live a life that is truthful and genuine. Children watch the behavior of their adult role models every day. What is done and said matters. Therefore, it is important for teachers and all other adults to practice honesty. With positive and honest role models, every child can practice honesty.

Teachers are not only role models for honesty; but are often asked to be on the "look out" for honesty in students. Adult guidance and individual soul searching are very important when children are deceitful. When dishonesty is observed, the teacher, family and often community leaders are called into action and bring this dishonesty to the attention of the student. If at all possible, the student is required to make the situation right.

Students who cheat on tests are not being honest, workers who steal office supplies from their company are not being honest, and government workers who plead innocence when they have done something devious, are not being honest. Falsifying papers, lying about a political event, adjusting test scores are other acts of dishonesty and are all too prevalent in American society.

MY SCHOOL STORY: Throughout my teaching career, I have had students who tell untruths or half-truths. Why do they do this? Generally, they know that what they did was wrong or embarrassing. As a teacher, I was not allowed to put my students under oath but did my very best to find the truth and explain to these students why telling untruths are wrong and how they harm other people. When children become adults, it is hoped that honesty will be one of their character traits. Always remember, someone is watching.

SOCIETY'S STORY: The dishonesty of a few teachers often overshadows all of the honesty that is taking place in the classrooms throughout the United States. One recent report suggests that the attendance of students had been falsified so the school could receive more government grants. Certainly the failure to report accurate attendance is dishonest and does not contribute to the education of students even though it presents a better image and brings in more government support.

MY STORY: The senior year in high school was rapidly coming to a close and senior pranks were out of control. The final Monday morning of classes arrived and crickets were in the hallways, classrooms and throughout the school. The administration, trying to identify the culprits, took the newly published yearbook to the local bait shop. One young lady was quickly identified and was called to the principal's office. She was asked if she was one of the responsible parties. She admitted her involvement in the prank. The real test was when the administration asked her to reveal the identity of the other culprits. She stated that she needed to be loyal to her friends and could not disclose this information. Loyalty to her friends caused her to spend the Saturday before graduation attending in-school detention. She was also warned about the possibility of not singing and not walking at her high school graduation. She maintained her integrity but also continued to be loyal to her classmates.

Honesty and Journalism

Journalists are men and women who work in the streets and offices to report news and other events in a truthful and unbiased manner. All news people should report only facts and, unless stated, leave their opinions to themselves. If citizens are expected to believe what they read and hear, they must be assured that the news commentators and journalists are honest. When journalists place honesty and objectivity into every news story they write, they should be saluted. They deserve the respect of their readers.

Biased media and a false political agenda, often test the meaning of honesty. Some journalists use the media to perpetuate their prejudices and have even been accused of producing "fake news". Some incidents may be exaggerated and untrue and unkind statements may be deceitful. Dishonest and false news are divisive and will not unite the citizens.

More than one journalist has lost his/her job or placed on leave because of dishonest reporting. When something has been misreported, an apology and correction is in order.

SOCIETY'S STORIES: Friday, Feb. 6, 2015. The news was filled with disappointment when it learned that a very popular and highly respected national TV anchor told some untruths about a visit to the war zone in Iraq some ten plus years ago. Week of May 11, 2015. Another popular news personality was criticized for not disclosing his contributions to the Clinton Foundation before participating in a biased interview. Although he apologized for not disclosing this information and withdrew his name from moderating a political debate, he lost integrity and respect. Can we trust the news media and journalists when they lie to us?

Honesty and Politics

Words from Winston Churchill: "Without integrity nothing counts. With integrity everything counts."

Just as journalists are held accountable for their honesty, politicians must also be held accountable for their decisions and actions. Politicians are the men and women who make the laws and communicate with their constituents. They are the role models who live in "glass houses" and their every move is watched. When politicians lie, they lose integrity and the trust of their supporters. Once someone has been deceived, trust must be regained.

Half-truths, twisted truths, lying under oath, and outright lies are dangerous and far too frequent in the political world. Honesty seems absent from the investigations of the IRS, NSA, Benghazi, and the Veteran's Administration. The possible overreach of the Justice Department in tapping the telephone lines and computers of members of the AP and Fox News is also a form of dishonesty. Being fair and honest eliminates the possibility of choosing winners and losers and making exceptions for poor behavior. Dishonesty destroys unity and the confidence of citizens. And we all remember, "What difference does it make?"

Some political leaders refuse to answer a question honestly---either by denial, taking the fifth-amendment or by telling half-truths. Once a lie is told, people continue to lie to cover up previous lies. Covering one lie with another is dishonest. It was not the acts of Presidents Nixon and Clinton that caused intense disgrace and almost removal from office; it was the fact that they both lied under oath.

It is shameful that government officials need to be sworn in at hearings to get to the truth. Everyone should be thankful for the committees that are willing to conduct honest and reliable investigations. Thanks should also be extended to all of the judges and justices that enforce the laws and uncover the lies of others. Truth should always win.

Deceit is a form of dishonesty. Some political events seem to suggest that the government is not being completely honest with the citizens. Politicians running for office, often take advantage of citizens by telling lies or by being deceitful. They want to win elections at all costs. Dishonesty and deceit are among the reasons that citizens are loosing confidence in their government. Credibility is lost when truth is replaced with a twisted "spin".

In the adult business and government world, integrity is highly valued and refers to employers and employees who are honest and trust worthy. They are role models that can be trusted in all matters. If honesty and integrity are virtues that are appreciated and expected of children, then it seems reasonable for politicians, community workers, teachers and family members to also practice honesty in their decisions and in their speaking. In order to preserve integrity in the business and political world, honesty must prevail. Honor is a result of trust and honesty.

Building trust with our allies is important for international trust. Our allies will never trust us if we lie. Politicians realize that children look to them as role models and their behavior must be honest so that they can be trusted.

SOCIETY'S STORIES: Some people feel it is okay to lie because the outcome is their desired outcome. Recently, a Senate leader was confronted with an untrue statement he made regarding a candidate's failure to pay income taxes. When asked about this he did not apologize, he merely stated: "We won the election, didn't we." These half-truths and spins are dishonest and greatly disturb teachers who are trying to instill honesty and integrity into the hearts and souls of children. Politicians, always remember, someone may be watching you

The American people were certainly deceived when the Affordable Care Act was passed in 2011. It was later revealed that an economist and Presidential advisor, on many occasions before the passage of the ACA, referred to the American people as "stupid" for falling for the lies. The Senators and Members of the House might also be considered "stupid" because they did not do their job in representing the people and passed a bill before it was read. It has been more recently discussed that the federal government was "not fully forthcoming" when the Affordable Care Act was presented and passed. Politicians, who were in favor or the ACA, lied when they promised that health care would be more assessable and affordable. These statements were not honest and truthful and certainly have created a headache and heartache for many citizens. It is evident that the people of the United States have been blindsided by some of the promises made and also some of the restrictions that are found in the law. This is costing many thousands of dollars of hard earned money. (Some say just the enrollment process has cost each taxpayer $12,000.)

QUESTIONS FOR SOCIETY: Is the Affordable Care Act a lie or just deceitful? Are political answers like: "I don't remember it", or "What difference does it make?" or "We won the election, didn't we?" really acceptable in the political world?

Honesty and Citizenship

Illegal immigration is a call for honesty. Our immigration system is broken when we have over twelve million people living in the United States without legal status and our government is looking the other way. (Some say it is as many as twenty million.) When visitors come to the United States without legal documentation and/or overstay their visas, they are not being honest.

Illegal immigrants lie when they are offered incentives to use entitlement programs and the privileges of democracy. Many do not pay taxes and yet they do not hesitate to enroll their children in the public schools and use the hospital emergency rooms for childbirth and family health care. Some illegal immigrants disobey laws and flee to sanctuary cities. This abuse of laws encourages further breaking of the laws and punishes law-abiding citizens. When laws are not enforced, the government is enabling dishonesty.

SOCIETY'S STORY: As of November 2012, it was reported that more than 4.3 million people were waiting in line to get family-sponsored green cards. If they play by the rules, endless paperwork, exorbitant attorney fees and unconscionable waits will be in their future. Some will need to wait for years for their "green card". Meanwhile, President Obama wants to give many illegal immigrants legal status by the "power of the pen". This action is not only unfair to people who have legally applied for citizenship, it is also illegal. When undocumented immigrants come into the country illegally, they are not only disobeying the laws of the country, they are being dishonest.

MY INTERNATIONAL STORY: In 1978, my husbands company transferred our family to Tokyo, Japan. We packed up our three children and awaited an adventure into a new culture. We were required to possess a "green card", went to the government office for finger printing and background checks, obtained a drivers license and fulfilled the requirements of working and living in Japan. We knew we could be asked at any time for our "green card" and carried it with us at all times. We knew we were not allowed to vote. Later we learned that my husband had been chosen for this assignment because of his integrity. This was an important lesson for our children because they also had to uphold the integrity of their family and also their country. They also learned the importance of obeying the rules of another country.

QUESTIONS FOR SOCIETY: Can we trust undocumented immigrants to become responsible citizens? Are we fair to legal immigrants when the illegal are allowed to skip the necessary requirements to citizenship?

6. Fairness

This chapter is dedicated to all coaches and sports personnel who value fairness both on and off the field. It is also dedicated to the Justices on the Supreme Court and all of the judges in the courts of law who understand The Constitution and practice fairness. Our children are watching you and relying on you as role models.

When behavior is offensive, don't look the other way.
No double standards in the classroom. We demand only fair play.
We need coaches who are fair and Justices, too.
Schools need to be fair in all that they do.
Fairness is vital when building character in children.

The voice of my mother: "Life is not always fair."

Quote: "It is interesting that when consistent fairness is practiced in the classroom, parents are in agreement until the teacher corrects their child---then it is not fair and the teacher is "picking on" their child." Anonymous

Fairness in Childhood

Understanding the difference between equality and fairness develops character.

Being fair does not always mean that everyone is created equally. Each person has a personality, different physical features, and different abilities. Some students have a greater ability to understand many different languages and are linguists. Others are math and science oriented. Discovering areas of excellence makes each person unique and distinguishes one person from another.

For some, the differences in capabilities may seem unfair. Individual differences are a reality of life. Fortunately, students generally love to learn in areas that hold their interest and excite them. Appreciating the different qualities of each individual will promote fairness on the streets, in the home, in the school and in the workplace. Celebrating the talents of others will produce an atmosphere of unity and co-operation. Recognizing the difference in capabilities and encouraging progress is a skill that is required of a classroom teacher.

Not everyone is born with a 'silver spoon' in the mouth. Students come from rich families and poor families. They come from families that value quality education and families that do not. Not all families can afford to send their child to a private school. Not every parent wants their child attending a church related school. Not every student has a parent who has the time or wants to put the effort into home schooling. Charter schools are not available in every community. Some public schools produce students who are better educated than others. Some students are raised with the American culture in their DNA; others are not. Some understand the importance of good manners; others do not. The list goes on.

Most teachers practice fairness in every way possible. Grades in school are often not fair. One student may put as much effort into a project as another person but the end results are not the same. No matter how hard a teacher tries to be fair there will always be some student who gets a good grade while others may not. Although some choices may seem unfair, all students in every school community have the responsibility of making the environment as respectful and principled as possible so true learning can take place. Most teachers do everything within their power to practice fairness; however, the home environment may outweigh the fairness of the teacher.

When students whine about unfairness, it is best to ask them if they have invested their time in meaningful learning, have they set goals and invested energy into attaining their goals, have they persevered when they met with adversity, have they developed the kind of social skills that encourage friendship? Have they allowed substance abuse to take over their logical thinking, have they been fair to their fellow students, do they have a moral code that makes a good citizen, have they put their very best effort into every thing they do? Many times students want instant gratification and do not think of the consequences that result from minimum effort. Until a student has invested his academic, social and moral skills into every area of his learning, there should be no whining about unfairness. Fairness can be in the eyes of the beholder.

Coaches of youth sports, college coaches, and professional sport coaches specialize in fairness. They practice fairness in the way they treat their players, fairness to the other team, and fairness in playing the game by using common rules and regulations. When coaches fail to provide a positive role model for their players and the players are out of control, it can be said: "the coach lost the locker room."

In sports, we often hear of "participation trophies". Everyone who participated in the event is rewarded in the same way. Competition has been taken out of the equation and the difference in ability does not come into play. As children mature, they realize that there is a difference in ability and also a difference in the effort that is put into the game. Older youth often want to compete and still seek fairness. They no longer need "participation trophies" for motivation.

Everyone has experienced some amount of unfairness. "Life is not fair" is a phrase I often heard from my parents when I wanted something that we could not afford.

SOCIETY'S STORIES: A young twelve year old took a timing device to school. He had created it at home and was anxious to share this recent invention with his teachers. He took the device to his English teacher and she followed the federal guidelines "if you see something; say something". She took the devise and the child to the school office; the police were called to investigate. The young boy and his timing device were escorted to the police station where it was determined that the device was harmless---end of story. Not so fast, the parents became involved and declared that the school was not fair and did not appreciate his ingenuity. Politics became involved and he was invited to the White House. More recently, it was reported that the family was filing a lawsuit against the school and community.

Case number two: A young second grade child took bites out of a "pop tart" to carve the shape of a gun. A teacher took the young man to the office with the "gun" because weapons were not allowed on school property. The young second grader was expelled from school for a few days because he had disobeyed the rule of no weapons on the school site.

AUTHOR COMMENTS: In either case, the teacher was being very watchful and accepting the responsibility of keeping the school safe. The teachers were attempting to be fair to all of the students. The younger child was punished for his creative carving. The twelve year old was rewarded with a trip to the White House. There is no question that schools need creative minds. I personally would have been much more impressed if the older student had written an essay for his English teacher and described the wonderful invention. He could also have asked permission of his science teacher to bring it into the school. If fairness is to prevail in the public schools, everyone must practice fairness. Teachers often feel helpless when they attempt to be fair to all.

MY SCHOOL STORY: It was my first year of teaching. I was assigned to a first grade classroom. In this classroom was a set of identical twin boys. Although these young boys looked alike, their academic ability in reading was quite difficult. "Jack" caught on very quickly and "Joe", struggled to become a fluent reader. It was time for report cards and "Jack" received a C and "Joe" received an A. (At least that is what the report card said.) In the evening, I received a call from a very understanding father. He informed me that I had perhaps given the wrong grade to the wrong child. Feeling that I could not have possibly made such an obvious error, I asked that the boys return to school the following day with their report cards in hand. Yes, I had made a very obvious and unforgiveable error. I gently spoke with the boys and we talked about fairness from a six-year-old frame of mind. To this day, I am deeply sorry for such a senseless mistake; but, am also grateful to both boys and their father for understanding fairness. I am also grateful that I had the opportunity to correct my error.

QUESTION FOR SOCIETY: Is it fair for the students who do their homework every evening and attend school on a regular basis to receive the same grade as students who do not attend school on a regular basis and do not do homework?

Fairness is Justice

"Believing a person deserves a defense is not the same as doing everything in your power to get him off scot-free." (Bruce, p. 271)

"Injustice anywhere is a threat to justice everywhere." Martin Luther King, Jr.

Everyone wants to be treated fairly. Prejudice, entitlements, double standards are all examples of political unfairness. It is not fair to those who work hard to achieve their goals while others do not work hard and feel entitled. It is unfair when someone's religion, race, gender or political preference interferes with his fair chance for success. Unfairness is practiced when the government has different laws for immigrants and other cultural differences. When the government picks winners and losers, fairness is not practiced. Laws become meaningless and inconsistent when fairness is not practiced.

If fairness is practiced to its fullest extent, there must also be justice. The judicial system in the United States is designed to promote fairness. A fair and honest judge must have a clear understanding of right and wrong. He will also remove any emotional attachment. When justice is fair, there is neither a double standard nor any social or political favors. When citizens and visitors disobey a law, there must be consequences. Once the evidence has been presented, the decision for punishment or acquittal should be fair and just. Fairness places huge responsibility on our courts and judges.

SOCIETY'S STORY: In Baltimore and in many other cities, young people demonstrate in the streets in the name of social justice. Rioting and looting often result. Even when there is disagreement with law enforcement officers, justice must prevail in the courts of law. Justice can only be accomplished when all the facts are available. The jury is still out regarding which group of young people will prevail (the lawless or the lawful). Baltimore and every other community, the young children of America are watching you.

QUESTIONS FOR SOCIETY: Is it fair that someone who does not drink, smoke, take drugs pay for the health care of someone who lives a careless life? Is there a difference between "man created fairness" and "true fairness?"

7. Positive Attitude

This chapter is a tribute to everyone who inspires others to be the very best that he/she can be---especially teachers, military men and women and law enforcement officers. A positive attitude brings inspiration and courage to others.

A positive attitude sure matters. Always think that you can.
Set realistic goals and make only reasonable demands.
Be the best that you can be; put arrogance aside.
Be humble, have hope, let courage be your guide.
A positive attitude is critical for building character in children.

Fredrick Langbridge: "Two men look out through the same bars; one sees mud, and one sees stars."

Anonymous: "Exchange negative attitudes with positive ones, replacing anger with compassion, arrogance with humility and stress with serenity can bring peace to any situation."

One of the goals of a quality teacher is to instill a positive attitude in the heart of every student.

How often has a teacher stood before his/her class and looked at a field of angry or defiant faces? No amount of knowledge or preparation can reach the minds of students if their attitude is tainted with anger and an unwillingness to learn. Some of these students may have missed some of the important "building blocks" and are therefore unprepared to move forward. Others may live in poverty and see no future. Still others may be victims of bullying or drug abuse. Many students come to school with "heavy baggage" and a less than desirable attitude. A positive attitude toward learning gives students hope to achieve; hope to rise above their plight; hope for the future.

The attitude of the students, teachers and families affects the learning environment in the school and the success of the students. When families complain about a teacher, are unhappy with a situation and relate this to their children, this attitude is often reflected in the student's attitude toward school.

Families who have a positive attitude believe their children can achieve academically. When students achieve, they personally benefit and no longer feel the need to depend on society for their very existence. Once success is realized, self-esteem and self-confidence replaces the negative attitude. A perfect world would be for all students to come to school ready and willing to learn. This can only be achieved with the positive outlook of families, students and teachers. It is important to always think like the *Little Engine that could*---"I think I can, I know I can."

Teachers must have a positive attitude when there is disrespect and undisciplined behavior in the classroom. It takes courage to stand up for principles and virtues. It takes courage to step outside the box and stand up for what is right. It also takes courage and a positive attitude for teachers to step forward and demand respect and co-operation from families who have moral principles that are counter productive to student learning. It takes a positive attitude to find the best in each student in order to gain respect. It takes a positive attitude to keep pushing forward.

Some students have lost hope because they do not have goals or have been unsuccessful in reaching their goals. Other students do not realize that they should have goals. Students must understand the importance of setting realistic goals that match their ambitions and talents. It is important to always put the best effort into whatever challenges are faced and choose realistic goals with a positive attitude. Setting and meeting realistic goals can be transforming in a child's life and gives the child hope.

MY STORY: When I was in high school, I wanted to play basketball. I made the team but being only five feet tall, I was given a defensive position and was limited to the defensive half of the court. Needless to say, there was no way that I could score at half court. As I neared high school graduation, I had thought of becoming an airline stewardess. This dream was also dampened when I found out that no one less than 5 feet 3 inches need apply. Consequently, I put on my high heels, headed off to college, decided to major in elementary education and become a teacher. My high school advisor discouraged this decision and said I would never graduate from college. I was determined. I did not want to be just any teacher. I wanted to be the best teacher I could be. I wanted to be a positive role model for my students and I continued to learn from my mentors everyday. Perhaps my first two goals and expectations were disappointing. They were also unrealistic because of my physical development. I decided to face my physical limitations and move on. Today I continue to be a life-long learner.

Moral of the story: Sometimes a positive attitude requires a change of goals and expectations.

QUESTIONS FOR SOCIETY: It has been reported that one in five students won't graduate from high school and in major cities; half of the students won't get a high school diploma. Are these statistics a result of mediocre schools or are the students victims of apathy, poor attitude and non-attendance?

Myrna J. Sanner

Positive Attitude and Courage

Aristotle: "We become brave by doing brave acts."

There are no braver citizens than the men and women who serve in our military to defend the freedoms that we enjoy. These young men and women take many risks while defending their country. They are willing to take this risk because they want a better life for all people. Their attitude reflects hope for the future for all mankind---foreign and domestic.

Cries of "police brutality" have invaded the law enforcement profession. These men and women display courage and have a positive attitude in spite of the adversity. They return to work every day and continue to defend the rights of those who wish to live in a free and safe society.

Perhaps all young people should be required to spend a year to two helping others, leading a disciplined life and helping enforce the laws. They might then have greater appreciation and respect for the benefits of rights, liberty and freedom. Society will benefit from their service and they will have contributed to the "life, liberty and pursuit of happiness" of others.

QUESTION FOR SOCIETY: Would the young people living in the United States have a more positive attitude toward the rights and responsibilities if they were required to give a year or two serving their country and the citizens who are less fortunate?

8. Effective Communication

This chapter is dedicated to all of the legal immigrants who have worked so hard to learn the English language so they can communicate and assimilate into the American culture. This chapter is also dedicated to TV and radio news commentators, to the newspaper correspondents, who practice outstanding communication skills and are outstanding role models for children.

**Communication is about English; using proper grammar, too.
It's about enunciating clearly and listening too.
It is putting away social media and speaking the truth.
It is sharing a common language, and educating our youth
Effective communication is fundamental for building character in children.**

For many years, English has been considered the universal language. More books are produced in English than in any other language. English is our common language and the ability to speak English is perhaps the most important social skill for any one living in the United States. Speaking the truth, speaking fluently in the English language with correctness and integrity, and listening to the viewpoints of others are imperative for communication.

The Ability to Communicate is a Social Skill

After the family, teachers have the primary responsibility of making certain that all children are literate in English. The ability to read, write and speak intelligently is perhaps the most important goal of education. Schools in the United States are committed to the literacy since literacy can provide the pathway to future employment and the ability to attend college. Much of the poor grammar and illiteracy is due to the lack of practice in an enriched English-speaking environment. If a student does not have the desire to learn English, the teacher's time is wasted.

Immigrants who come to the United States are at a great disadvantage if they cannot speak and understand English. The ability to communicate and to understand rules and laws are reasons that the US government requires some knowledge of English on the citizenship test. If a citizen or an immigrant cannot speak and read English, they may not have an understanding of the universal laws, common language and the moral principles that exemplify the American culture. This is also the reason that that there is generally a five-year waiting period before citizenship is granted.

Verbal communication demands both listening and speaking. Verbal communication is perhaps most effective when two or more people are engaged in face-to-face conversation. Many students want a teacher who listens to his learning and concerns---students want feedback. Many people want a physician who listens---patients want feedback. Many clients want a lawyer who will listen to their side of the story. Everyone wants a listener. The ability to communicate in person with eye contact and body language can promote understanding. I recently heard of a child who asked his mother to "listen with your eyes".

Poor grammar and illiteracy are usually not the fault of the schools since every school teaches proper English grammar and writing skills for thirteen years. If the child does not learn to read and speak English sometime during the elementary school years, high school academic achievement (notice: I did not say graduation) is out of reach to say nothing of attending college. In order to eradicate poverty, elementary schools in the United States must concentrate their effort on teaching children to read, write and speak in English. Verbal and written communication are essential in most jobs, schools, military and government occupations.

In the United States, anyone who cannot read, write and speak the English language is considered illiterate. Statistics tell us that illiteracy is the primary cause of poverty and a reason that many people remain unemployed. Therefore, illiteracy and poverty put the child at risk.

Responsible young people immigrating to the United States want to learn English as fast as they can so they can integrate into the American culture. Their parents should also share this desire.

In many communities schools are also committed to the English literacy of adults who are the caregivers and role models for children. Some adults resist learning the English language and do not want to integrate into the American culture. In some communities improper grammar can be heard in the workplace and on the streets. Resistance to learning the English language and speaking proper grammar limits the ability to gain employment and often keeps children from reaching their goals. It is the responsibility of the adults to use the literacy programs that are available so they might assist in preparing their children and themselves for being employable.

AUTHORS COMMENTS: The government often suggests the necessity of providing free community colleges for everyone. They feel that there are too many young people graduating from high school who are deficient in the art of listening, writing and speaking in English. It is my opinion that since public education is free for everyone between the ages of five and eighteen, there are ample opportunities for students to excel in the area of language arts before they graduate from high school. If students have not taken full advantage of the opportunity to learn English, they should continue to attend the public high schools or after school classes until they are literate. GED (General Education Development) certificates are offered and can be earned after school hours in the local high school. There is no excuse for the average student to not possess English-speaking skills by the time he/she exits high school. The opportunity is there; it must be accepted and appreciated.

Common Language

A common language is an essential bond of cohesion in a civilized nation and is necessary when integrating into the American culture. The ability to speak, write and understand English is perhaps the greatest social skill that unites the citizens of the United States. When members of a community do not share a common language, they will not understand each other. When people do not share a common language, they may not understand laws and rules. A common language is important when understanding the laws and the consequences that result from harming or offending others. It makes common sense that in order to communicate and function effectively with work associates, neighbors, friends, community and government leaders, a common language is necessary.

Communication can be speaking, writing or just listening. One-way communication is not really communicating---it is giving knowledge and opinions without feedback. Communication is a two way process and listening is just as vital as speaking. True communication cannot happen if both parties do not speak and understand the same language. When there is a lack of communication, there is also a lack of trust. The lack of trust encourages disrespect for adults in authority who are then accused of unfairness and prejudice. Communication provides an opportunity to express what we believe, what we feel and what we value. The Biblical Old Testament story of The Tower of Babel is an example of how quickly unity can be destroyed when every one speaks a different language.

A common language is needed in all schools. It is often heard that the ability to speak and write in English, with good grammar and proper spelling, is the number one asset that every employer desires when hiring an employee. It is also the number one asset that all teachers desire in their students. The desire and ability to communicate create understanding.

AUTHOR COMMENTS: The mass immigration of illegal children is one example of how political correctness has hampered the ability to have a common language. Teachers and principals are being asked to fulfill the government mandate of teaching English and making these children literate within two or three years. If all children have the right to attend any public school, those same children and families have the responsibility to make every effort possible to learn English.

LOST IN TRANSLATION: When our family lived in Japan, many of our neighbors had maids---some lived with the family and others came during the day. The story is that whatever the lady or man of the house requested, the maid would always reply "hi" which meant "yes" in Japanese. However, the lady of the house was never sure if this reply meant: "Yes, I hear you", "Yes, I understand what you are saying" or "Yes, I will do what you ask". Since there is no word for "no" in the Japanese language, all was lost in translation.

BOOK CONNECTION: Arthur M. Schlesinger, American historian, social critic, public intellectual and author of *The Disuniting of America: Reflections on a Multicultural Society,* frequently wrote about the importance of speaking and understanding the English language in the American culture.

Technology and Communication

Computers, i-phones, TV and all forms of technology play an important role in connecting the larger world. However, its overuse can be detrimental to the well being of others. Some users love the game of hating and enjoy saying hateful things because they are seemingly invisible. When technological communication is out of control, bullying, making fun of others, spreading false information, etc. become problems for society. In fact, some are suggesting that the Internet and social media are promoting a culture of hatred and sarcasm.

In the world of i-phones, texting, and computers, young people do not often engage in adult conversations. It has been estimated that the average young person, between the ages of six and twelve, spends about seven hours each day on the computer, in front of the TV, on i-phones, etc. Since young people of similar age should sleep an average

223

of eight hours each night, only nine hours remain for learning in school, communicating with parents, and taking care of life essentials.

The overuse of technology in the classroom can be detrimental to the education of students. Some teachers sit at their desk and flash worksheets, notes, etc. on the screen without verbally interacting with their students. Teachers may allow figures on the smart board to dance before the eyes of their students but are unaware of which students understand the material and which students need to be re-taught. The overuse of technology in the classroom limits the availability to communicate on a one-on-one basis. Technology also diminishes eye contact.

We may soon be living in a no-eye contact world. Social media often replaces one-on-one communication and invades the privacy of others. Social media allows students to express their own emotions and thoughts but does not allow an opportunity to listen to the thoughts of others. One-way communication is not really communicating---it is giving knowledge and directions without feedback. Communication is a two way process and listening is just as vital as speaking.

Unfortunately, social media has created an avenue for hurtful and rude comments. Hateful communication creates distrust. When people are not made accountable for their words, the self-esteem and safety of the victims is damaged. If people want the right to use social media to communicate, they must also accept the responsibility of using social media for appropriate and positive purposes.

Many parents have imposed an "electronic free zone" at their dinner table each evening. They want to understand the attitudes and feelings of their children. They want to discuss what went wrong during the day and what went right. This allows the young person to communicate his/her feelings and foster positive attitudes and values in the child.

TV personalities and especially the news commentators have a responsibility to tell the truth and to communicate in an intelligent and knowledgeable way. Everyday these "TV faces" visit millions of homes and are role models for children.

Communication and Profanity

The voice of my father: "When someone finds it necessary to use profanity, they have a very limited vocabulary."

Inappropriate language is quite common in the American culture. Profanity is not communication; it is an emotional reaction that is often mean and irreverent. People using profane language have not developed a vocabulary with sufficient words to express feelings of anger, disappointment, etc. Profane language often wishes harm on someone. Many students, especially high school students, have role models who encourage obscene language. They use profanity as part of their everyday vocabulary. Foul language is prohibited in many schools and it should be. The misuse of words and using profanity are totally unacceptable.

Many TV stations have a three second delay so that profane language can be bleeped out of the conversation. Some newscasters have been reprimanded and taken off the air for periods of time because of an improper word had been interjected into the conversation.

AUTHOR COMMENTS: The sole use of i-phones and i-pads creates a concern for preserving communication on a personal basis and for educating our youth. Young people often feel everything they need to know can be found on computes and TV. If non-educated youth and non-English speaking students feel they do not need teachers and schools, perhaps they should lower their expectations for citizenship and educate themselves. Then they can no longer blame the school and the teacher. If they are serious about learning, they will soon discover that the ability to communicate is essential for college attendance and nearly every occupation.

SOCIETY'S STORY: When President Obama announced that he wanted high-speed Internet service in ninety-nine percent of all schools in the United States, I spoke with teachers. The best and most ambitious teachers felt that high speed Internet service is one of the last items on the list. They would like more willing hands and more creative thinking assistants helping educate their students. Most teachers would prefer ninety-nine percent literacy and well behaved students.

MY STORY: During a recent trip to Washington DC, it was noted that school groups did not allow the students to have any electronic devices with them while in the public. On the other hand, while having dinner at a local restaurant, at a nearby table all family members were texting and not communicating with one another. Teenagers and adults are rude when texting and talking on a phone wile eating dinner. They are ignoring the company that has joined them.

QUESTIONS FOR SOCIETY: How can an employee, who cannot speak English, expect the same monetary reward as someone who has worked diligently to master the necessary literary skills? How have computers, face-book and other social media affected the learning of the English language and privacy?

9. Strong Work Ethic

This chapter is dedicated in loving memory to my hard working parents and in-laws. The education and success of my husband and myself can be credited to the perseverance and the work ethic of our ancestors. We are hoping to pass this work ethic on to their grandchildren and great grand children.

Complete your homework on time. Attend school every day.
Go above and beyond, learning the American way.
Show up at the job site, set goals just for you.
The oval or corner office will soon be waiting for you.
A strong work ethic is basic for building character in children.

Sign posted at Brother Rice High School in Bloomfield Hills, Michigan: "The difference between being good and being great is a little extra effort."

Ben Carson often talks about his mother who worked two jobs and long hours to provide for him and his brother. Carson grew up in poverty and became an outstanding physician and a candidate for President of the United States. As he grew up, he "found very little difference between people from the lower-middle class all the way to the upper echelons of the upper class in terms of financial values and belief in a strong work ethic".

Schools and a strong work ethic

Anonymous: "Sometimes it is important just to show up."

Almost all teachers realize the importance of being on the job everyday. Teachers, have the responsibility of being regular in attendance, being well prepared for the lessons, and arriving in the classroom with enthusiasm and competence. In fact, many teachers attempt to never miss a day so student learning can progress uninterrupted.

School attendance is especially important in the pre-school and elementary school because many of the skills taught in the first twelve years of a child's life are basic for all future learning. Some things must be memorized and stored in the brain---especially reading and math skills. Elementary students often need to be told how to do a task. If there are extensive gaps in the learning process, the child becomes confused and falls behind. The child may never catch up.

Just "showing up" at the school door creates student potential for academic learning. Many low achieving students are either late for school or think nothing of attending school on an irregular basis. Elementary teachers have experienced the tardiness of students who arrive late for school everyday, receive free breakfast and often begin to attend to their schoolwork when it is time for lunch. Some students leave one school and move to another and may miss many days of instruction while they are relocating. In some cases, children have been dropped at school and when asked their name, have no idea of who they are, let alone where they live. When they leave the classroom in the afternoon, the teacher may not know where they are going or if they will ever see them again.

Teachers realize that a strong work ethic and regular attendance gets positive academic results. Some students feel they are entitled to an education but refuse to devote quality time to learning. They may also feel that if they sporadically occupy a seat in a school, they will graduate and be able to find a great job.

It has often been said that school is a child's work. Learning requires not only hard work but also perseverance. Learning requires initiative and a willingness to learn. As children mature, they become more independent. They set their own goals and find answers to their questions. They are willing to put away the distractions of social media and concentrate on the work at hand. Teachers provide guidance to persevere and achieve these goals.

Advisors and teachers must also be careful not to discourage students from setting goals and attempting to be successful. Success does not usually come without hard work, initiative, ambition, and perseverance. Some students might think that teachers, families and communities have failed them. We might ask, are our students failing our schools or are the schools, families and communities failing our children?

MY SCHOOL STORY: I recently spoke with a high school English teacher who was teaching *Romeo and Juliet* (a required reading) using comic books. She said that there was no continuity in the learning since many students only attend class two or three days of the week. These students are neither punctual nor hard working.

MY OTHER SCHOOL STORY: There are middle schools teachers who have searched the halls, closets and restrooms for students who were dropped off at school but did not report to their assigned class. These students came to school but had no desire to learn. These students were found in broom closets, restrooms, and in lockers. The cost was high to the students because they were missing an opportunity for learning and also costly to the school because time was wasted when teachers found it necessary to play "hide and seek".

Initiative, ambition and perseverance

The voice of my father-in-law: "If you wait to be told what to do, you will be told what to do the rest of your life."

Quote: "The dictionary is the only place where 'success' comes before "work".

Nearly every poverty-to-success (rags to riches) story contains at least one chapter about initiative, ambition and perseverance. Some of the earliest emigrants from Ireland were required to live in slums and do manual labor to gain citizenship. Many of the emigrants from Germany cleared woodland and plains to establish farmland. Italian immigrants also did manual labor to gain respect and earn a livelihood on the East Coast. African slaves were brought to America against their will and worked hard in the fields of the south without pay. All of these immigrants were at the mercy or their masters or employers. Many of these immigrants persevered in spite of the way they were treated. They understood hard work and were the very people that strengthened the work force and made America great. They took the initiative to begin a task and follow it through to the end. These are the people who persevered and realized the American Dream.

Meeting the requirements of any job takes initiative. Some people want a desk job that only requires punching the keys of a computer or calculator. Some want jobs that require very little thinking. Many people do not want to do "grunt work".

Many manual labor jobs are referred to as a "job nobody wants". These are jobs outside the home that require manual labor. They are necessary to keep communities safe and clean. Many homemakers, both male and female, find a great deal of satisfaction in maintaining a clean home, preparing healthy meals for the family, providing clean clothing. All jobs are important and everyone should take pride in their work and respect the work of others.

There are generations of people who have learned that if they do nothing but whine and complain, everything will be done for them. They grow up with a sense of entitlement and rely on others to do their work for them. Their work ethic may be destroyed. Many may have lost their integrity, their job and ended up on welfare. Some cannot find employment because their former employers are reluctant to recommend them for other jobs. This attitude of entitlement is often passed on to their children. People who feel entitled will perhaps never achieve their goals nor gain financial stability.

A strong work ethic does not always result in great financial gain. Teachers, police officers, firemen, veterans and military personnel deal daily with the preservation of the health and safety of others. They are paid a pittance when compared to the enormous salaries of more popular and seemingly more important people. Many sport and entertainment personalities enjoy enormous salaries when compared to the average worker. Many businessmen are paid many times more than their staff. Some politicians might be added to the list of overpaid personnel. They have huge staffs paid by the government and many are well reimbursed for speeches they give after they leave office. They may receive three to four times the average salary of the taxpayers.

There is sometimes an unwillingness to work up through the ranks. As one executive put it "The young people do not only want my job, they also want my corner office." Success is rarely a result of laziness. Success requires continual education and hard work.

There is human dignity in work. Capitalism works very well for a highly motivated and energetic person. It does not work so well for citizens who are complacent and feel no need or desire to contribute to the well being of society. These unmotivated people have a sense of entitlement and want to enjoy the efforts of others.

AUTHOR COMMENTS: There is a political movement to provide free community college education for all young adults. This will add millions of dollars to the already high cost of education. Many people who support this action have also suggested that students be passed from grade to grade before they can read, write and do math. In other words, these young people feel that they need more time to learn the basic skills. They feel they are entitled to spend more tax money on education. They may have attended school but did not take advantage of the opportunity to learn. Really? If students have not been successful in high school, they might flip hamburgers for a while or join one of our armed services, if they qualify. They would soon learn the importance of hard work.

SOCIETY'S STORY: The life story of the late Dave Thomas, founder of the Wendy's fast food chain, comes to mind when talking about going "from rags to riches" and perseverance. Dave was an orphan and never gave up on his dream of providing fast food service for millions of Americans. He was also a very generous man and never forgot about caring for others. His values are great lessons for young children. During a recent visit to Wendy's, I read that there are over 100,000 homeless children waiting for permanent homes. The Wendy's Foundation and restaurants continue to find permanent homes for homeless children.

MY STORY: As a senior in high school, I decided that I wanted to be a teacher. My high school advisor and Latin teacher (who is now deceased) advised me that there was no way that I could ever graduate from college. I decided to apply and was accepted. The rest is history. When I was of college age more that half of my classmates worked during the summer and/or had part time jobs while in school. This was the norm rather than the exception. At the age of eighteen, we were able and willing to work hard to achieve our life goals. We did not expect the government to pay our way or make excuses for our lack of learning.

Moral of the story: Determination, ambition and initiative demonstrate a strong work ethic that will reap positive results.

QUESTIONS FOR SOCIETY: Should tax payers pay for the additional education required to remediate the students who have put little or no effort into their own education? Should students be promoted and given diplomas for attendance but not for knowledge acquired?

10. Knowledge, Wisdom and Common Sense

This chapter is dedicated to schools that impart knowledge, homes where experience brings wisdom, and streets where common sense prevails.

Knowledge

"We must remember that intelligence is not enough. Intelligence plus character; that is the goal of true education." (Bennett, *The Educated Child*, p. 523).

When knowledge is stored and wisdom is gained
Common sense always rules when the mind is well trained.
Artificial intelligence gives answers when knowledge is in vain.
But the wisest human knowledge is stored in the brain.
Knowledge is important for building character in children.

The voice of my father: "You can lead a donkey to the trough but you can't make him drink."

Knowledge is most often gained through education. Gaining knowledge or intelligence is a key reason for attending school. People who have a thirst for knowledge do not attend school because it is a requirement; they attend school because they want to know more about a particular subject and they want to learn. The more knowledgeable one is, the more capable he is in completing tasks and understanding basic information. Knowledge is necessary before one is able to get a job, attend college or join the military service. Most knowledgeable students are life long learners.

Knowledge is the ability to retain facts and store them in the brain for future application. People need basic knowledge to reflect on and apply information they already know. Knowledge is putting basic skills into use. Therefore, knowledgeable children need the basic building blocks of language arts and math in place before future learning can take place. This broad base of built-in knowledge will allow for immediate recall, which is more effective and faster than calling out to Google. Children need basic knowledge to complete actual tasks that are associated with critical thinking and solving problems. These tasks require higher thinking skills.

No child can think critically or conceptually about U.S. history, without the knowledge of certain historical events. Knowledge of The Constitution is necessary before students can understand the importance of the Bill of Rights and patriotism. Knowledge of factual information is necessary when drawing conclusions about an event in history or a scientific experiment. Knowledge is the ability to use math to balance a budget and use English to communicate. Without basic information, everything that is left is an uninformed opinion.

Some people feel that storing knowledge is not as important as it used to be because i-phones, i-pads, the Internet, and other technological devices allow immediate access to information. Information is available in schools, at home, in the work place, and everywhere with the flip of a wrist or the tip of a finger. Many people feel that the ability to assess all available information will make them knowledgeable. Knowledge is required to put accessed information to use. In truth, technology often encourages instant gratification without the use of mental faculties.

I was fascinated by the word, "mindfulness" as the ability to focus and concentrate on one thing at a time. Knowledge might also be the ability to concentrate and focus. Electronic devices, TV, i-phones, i-pads, etc., are often distractions that interrupt the ability to concentrate. When people become too involved in the social world, they often have very little knowledge about what is happening in the real world. It may be necessary to block out social media and become more mindful in order to become knowledgeable of the real world. In truth, relying too heavily on technology may encourage mental laziness and diminish humanity.

When relying too heavily on technology, humanity may suffer. The truly intelligent person is deeply humanistic and posses qualities such as being affectionate, industrious, and likeable. Only humans can learn behavior skills, have emotional capacities and moral intuitions.

The opposite of being intelligent is being ignorant. Ignorance is sometimes due to laziness. It can also be a result of misinformation and the lack of knowledge and wisdom. Ignorance can also be the result of not wanting to learn and persevere.

QUESTIONS FOR SOCIETY: How many students have the ability to block out all social media for hours? Could students acquire more knowledge if they would only concentrate on the information being taught?

Wisdom

The Serenity Prayer: "God grant me the serenity to accept the things I cannot change, the courage to change the things I can, and the wisdom to know the difference."

Many people use wisdom and knowledge interchangeably. Knowledge is the accumulation of facts. Wisdom comes after knowledge and combines knowledge with experience. Wisdom is a more thoughtful process and more proactive. Wisdom follows applied knowledge.

Wisdom is perhaps the most important ingredient when undertaking a successful task. It is evaluating all of the options and making an informed decision. Wisdom comes with understanding and helps discern what action might be pursued. Wisdom teaches us not to travel the same path again when some past event has not been successful.

Common Sense

Einstein: "The definition of insanity is doing the same thing over and over again and expecting different results."

There is a fine line between wisdom and common sense. Once wisdom is gained, common sense takes over. Many young people have not accumulated enough knowledge and wisdom to make common sense decisions. Common sense decisions take maturity and are based on past experiences. Common sense allows one to act appropriately and make informed decisions. In a free society there is a need to practice common sense regarding laws, language, and academics.

Common sense requires thinking before speaking and acting. Common sense is the ability to immediately assess a situation and make a decision that agrees with the inner conscience. Common sense is making good judgments of what is right and wrong. Common sense experiences help youth continue to gain knowledge and wisdom. Common sense is needed to make appropriate and intelligent decisions.

AUTHOR COMMENTS: When only registered citizens are allowed to vote and only one vote is allowed for every person, common sense tells us that voter identification might be needed at polling places. It is common sense to have a national language where everyone can understand, speak and communicate. Common sense also tells us that when we, as a united nation, agree on common moral principles our country will be a safer place to live. It is only common sense that the government cannot continue to have a national debt of trillions of dollars without bankrupting the country. It is common sense that the availability of monetary resources is not a "bottomless pit". It is common sense to live within financial means.

SOCIETY'S STORY: It was reported that students at George Washington University passed a petition to fellow students suggesting an even exchange of one United States Citizen for every undocumented illegal immigrant. More than 2/3 of the students signed the petition. How many of these students would actually like to be exchanged for an undocumented immigrant? Either the students did not read the petition or they lacked common sense. Could it be that when someone makes emotional rather than rational decisions, they many lack common sense?

MY STORY: In order to gain knowledge, many children and young adults go through the process of attending kindergarten; elementary school, high school and some even choose a college education. I attended all of these schools to gain knowledge. It was not until I began to teach that I put all of this knowledge into practice. Each year, as I taught my students, I gained wisdom about the curriculum, student achievement, behavior expectations, etc. Later, I gained additional knowledge when receiving a graduate degree and also completed National Board Certification. Teaching and going to graduate school became easy because I could build on my base knowledge.

I have taken no courses in parenting or grand parenting. I often rely on the knowledge and wisdom of my parents and other adults to help me through the process of rearing children. I continue to gain knowledge and wisdom; however, today, most of my decisions are based on common sense---my previous experiences and wisdom.

BOOK CONNECTION: *Things That Matter* by Charles Krauthammer, shares some wonderful examples of how knowledge can be the forerunner of wisdom and common sense.

Below are some common sense applications in life:

What goes up must come down, (law of physics)

Anything on line or in cyber space is public knowledge to all (experience IRS, NSA)

If laws are not enforced, more crimes will be committed (number of people in jail)

If you do not attend school, you will not be educated (the inability to find employment)

If you want to be trusted, you must be honest in all things (life experience)

You cannot pay your bills without putting money into an account (bounced checks)

You cannot be healthy if drugs are abused (number of people who need rehabilitation)

You cannot get a job if you are not willing to work (nobody wants a lazy employee)

You cannot live in cleanliness unless you clean (messes must be cleaned up)

You cannot communicate unless without a common language (must understand others)

You cannot expect life necessities unless you are willing to work (there are no free lunches)

If you don't maintain your home, it will fall apart (home ownership is hard work)

If at first you don't succeed, try; try again (never give up---there is light at the end of the tunnel)

Artificial Intelligence

QUOTE: "Man is not rewarded for having brains, but for using them."

David Brooks, noted columnist, recently referred to AI (Artificial Intelligence) because so much knowledge is stored on electronic devices and not in the human brain.

Artificial intelligence is becoming more common every day. The ability to access information is evident when observing the public. Everyone is in touch---on the streets, in the cabs, in the schools, and in restaurants. Technology is everywhere. Students have knowledge at the tip of their finger or the stroke of their thumb. Swiping an i-pad or i-phone or pressing the key of a computer can retrieve almost any information. The use of a computer provides immediate gratification to find all answers. However, many students do not want to spend the necessary time to learn and store knowledge.

Technology has become indispensible in the lives of the young. There is a "push" for more technology in the schools, in the government, in businesses, and on the streets. Every one is looking for more apps to experience instant gratification. As technology becomes a part of everyday life, it seems that stored knowledge is diminishing. This might be one reason for the decline in SAT and ACT (leading college admissions tests) scores. This might a reason that many students rely on artificial intelligence rather than stored knowledge. As technology becomes the sole source of information, stored knowledge may soon disappear.

AUTHOR COMMENTS: With "artificial intelligence" becoming more prevalent, perhaps the educational goal of President Obama and the Department of Education, having access to high speed Internet in every school, should be re-examined. Common sense tells us that if we want educated children, perhaps we should invest money in teachers, who improve literary intelligence and creative intelligence, rather than in computers that become obsolete in less than three years. Having stored knowledge is more important than knowing about the greatest golfer, rock star, etc. It is more important than knowing what someone had for breakfast or what social activity was recently attended.

QUSSTIONS FOR SOCIETY: What would happen if we had a cyber attack that lasted a period of time? Would we still have knowledgeable people or would we experience the "dumbest generation"?

11. Compassion

This chapter is dedicated to the doctors, nurses, and caregivers who daily show compassion by their thoughts, words and deeds. They are the citizens that work long hours, many times without pay, to assure that health care is available to our very youngest and oldest citizens.

Give of yourself---time, talents, and treasure.
When showing compassion, give without measure.
Have empathy for others; show sympathy, too
Show kindness and caring, stand in another's shoe.
Compassion is critical for building character in children.

Compassion is a feeling and an emotion. Compassion is the sympathetic consciousness of others' distress, together with the desire to alleviate it. True compassion is becoming involved in the emotions and respecting the feelings of others. It is active and does not wait for others to act. It is consistent and never walks away. Compassion is a virtue that requires sharing and trust. True compassion is being generous with compliments, actions and support. Compassion is about giving and expecting nothing in return. It is giving of ones self--- time, talent, and treasures. Compassion includes having a kind heart and caring about others. Compassion builds character.

Empathy and sympathy are emotional forms of compassion and create a feeling of caring and unity. Empathy is the ability to understand the reality of the inner life of someone else---the emotions, as well as external circumstances. Empathy is the ability to walk in the shoes of another

In the elementary classroom, kindness and caring are words that are associated with compassion. Administrators, counselors and teachers, when teaching positive behavior and moral principles to children, often use these words. They are attributes that promote a feeling of unity in a classroom.

In a child's world, words like "I'm Sorry" show remorse and are encouraged in the schools when someone has wronged another. A responsible teacher speaks to the offender and explains how to become more compassionate. Looking the other way and hoping for positive results is not realistic. When possible, it is important to make the wrong, right. Compassion has a giver and a receiver.

Compassion is an emotion. Governments are not capable of having feelings of empathy and sympathy. The government cannot show love and compassion because these are feelings. The government may want a different outcome by giving away entitlements and money but this is not a feeling. When the United States government attempts to be all things to all people, both at home and abroad, it often asks for more money for entitlement programs. Money and entitlements without human understanding are often misused and provide little benefit. When humans give, they give with compassion and feeling.

AUTHOR COMMENTS: Each year the government shares its financial resources with hundreds of countries to improve their social, economic and physical conditions. When this money is not monitored, it often falls in the hands of those who practice illegal activities and politicians who pad their personal pockets. Foreign governments often take advantage, not only of their children, but the generosity of the American people when they do not use the assistance for the intended purpose

MY STORY: The day I returned from Thanksgiving break, I received word that a dog had mulled one of my students while he was out of town celebrating Thanksgiving. He had 22 stitches in his head from the injury. Because of the possibility of an infection, he would not be allowed to return to school for at least two weeks. My initial concern was for his health and all of the students made "get well" cards for him. I also contacted the family to determine his ability to receive assignments to keep him abreast with the academic learning. It was arranged that each day after school, I would deliver his work for the day and also pick up any completed work. In this manner, I could be in touch with his learning and help him stay current with the academic program. The "get well" notes and the daily visits were appreciated. When spring conferences arrived, his father and mother both attended conferences and informed me that the family had been transferred to another location. The father particularly wanted to express his thanks to the class and me for the compassion we had shown his son. For me the beauty of the story is that at the time I did not know that the father would become NFL coach of the year and the son would become a physician. Yes, compassion is active and does not wait for others to act. It is consistent and never walks away.

Thank you coach for sharing your kindness and gratitude. You will always be a winner.

MY INTERNATIONAL STORY: There are many non-profit organizations that provide education and financial support for children throughout the world. They encourage adults to adopt a child who is living in poverty. By donating money and corresponding on a regular basis, these young children can realize their educational goals and develop a relationship with someone who cares about them. One reason that many of these organizations are so effective is that the well-monitored funds go directly to the people in need. The local government is not involved.

SOCIETY'S STORY: While in the United States, Pope Francis often spoke of the necessity of having compassion for others. Compassion plays a role in caring for the poor and elderly. Compassion reaches out to children who are suffering and people who are persecuted. Compassion is about giving---it is not about receiving or greed.

QUESTION FOR SOCIETY: How do we build a generation of students who show compassion and love? Can any government show compassion?

12. Love and Friendship

This chapter is dedicated to everyone who loves their neighbors as themselves. It is also dedicated to all volunteers and members of Young Life who give so generously of their time, resources and talents to those who need mercy and love. There is no other country on the planet where people have been so blessed and in return give so much to their fellowmen---both at home and throughout the world.

Put love in your friendships. Fairness is a must.
There is nothing more faithful than a friend you can trust.
Nurture those friendships; they cannot be replaced
Peace goes beyond, sex, religion or race.
Love and friendship are obligatory for building character in children.

Maya Angelou: "I've learned that people will forget what you said, people will forget what you did, but people never forget how you made them feel."

I would like to open this chapter on love and friendship with a quote by Bruce B. Wilmer. It is on a plaque that rests in my study. It was given to me over 25 years ago by one of my third grade students. Pete, this one is for you:

You're Special to Me by Bruce B. Wilmer

You're special to me---You're someone I trust.
I treasure the topics that we have discussed.
I'm thankful for times you have summoned a smile.
I'm grateful our paths have converged for a while.
I'm pleased by each confidence you have displayed.
I cherish those moments you've sought to persuade.
I'm touched by the gestures of kindness you've shown.
I've noticed how fast, all our hours have flown.

500AD Chinese Proverb: "All the children who are held and loved will know how to love others. Spread these virtues through the world, nothing more need be done."

When you were growing up, who loved you? Hopefully, the answer will be "my mother and father". An answer to that question can be very revealing when working with young people who have been neglected or come from dysfunctional homes. There are many people in a young person's life that can also provide nurturing love. It might be a grandparent, an uncle or an aunt; a sibling, a friend, a community worker or it might just be a special teacher who took a special interest. It might also be community volunteer who has shown love and kindness. Teachers and community helpers can make a difference but caring families can make an even bigger difference.

The Bible teachers "love your neighbor as yourself". Love is practiced in nearly every religion and is a virtue that is fundamental to The Constitution and The Ten Commandments. People who love their fellowmen are kind and caring. They always do what is best for others and have no selfish desires. Love, like compassion, is giving generosity of time talent and treasure to others. Love overshadows all.

Teachers and community workers give generously with a loving heart. They realize that there may be children in their class who have not been loved since birth. They look for the good in each individual and often give freely of their time for academic, social and emotional counseling. They help young people make decisions between what is right and wrong, between love and hate, honesty and lying, fairness and bullying, using drugs and refraining, hard work and laziness, positive attitude and defeat, respect and rudeness, responsibility and blame, arrogance and humility, fairness and prejudice, etc. They are outstanding role models and look for that special child who is in need of extra care and kindness.

Nelson Mandela: "People must learn to hate, and if they can learn to hate, they can be taught to love."

Hate is the opposite of love. There is no room in the American culture for hatred, anger and violence. These characteristics are not the part of any religion and certainly not a part of any civilized society. Hatred is more than race, guns and mental health. Hatred is a disease of the heart and soul. Any massacre, whether in Charleston, South Carolina, Sandy Hook, Connecticut, or Columbine High School in Colorado, must qualify as a "hate crime". Love was definitely missing from the hearts of those who committed these brutal crimes.

Some young people have not yet found the value of each member of society and have learned to hate rather than love. Teachers, parents, volunteers and community workers can all participate in an intervention when a child displays the characteristics of hatred. When a student is disrespectful, verbally abusive, defiant and filled with hatred, teachers attempt to find the good in the student. They attempt to instill love and a moral conscience into the heart and soul to eradicate these negative behaviors. They know that by putting a filter on the actions, words and deeds that foster hatred, they can help the student live peacefully. Communities will never be safe until every person feels love in his heart. Peace and love will also provide unity in the community. Love must abide.

SOCIETY'S STORY: It is between the ages of 9 and 10 that children are most influential and can be indoctrinated with love or hate. Recent reports out of Syria found that ISIS is recruiting young children as young as 9 years old. They are teaching them brutal behavior. Certainly, these are crimes of hatred and terrorism. If we are going to indoctrinate our children let it be with love rather than hatred.

The Importance of Friends

"School systems throughout this great nation of ours are making sure every pupil has a computer and becomes proficient in computer skills...I wonder if schools shouldn't also make sure every kid has a friend and is proficient in nurturing friendships and intimate relationships." (The News-Press, Sunday April 12, 2015 "Technology may be our downfall" by Dan Warner)

Quote: "God evidently does not intend us all to be rich, or powerful, or great, but He does intend us all to be friends.

Bob Goff author of "*Love Does* "A friend knows what you need even before you ask. A friend doesn't just say things, a friend does." (Groff, p. 73)

Having friends is only half of the story. Being a friend is the other half of the story. It takes two people to form a bond of friendship. Friendship often rises out of mutual interests and common goals. Friendship is an expression of love, kindness, fidelity, acceptance, loyalty and generosity. Loyalty and friendship respect confidences and privacy. Loyalty is remaining faithful even when you disagree. Friends love each other and protect each other.

The choice of friends is critical for every child. Some troubled young people have made poor choices in their friendships. They have chosen friends who have allowed negative influences such as substance abuse, dishonesty, hatred, addiction to social media, violent movies and video games, lack of respect, lack of responsibility, a poor attitude, etc. to dominate their world. The influence of these friends may cause harm and lower self-esteem.

All children need friends---good friends that lift them up and understand. Children at the ages of 9 and 11 are very influential and can be taught to give compliments and help build self-confidence and self-esteem in others. Young children may be asked to befriend someone who has been treated unfairly. This can form a lasting and loving relationship.

If a child makes a mistake, families, friends and teachers remain loyal and help him/her through difficult times. With parental and loving adult guidance, children can understand the difference between friends who are good role models and those that are poor role models. At a very young age, children can be taught that peer pressure is not friendship.

SOCIETY'S STORY: Young Life is a non-denominational organization that reaches into the community to help all youth practice kindness and love. These dedicated college students visit high schools throughout the country and encourage good social skills and moral values. Leaders stress the importance of good behavior and moral principles. Young Life shows a genuine interest in changing the hearts and souls of young adults. They take personal interest in young people and treat them as individuals with respect. These young college leaders believe in reaching one teen-ager at a time.

13. A Moral Conscience

This final chapter is dedicated to all of the pastors, priests, rabbis, amahs, monks and leaders of all religious denominations. These leaders are servants of God and practice religions of love and peace. Perhaps you are also one of God's servants.

A moral conscience is essential, put impulsiveness aside.
Think through your decisions; let your conscience be your guide.
Before you take action, ask for guidance from above.
May all of your actions be for peace and with love.
A moral conscience is compulsory for building character in children

The Ten Commandments and the Constitution

John Adams: "Our Constitution was made only for the moral and religious people." (Carson, One Nation p. 41-42.)

The Constitution of the United States and democracy are founded on the Ten Commandments and Judeo/Christian principles. Most citizens of the United States have been raised in Jewish or Christian households and follow the moral code of The Ten Commandments. Judeo/Christian values have guided the moral lives of millions of people in the Western Civilization for centuries.

The rights of "life, liberty and the pursuit of happiness" are "endowed by our Creator". These words are clearly stated in the Declaration of Independence. United States coins all contain the words; "In God We Trust". "One Nation Under God" is said everyday when reciting the Pledge of Allegiance. Some citizens and visitors would like to eradicate "In God We Trust" from the coins and take "one nation under God." out of the Pledge of Allegiance. There are also some who would like to take "Christ" out of Christmas. Religious freedom allows everyone to practice the religion of his choice without interference.

An oath of allegiance is pledged when people receive citizenship. The President of the United States and members of Congress hold their hand on the Bible as they are sworn into office. Many other government officials and workers are also sworn into office with their hand on the Bible. With this oath, they swear to uphold The Constitution. They swear to obey the laws.

The first Amendment guarantees freedom of religion and is the primary reason that many Europeans immigrated to the United States. The Continental Congress agreed that the government should play no role in dictating any particular religion.

Since The Ten Commandments are the foundation of The Constitution, a review of The Ten Commandments may serve as a guide to parents and teachers when rearing and teaching young children the moral values of the United States. The first three commandments speak about a relationship with God. Commandments four through ten teach us how to treat and love our neighbor and fellow citizens. People of all religions are our neighbors.

The Ten Commandments
First Commandment: Thou shalt have no other gods before Me.
Second Commandment: Thou shalt not take the name of the Lord, thy God, in vain.
Third Commandment: Remember the Sabbath day, to keep it holy.
Note: The first three commandments deal with our relationship to God.
Fourth Commandment: Thou shalt honor they father and they mother.
Fifth Commandment: Thou shalt not kill.
Sixth Commandment: Thou shalt not commit adultery.
Seventh Commandment: Thou shalt not steal.
Eighth Commandment: Thou shalt not bear false witness against they neighbor.
Ninth Commandment: Thou shalt not covet they neighbor's house.
Tenth Commandment: Thou shalt not covet they neighbor's wife, or his manservant, or his maidservant, or his cattle, or anything that is thy neighbor's. (Luther's Small Catechism)

God In the Schools

Noah Webster: "Education is useless without the Bible."

"After liberals booted Christianity from public school, they had to replace it with something when they observed student behavior and effort steadily decline, including lower standardized test scores, increased dropout rate, more instances of teen pregnancy, proliferation of drug use, multiplication of discipline referrals and higher absenteeism. These are perfect problems for the liberal, who can propose extending the day and school year as well as institute various programs of indoctrination, such as character education to "help" children." (Wick p. 111)

Years ago, in America, biblical morality was accepted as central to a holistic education. The moral basis of The Constitution was taught in every school and society required that education encourage the development of moral character. Today, many parochial and private schools still insist on a moral code that is aligned with The Ten Commandments. In the public schools, the religious convictions of teachers are held at bay because of the division between church and state. Teachers hesitate to talk publically about their faith for fear of offending others.

Teaching the Ten Commandments, public prayer or even having a Bible visible in a public school has not been permitted for many years. Coaches have been reprimanded for having prayers in locker rooms. Public school teachers, attempting to discuss the principles of morality, often receive reprimands from the administration and criticism from the parents. Teachers in public schools are expected to be politically correct and promote social justice, which often creates a double standard and confusion when enforcing the rules of the school.

Fortunately, teachers can reach the hearts and souls of students by practicing exemplary virtues and being outstanding role models. Positive principles displayed daily in the schools will provide a successful learning environment. Positive social behavior will allow every teacher uninterrupted time to teach the academics and build character in the students. The ability to educate the heart and soul will result in mutual respect, moral responsibility and exemplary behavior. The more support the school receives from the home, church and community, the more engrained these principles will become. When applying these virtues in daily living, a moral conscience can be formed in the heart and soul of every child.

Many parents, who recognize the absence of principles in the public schools, are escaping to charter, private and parochial schools. Some are even resorting to home schooling. These parents appreciate the freedom of choice and want their children to live principled lives that agree with the moral values of The Ten Commandments and The Constitution. When the community agrees on a set of positive principles, it presents an opportunity for all families to interact with all teachers and other members of the community in a unified and positive manner.

MY SCHOOL STORY: As a public school educator, I have always been very tolerant of other religions and made a conscious effort to never inflict my religious views on anyone---especially my students. I have always had some very important principles and behavior expectations for my students that are in agreement with The Constitution and the moral code of the United States. I do expect my students to obey the rules of my school. I also expect the community to support me when I find a student who is being mistreated at home, brings drugs to school, is disrespectful, dishonest, or does not abide by the moral codes of society. I further expect the support of my community to make certain that I am allowed to teach the assigned curriculum in a manner that is safe and helpful to my students. It is up to those who work for the government to not only support the schools financially, but also support moral behavior and academic literacy.

God and Politics

Ben Carson boldly speaks out about government decisions regarding evolution, homosexuality and abortion that have divided our nation and ignore the Judeo-Christian principles. He addresses government decisions that have gone against the teachings of the Bible and have divided our nation. The interpretations of social issues such as marriage, homosexuality, gambling and the use of drugs and alcohol may vary and should be left to the individual (moral conscience) rather than the government. (Carson, *One Nation*, (p. 192-199)

In a democracy there is a division between church and government. No matter how hard the government may try to eliminate God from politics, they must recognize that The Constitution was founded on the Judeo/Christian principles. Many of the mid-eastern countries have no separation between religion and government. They do not live in a democracy; they live in a theocracy where religion is their constitution. Their religion is their law.

When people practice brutality, disrespect, dishonesty, and intolerance, in the name of religion, their religious convictions must be questioned. When their behavior interferes with peace, freedom and liberty, which are part of The Constitution, their behavior must be questioned. Religious tolerance is a two way street. If citizens of the United States tolerate all religions, all other religions must respect and abide by the moral code of the Ten Commandments and The Constitution. All religions must unite and demand compliance to the laws of the country and rules of society.

Some people, who treasure the values found in The Ten Commandments feel that the government is attempting to force God out of their lives. They feel freedom of religion is under attack in America. As the United States becomes more multi-cultural, many devout members of many different faiths feel that some government decisions (including decisions made by the Supreme Court) are interfering with their moral beliefs and practices. They feel that political correctness and policies conflict with the teachings of many Western Civilization religions.

Decisions made in the name of social justice and political correctness should never prevent an individual or group of individuals from practicing their faith and for standing up to behavior that does not agree with The Constitution and The Ten Commandments. As a nation, we cannot allow political correctness and double standards to divide us. We must be a united country in what we believe and what we practice

Recently some foreign terrorists have taken on barbarian and inhumane behavior such as crucifying, beheading, and other forms of brutal behavior. Brutality, hatred, disrespect, dishonesty and persecution are against the very core of American values and The Ten Commandments. This behavior certainly goes against the principles of the United States. It cannot be condoned nor can it be supported. Some also feel that the United States should not support countries that do not practice religious freedom. They feel that this continued support only encourages the persecution of others.

AUTHOR COMMENTS: I believe that the inner soul of every person desires love, hope, peace, justice and truth. These are principles that define the United States as a compassionate nation, a nation of international understanding, a nation of love and generosity, a nation of fairness and honesty, a nation of rights and responsibilities, a nation of respect and manners, a self-disciplined and hard working nation, a nation of knowledge and wisdom. I believe that obedience of The Ten Commandments will be the saving grace of the American culture. These principles are taught in the homes and in the schools through codes of conduct and behavior expectations. These are all principles that should be instilled in the hearts and souls of young children. These principles build character in children. As a country, we will only have a safe haven when all citizens unite in obeying The Constitution and The Ten Commandments. Faith must be LIVED and be allowed to LIVE.

SOCIETY'S STORY: It is not only the government that sometimes interferes with the public practice of religion. It has been reported that the American Civil Liberties Union is suing a high school principal in South Carolina for saying "God Bless You All". Lawsuits have been filed for having prayer or Bible readings at graduation ceremonies, sporting events, and even baccalaureate ceremonies. Individuals generally voice these complaints and the Supreme Court often decides to restrict the rights of a large majority. When the moral values of the Bible, The Ten Commandments are removed from the laws of the land, society is not only removing God but also The Constitution.

QUESTIONS FOR SOCIETY: Do citizens of the United States really want to remove The Ten Commandments and God from their lives? When people are beheaded, persecuted or slandered in the name of religion, is that a religion of love? Does your religion practice love, kindness and truth? As a country, are we willing to accept poor moral principles or are we willing to stand up for what is right?

God and Religious Freedom

"We have been favored by God because we have acknowledged him, but as the forces of political correctness attempt to push God out of our lives, we must have the courage to resist them. That does not mean that we should retaliate or manifest the same intolerance they have shown. It does mean, however, that we must stand up and be counted. If they do not wish to accept the godly principles that we choose to live by, we should make no attempt to force them, but by no stretch of the imagination should allow them to force their beliefs on us. For the God in whom we place our trust has entrusted each one of us with the freedom to choose our beliefs---as well as the mind to speak up for what we believe to be right." (Carson, *America the Beautiful*, p 190)

Freedom is the birthright of all Americans; however, a democracy cannot exist without common values and lawful obedience. In the United States, all people look to the civil laws and rules to guide their decisions regardless of their religious beliefs. Everyone living in the United States is expected to obey and respect the laws of the country. These civil laws agree that murder, dishonesty, cheating and theft and many other unlawful acts violate their moral conscience.

Almost everyone, regardless of religious affiliation, living in the United States wants to live in an atmosphere of peace, love and respect. Religions that reject these Judeo-Christian values and do not support The Constitution can be (and have been) divisive. Moral values and behavior can create contention between people of various ethnic groups and religions. When laws are not enforced, chaos will result. When laws are obeyed, peace and harmony will exist.

Faith, family, fairness and truth are just a few of the moral virtues that are becoming causalities of the American culture. These values have been diminished in our schools, in the government and often in the home. Every citizen, church and community has the responsibility to stand up to the government when political correctness and social justice stand in the way of practicing their moral convictions.

It sometimes seems the United States has two different codes of conduct---one for responsible citizens and guests, the other for the irresponsible. Americans can find unity in defining moral values when they rely on the Judeo/Christian values that define The Constitution. These values, once defined and encouraged, will promote a society of well-behaved and well-mannered young people. When all parties abide by the same rules, the citizens of the United States will be united. Lives are more enriched when virtues are in place.

God is alive in a Democracy:

"A human being without faith, without reverence for anything, is a human morally adrift. Faith adds a significant dimension to the moral life of humanity worldwide." (Bennett, *Book of Virtues* p. 741-742)

Being a member of a religious group is a statement of belief and values. Most religions believe in a higher power---someone much greater than themselves. Their leaders teach love, kindness and peace. They are the Billy Grahams, the Pope Francis, the pastor of your parish or congregation, the soup kitchen and Red Cross volunteers, etc. They are the members of Young Life and other youth organizations, who fearlessly face the negative influences of society and give freely of their time and talents to encourage others to lead a moral and principled life. These are the people who help others practice what is right, what is truthful and what is generous. These are the people who believe that spiritual guidance can create a moral conscience in the heart and soul. Believing in a higher power brings humility and humility makes us human.

God is good and represents everything that is good. God is not evil. God is respectful and responsible. God is honest, fair and perseveres. God is knowledge and God is wisdom. God is compassionate and loving. The God of Love helps decide between right and wrong. All gods must be gods of good rather than evil, gods of love and not hate, gods of truth and fairness.

Within all religions, there should be an opportunity to practice love, forgiveness and self-reflection. Through the years, many religions have shown compassion and have taken on many social responsibilities like feeding the poor, caring for the sick, and offering shelter to the homeless. As time evolved, the government has taken on many social issues and in some cases, has diminished the moral conscience of the religion. When moral codes and civil laws are violated, people of religious convictions must be willing to stand up for what they believe. They want freedom to practice compassion, love, truth, honesty, etc.

A moral conscience is at the heart of nearly every religion. A moral conscience is grounding and helps define a person. A moral conscience will guide decisions between right and wrong. A common moral code that includes justice, honesty and mercy, will unite the citizens of any country. When moral values and principles are in agreement, peace and unity will exist. The future of our free nation may depend on rediscovering the truths of morality and restoring them to the elementary, secondary, and higher education classrooms.

Myrna J. Sanner

Dennis Prager: *Still the Best Hope,* p. 43-48)

- **No God, Life is Absurd**
- **No God, No Wisdom**
- **No God, No Free Will, No Punishment**
- **No God, No Good or Evil**
- **No God, No Beauty**

AUTHOR COMMENTS: When the government begins to interfere in religious beliefs and practice, there is often a conflict in interpretation and practice. Tolerance is a two way street. If The Constitution truly practices the division between church and state, then individuals within a faith have the right to practice their religious teachings and convictions. If a religion believes that the death of a fetus is against the teachings of The Ten Commandments, then that religion should be allowed to oppose abortion in practice. If gay marriage goes against the teachings of a religion, the members who oppose gay marriage should be allowed to decide who can be married in their church. Businesses and individuals, who practice certain religious beliefs, should be allowed to make decisions that agree with their moral conscience as long as it does not infringe on the moral principles of society.

Grace, Mercy and Love Flows

Quote: "Love God passionately. Love others intentionally."

"The rights of man come not from the generosity of the state but from the hand of God." (John F. Kennedy, Inaugural address, January 20, 1961.)

SOCIETY'S STORY: On Thursday, June 18, 2015, Charleston, South Carolina, America awoke to the news that nine American citizens, who were participating in a Bible Study at the historical Emmanuel AME Church, were murdered by a lone gunman. Race seemed to be the primary motive. Religion may also have been a motive since the shooting took place in a church. The entire nation united in mourning the deaths of the three pastors and six other victims. Three days later, the nation united in prayer for the victims and their families. Many family members offered forgiveness to the young killer. They prayed for mercy and grace for his soul. Unity and grace were shown in the hearts of the survivors of these brave Christians.

These families recognized that their lives would never be the same. They also recognized that according to God's law and civil laws, this kind of behavior is not acceptable. These families chose to use this incident as an opportunity to express their faith. They would allow justice to be done in the courts of law.

Out of Charleston came testimonies of mercy, grace and forgiveness. When these Christians faced adversity, their faith moved them above the adversary. The survivors of these nine victims expressed their love of God and fellow men. They did not seek revenge; they sought pardon and mercy. They spoke of forgiveness and love. They spoke to the teachings of a moral and just nation. They practiced the principles of Christianity. Their words touched the hearts of all Americans.

In the morning of October 1, 2015, American experienced another mass shooting at a community college in Oregon. Nine people were killed and seven injured. Christianity seemed to be the motive in this situation. The murderer asked each victim if he/she was a Christian. Those that claimed to be Christians, he shot in the head. Those that did not answer or gave a different religion were shot in the leg.

More than one news commentator commented "If we cannot be safe in our churches, where can we be safe". At the time of the Sandy Hook massacre, these same commentators said, "If we cannot be safe in our schools, where can we be safe". Perhaps there are no safe havens without the realization that there is a heart and soul in every person that must be listened to, nurtured, respected and loved. Then hope, peace, justice and truth will live.

To believe in a higher being is to put trust in something greater than ones self. The Christians in Charleston had faith in God and they were assurance that God would see them through this tragedy. They relied on God for their strength and wisdom. Their actions raveled that they truly believed God's word and felt His love. Thy recognized that inner peace comes from God. Their faith gave them hope. Hope is the oxygen of the soul.

AUTHOR COMMENTS: The members of the AME church certainly raised the moral tone of society. They demonstrated the ability and willingness to forgive and were true to the teachings of the Gospel. Grace is not possible without the love of God in the heart. With God there are no "winners and losers", every person is one of His precious creations.

Peace, love, honesty and fairness are a part of almost all religions and all cultures. They should be honored and lived. It is necessary to put emphasis on the principles that unite rather than on the principles that divide. These common principles will allow every one to live in peace and harmony.

Prayer for Peace St. Francis of Assisi

Lord, make me an instrument of your peace.
Where there is hatred, let me sow love;
Where there is injury, pardon;
Where there is doubt; faith;
Where there is despair, hope;
Where there is darkness; light;
Where there is sadness, joy.

Summary

I took on the task of identifying the thirteen positive principles that I felt would create a moral conscience in young people. Since there is a great deal of overlap and one principle often promotes another, others may choose different virtues. All virtues that are aligned with The Constitution and The Ten Commandments will promote unity and peace.

Children need a moral conscience in order to accept moral and ethical accountability and responsibility. Teachers and parents encourage personal responsibility, social civility and principled living by providing consistent and constant guidance. Therefore, I would encourage every school, every community, every family to discuss and disclose a moral code that it desires to instill in the hearts and souls of their young children. The virtues may vary from community to community, from school to school and from home to home. The important ingredient is a commitment to educate the hearts and souls of children. The ultimate outcome will be a community that eradicates illiteracy, possesses positive social behavior and outstanding moral principles, and practices patriotism and loyalty to The Constitution.

Every adult, every child, every parent, every teacher, every community worker, every business man, every politician, in other words EVERYONE can look in the mirror and see what he has done to promote moral principles in the heart and soul of every citizen. He can also look in the same mirror and realize that he has very possibly not done EVERYTHING to promote positive behavior

After studying the importance of positive principles and negative influences, this is my advice and dream for all young children:

If You Want Respect by Myrna J. Sanner
If you want respect, you must be respectful
If you want to be trusted, you must be honest
If you want human rights, you must respect the rights of others
If you want peace, you must obey rules and laws
If you want to be treated fairly, you must be fair
If you want to learn, you must study
If you want a job, you must put effort into your work
If you want good health, you must not abuse your body
If you want to have friends, you must be a friend
If you want to be loved, you must love.

Chapter III

Building Character in the American Culture

The goal of education is to build character from within
Educating the hearts and the souls, make boys into men.
When moral principles are in place and we all speak the truth,
Women are ladies and children become responsible youth.
Quality education is essential for building character in all children.

Abraham Lincoln:
"You cannot build character and courage by taking away people's initiative and independence."
"You cannot help the poor by destroying the rich."
"You cannot strengthen the weak by weakening the strong."
"You cannot bring about prosperity by discouraging thrift."
"You cannot lift the wage earner up by pulling the wager payer down."
"You cannot further the brotherhood of man be inciting class hatred."
"You cannot help people permanently by doing for them, what they could and should do for themselves."

Character education is found in many schools and instructs students on a variety of positive traits, such as integrity, forgiveness, tolerance and many other virtues. When moral principles are integrated into the education process; children realize that they are obligated to become educated and informed citizens. They realize they are part of a bigger picture---the American culture and citizens of the United States.

Character building is defining the virtues that unite and eliminating the negative influences that divide. Character building looks at children as human beings and addresses them more fundamentally and personally than race, gender, religion or political affiliation. Character building does not place citizens into any "isms" category, which divides, rather than unites, a country. Character development brings children from the realm of innocence to the responsibilities of adulthood. In the United States moral character also includes upholding the principles of citizenship and the American culture.

As we look at the demographics of the Untied States, character varies from culture to culture, state to state, family to family and individual to individual. The teaching of a moral conscience and building character should not depend on political and religious backgrounds. Good people can be conservative and good people can be liberal. Building character does not depend upon religion because there are virtuous citizens who practice Christianity, virtuous citizens may be Muslims and virtuous citizens may be Jewish. There are even many virtuous citizens who belong to other religions or no religion. Building character does not depend on political affiliation; there are Democrats, Republicans, Libertarians, and Independents who are virtuous. In order to build character, we must focus on the virtues that unite us as a country.

When there is confusion or disagreement in understanding the qualities of good character in the American culture, The Constitution and Bill of Rights must be consulted. Many character-building virtues are embedded in these documents and they are the foundation of patriotism and citizenship. Every coin is inscribed with American values---"Liberty", "In God We Trust", and E Pluribus Unum". When students have consistent guidelines to reinforce their understanding of what is expected of them as a United States citizen, they will begin to understand the American culture.

Can Character Building Happen in the American Culture? I certainly hope so!

First of all, it is important to recognize that some cultures do not appreciate the American culture. There are some cultures that are envious of the freedom and liberty that can be found in America. There are some cultures that do not respect our laws and Constitution. There are cultures that practice brutality, suppression, persecution and other evils. If allowed to infiltrate the American culture in great numbers, negative influences may enter the hearts and souls of the youth and destroy the American values and democracy.

Understanding and tolerating all cultural has long been one of the attributes of being an American. However, this understanding and tolerance does not necessarily mean accepting the behavior and practices of other cultures. In fact, it would be impossible for everyone to abide by the laws and rules of all cultures. Not only would it be impossible, it would create a culture of disunity and chaos.

Then what is the American culture? The American culture embraces the English language, moral principles that are found in The Constitution, and patriotism and loyalty to the United States of American. In order to build character, all of these must be present in the heart and soul of every citizen.

Building Character Requires a Positive Learning Environment: If virtues are not present in the home, character development must begin in the schools and in the community. Public schools, by their very nature, have the responsibility of accepting all children and cannot refuse entrance for any reason---even the lack of citizenship, lack of literacy, the lack of patriotism and the lack of good moral character.

A positive learning environment is present when students have a strong moral character. Among the outstanding principles that promote a positive learning environment are respect, responsibility, fairness, honesty, strong work ethic, self-discipline, manners, positive attitude, good communication skills, compassion, love---the list is endless. Once a moral conscience is in place, students will have the ability to make principled decisions and practice self-discipline. Students with good moral character will become role models for their peers and hopefully, these qualities will be carried into adult life.

A positive learning environment requires a quality curriculum with benchmarks and standards that are reasonable and the same for all students. There will be no "watered down" curriculum that rewards the lack of initiative with a high school diploma. There will be no "double standard". Under-achieving students will not rely on computers and calculators for basic knowledge. All students will be given mandatory homework and an opportunity to receive help during after school sessions, Saturday school and summer school. Families will be responsible for daily attendance. Homework will be assigned, completed and returned. Students will be given enrichment and remediation as needed but all must meet minimum expectations.

Underachieving students will be asked to rely on their personal ambition and integrity. Underachieving students will be given the same tests and the same material for reading and understanding. These will be evaluated and the reason for underachievement recognized. Once students are motivated, they will have a thirst for additional knowledge. A positive learning environment is present when children have a passion for learning.

A positive learning environment requires fairness. Quality learning may suffer and will not take place when all students are not treated equally and fairly. Making excuses for immoral behavior and not learning has divided many communities and public schools. Perhaps the most divisive of all are the exceptions made for race, religion, culture, gender or political affiliation. According to The Constitution, "all men are created equal." All students will abide by the behavior code of the school and everyone will practice loyalty for our country. When behavior is unacceptable and students resist learning, removal to a more controlled environment may be warranted. Double standards are not acceptable because they divide rather than unite.

Often, the education that a child receives depends on his character and his willingness to learn. Certainly, students have different abilities. Meeting the requirements of benchmarks and standards does not require a genius. Expectations often require only a third grade knowledge of English and everyone should know basic math. It does not require a genius to abide by the behavior code and practice patriotism. If at the close of elementary school and six or more years in education, students have not been successful, certainly, ability testing will help teachers again assign students to the appropriate remediation program; however, certain basic requirements will always be necessary. After thirteen years of free education, if the basic requirements for graduation are not met, remediation can be continued at the local high school until honorable graduation requirements are met. There should be no free higher education until the student has met the requirements of a high school education.

Since the federal government makes equal demands of all teachers, regardless of student will and character, then all students must be treated equally and fairly and meet the demands of a quality education. Perhaps equal demands sounds a bit harsh in the present education world of "choosing winners and losers", "watering down" the curriculum and creating a "double standard". However, if we truly want successful and quality education, everyone must accept personal responsibility for his/her learning. A quality-learning environment demands quality learning. In this environment, teachers will be encouraging and supportive of all students. We are all Americans and everyone will be educated equally and contribute to prosperity and freedom.

Building Character requires English literacy: The ability to communicate and share thoughts by understanding a common language builds character. The ability to communicate helps build self-confidence and self-esteem. English literacy allows students to integrate into the American culture.

Without literacy, children will find it almost impossible to integrate into the American culture. Without literacy, children cannot understand nor read the laws. Without a common language, there is little hope of tolerance and understanding. The illiterate do not qualify to be candidates for citizenship.

Think outside the political box about a classroom filled with literate students and all share ideal social skills and moral values. There would still be a variety of abilities, interests and achievement; however, the atmosphere would be one where everyone is receptive to the information being taught and where respect and responsibility abound. It is the character of the students that can make a difference in the academic learning that is taking place.

Building Character Requires Moral Principles: There does not seem to be enough political will and courage on the part of the federal government to define and encourage a moral conscience. Therefore, the responsibility of building character in children has been primarily left to the local community and families. Since children are not born with the knowledge of right and wrong, principles must be taught. Principled children recognize traits such as honesty and compassion and vices such as deceit and cruelty. In the United States, moral character requires moral principles that uphold the principles of The Constitution, citizenship and the American culture.

It is in the local community, where the role models of teachers, parents and other community leaders can filter down to the students. It is in the home and school where the individuality of the students can be more easily recognized. If demanded and taught, the principles of proper behavior and moral values can become part of the character of the students. When building character, these virtues must be entrenched into the heart and soul. Without principles, children may disobey the moral code of society and reject the American culture. Without acceptable social skills; children may become disruptive and disrespectful.

Moral principles will replace the troubling influences that encourage negative behaviors in the school and community. Starting from the inside out and educating the heart and soul of the individual child will do far more character building than the top down mandates of the federal government. The assimilation of a moral conscience takes time and patience. Teachers find it nearly impossible to teach and students find it impossible to learn if constructive principles and morals are missing. Principles and moral values are nouns. It is time to turn these nouns into verbs. Verbs are action words that show the steps children can take to ensure that their hearts and souls are also being educated.

Building Character Requires a Behavior Code: Some feel that building character is not a social issue but a moral issue. It is possible that there are two issues at stake here and we have a paradox. First, the lack of moral values produces students who lack good behavior and social skills. The social skills that students possess are most often a result of the moral values that have been instilled in their hearts and souls. Forming a good moral conscience will help a young person live a principled life. When these principles are put into practice in the public school, they are often called "codes of conduct" or "rules of behavior." These are the principles that build character in young children. Principled behavior will dictate the decisions of the students and be carried into adult life.

Teachers do not expect perfect children in the classroom. They love children with all of their attributes and flaws. Once the moral code is in place, students will have the ability to make principled decisions and practice self-discipline. This will make the school and home environments not only safe but also provide an atmosphere that promotes quality learning.

Building Character Requires Lawful Obedience: Lawless behavior is becoming a norm in some communities. Some citizens and politicians think they are above the law and allow political correctness and social justice to take precedence over common sense, moral principles, and the enforcement of laws. Practicing wrong without knowing what is right breeds a society of lawlessness. Laws without enforcement create turmoil. A free and just culture must be fair to all people and all citizens must abide by the same rules and laws. People of good character obey the laws.

As children mature, they realize that a democracy is filled with rules and laws---traffic laws, school rules, rules in the home, and laws on the street. These laws and rules are the very principles that keep citizens safe and keep them from harming others. Teachers, parents, community and government leaders can promote obedience to the laws and rules. Once the laws and rules are explained and put into practice, students will begin to practice only positive behavior. When children have adopted positive principles and have learned to reject the negative influences, common sense and self-discipline take over. Children will then be responsible for their behavior and make moral and conscientious decisions. Self-disciplined children know right from wrong and abide by all rules and laws. Self-discipline allows students to practice the positive and eliminate the negative.

With the national variance in expectations, abilities, and personal opinions, it might be best for schools to return to local control where family support and values and morals are similar. In the local community, teachers can communicate with parents on an individual basis and student learning is a high expectation. Defining and demanding virtues and principles will offer consistency to teachers when educating young students and for parents when rearing their children. The laws will be universal and can be enforced uniformly.

Building Character Requires Practicing Patriotism: Freedom without virtues is chaos. Rights without responsibilities create a society of entitlements. When teachers insist on virtues that build character, they are sometimes accused of prejudice---race, religion, sex, political, etc. and therefore, often shy away from insisting on a moral conscience for fear of being socially incorrect.

There is no room for behavior that defies patriotism and the American culture. Patriotism requires students of civics to know that one of the responsibilities of the President of the United States is to enforce the laws of the country. The President appoints an Attorney General who assists him in making certain that all laws are obeyed and are enforced in a fair manner.

Building Character Requires Positive Role Models: Children are not born with a conscience. They learn far more from what they observe than what they are told. A moral conscience cannot immediately appear into the hearts and souls of young children through osmosis; however, role models with good moral character can implant a moral compass in children. Good moral character can be taught.

When families fail to provide good role models and teach moral principles, the responsible rests on those next in line. This might be a social worker, a teacher, a law enforcement officer or a friend in the community. Everyone that a child comes into contact with can have a positive influence on character development. Good character and the willingness to learn are perhaps two primary factors necessary when building character in the schools.

As the child matures, his world expands into the adult community. Businessmen, politicians, TV personalities, rap stars, sport heroes, and religious leaders are among the many popular role models. When role models display exemplary behavior, children will imitate this behavior. They will distinguish right from wrong and understand their responsibilities as well as their rights. Young children begin to recognize virtuous characteristics in themselves and others when positive role models are present.

Most families begin teaching virtuous principles at birth. When children associate with peers who do not share the same principles, parents may seek refuge in schools that are principled. This is evident when parents withdraw their children from public schools and enter them in charter schools, private schools and parochial schools.

The Results of Character Building: Today, in the United States, total agreement on moral values and social skills does not seem to be a priority of the federal government nor the families. Many seem to want every right of citizenship but do not want to take the responsibility of obeying the laws. They may forget that with every human right there is a responsibility. Some may want the freedom and liberty but do not want to be patriotic. For some even the ability to communicate in the English language is not a priority.

Character can be molded and character can change. Character building should be one of the missions of every family, teacher and community leader in the United States---encouraging children to do good and not evil. Character is being able to differentiate right from wrong. Character is accepting responsibility for behavior. The character of all citizens should be upstanding and complimentary to the rules and laws of society.

It is imperative to instill positive principles at a very young age, during the formative and developmental years. Waiting until young adulthood might be too late because negative influences may be too permanent. Children with good character will realize that they must contribute to the welfare of everyone, rather than relying upon others to support them. If character can be changed with the addition of principles, virtues, moral values and behavior skills, let's get to work. The time for building character in young children is NOW!

Jeffery Wick, author of *Public Education* suggests that character in children can improve when schools are allowed to teach character development with consistency. He suggests: "Each month a new characteristic is highlighted as the word of the month. Bulletin boards, lesson plans, and announcements are dedicated to defining the trait and explaining its value to the student body. Again, this initiative, through altruistic in nature, is a poor substitute for the absolute morals Christianity imparted in public schools for many decades." (Wick, p.111)

BOOK CONNECTION: William J. Bennett's *The Children's Book of Virtues,* is an excellent book for both children and adults to help them understand the "dos and don'ts" of moral behavior and form good social habits that result in good character. Bennett's list of ten virtues includes: self-discipline, compassion, loyalty, responsibility, friendship, work, courage, perseverance, honesty, and faith. The book contains timeless stories, poems and essays that show the value of moral and socially responsible behavior and could be used in every home and school to teach children virtues.

MRS. OBAMA'S GARDEN: When looking back on the moral principles and negative influences, I can think of no better analogy than the White House garden that is planted every spring. When the Obamas moved into the White House, an area of the lawn was prepared for planting. Many school children from Washington DC were invited to the garden to plant seeds for fresh vegetables and TV cameras were rolling. I do not recall hearing how this garden was nurtured. However, I would suspect by fertilizing, weeding and watering. Did these school children return to the garden every week to care for these seedlings? When the vegetables were mature, who harvested the vegetables and how did they flourish? And who picked the vegetables from the vines? Who is responsible once the harvest is complete?

When the seeds of a young child are planted, in most cases the parents involved are very excited. The child is brought into the world and the pictures of the darling baby are abundant. As this child grows, this child also needs fertilizing and watering (the nurturing of the parents by speaking English and providing a positive moral role model). Water and fertilizer must be applied on a regular basis or as needed to produce vegetables that are healthy and mature. Weeds (troubling influences) soon appear in this garden and if not taken out, will overcome the good plants. Without nurturing the plants will not flourish or will eventually die.

It is often the teachers who need to weed the garden and take out the negative influences. When families allow these negative influences to continue to grow in the home, it is almost impossible for the teacher to have a healthy and knowledgeable classroom. Teachers often ask: Who cares enough to make certain these young people are educated and grow into responsible adults? Are these young people ready to enter the world of working and responsible adults?

I think you get the picture. The easy part of having a garden is planting the seeds and the excitement that comes with seeing the first seedling peek through the earth. When weeds (the negative influences) overcome these plants, they (young children) will not grow into strong, mature plants. Therefore, constant weeding (taking out the bad) and watering (nurturing the good) are necessary for good vegetables to contribute to the healthy meal. How does your garden grow? Are you just planting seeds or are you taking time to nurture and remove the negative influences in your child's life? Or are you leaving the hard part to someone else in your community? Fathers and mothers, you conceived your child with pleasure and desire, please complete the process with love, compassion and discipline.

TAKE TIME Author unknown
Take time to work. It is the price of success.
Take time to read. It is the fountain of wisdom.
Take time to pray. It is conversation with God.
Take time to laugh. It is the music of the soul.
Take time to listen. It is the pathway to understanding.
Take time to dream. It is hitching your wagon to a star.
Take time to worship. It is the highway to reverence.
Take time to love and be loved. It is the gift of God.

MY FINAL STORY: "I have a dream that one day all students will be successful in the schools. I have a dream that all children brought into this world will be wanted and nurtured. I have a dream that all people will be honest, respectful, kind, hard working, and have a positive attitude. I also dream that all children will have the academic knowledge, moral principles and social skills to contribute to the safety and welfare of all of the other citizens in the United States.

Bibliography

Bauerlein, Mark, *The Dumbest Generation*, (Tarcher/Penguin Books: New York, 2008)

Beck, Glenn, *Conform*, (Threshold Addition/Mercury Radio Arts: New York 2014)

Bennett, Wm. Edited by William J. Bennett, *Book of Virtues* (Simon and Schuster: New York, NY, 1995)

Bennett, William; Chester E Finn; John T. E. Cribb; *The Educated Child: A Parents Guide From Pre-School Through Eighth Grade*, (Touchstone: The Free Press a Division of Simon and Schuster, Inc. 1230 Avenue of the Americas NY, NY 10020, 1999)

Braun, Adam, *The Promise of a Pencil*, (Scribner: New York, 2014)

Bruce, Tammy, *The Death of Right and Wrong*, (Prima Publishing: Roseville, California, 2003)

Carson, Benjamin MD and Carson, Candy, *America The Beautiful*, (Zondervan: Grand Rapids, Michigan 49530, 2012)

Carson, Benjamin MD and Carson, Candy, *One Nation*, (Sentinel, Penguin Group: New York, NY, 2014)

Luther's Small Catechism, (Concordia Publishing House, St. Louis, Missouri, 1943)

Goff, Bob, *Love Does,* (Thomas Nelson: Nashville, TN, 2012)

Krauthammer, Charles, *Things That Matter,* (Crown Publishing Group: a division of Random House LLC, a Penguin Random House Company, New York, 2013)

Murray, Liz, *Breaking Night,* (Hachette Books: New York, NY, 2006)

Nelsen, Jane and Erwin, Cheryl, and Duffy, Roslyn, *Positive Discipline* (Harmony, Penguin Random House: New York; NY 1981)

Parrett, William H., and Budge, Kathleen, *Turning High Poverty Schools Into High Performing Schools.* (ASCD Books and Publication: Alexandria, Virginia, 2011)

Pauley, Jane, *Your Life Calling: Reimagining the Rest of Your Life,* (Simon and Schuster, New York, NY 2011)

Peterson, Paul E. *Saving Schools,* (The Belknap Press of Harvard University Press: Cambridge, Massachusetts 2010) LA226.P44 2009043592

Prager, Dennis, *Still The Best Hope*: *Why the World Needs American Values to Triumph,* (Broadside Books: An Imprint of HarperCollins Publishers, New York, 2012)

Rath, Linda K., and Kennedy, Louise, *The Between the Lions Book for Parents* (HarperCollins Publishing Co: New York, Jan. 6, 2004)

Reynolds, Glenn Harlan, *The New School* (Encounter Books: New York NY, 2014)

Ripley, Amanda, *The Smartest Kids in the World,* (Simon and Schuster: NY, 2013) L:B43.R625

Ryan, Paul, *The Way Forward* (Hachette Book Group: New York, NY, 2014)

Schlesinger, Jr., Arthur M.; *The Disuniting of America* (W. W. Norton: New York, NY, 1991)

Thompson, Clive; *Smarter Than You Think: How Technology is Changing Our Minds for the Better,* (HarperCollins: New York, NY, 2013)

Whitmire, Richard; *Why Boys Fail* (AMACON, Division of American Management Association: New York, NY, 2010)

Wick, Jeffrey; *Public Education,* (Wine Press Publishing: Enumclaw, WA, 2011) 2011921212

Willis, Judy, MD; *Researched Based Strategies That Ignite Learning* (ASCD: Alexandria, Va. 2006)

ADD...................Attention Deficit Disorder
AFT....................American Federation of Teachers
AI.......................Artificial Intelligence
ASIJ....................American School in Japan
CCC....................Common Core Curriculum
CCSS..................Common Core State Standards
CCSSO................Council of Chief State School Officials
ESSA..................Every Student Succeeds Act
FSA.....................Florida State Assessment
GED....................General Education Development
HHS....................Department of Health and Human Services
HUD...................Department of Housing and Urban Development
IEP......................Individual Education Plan
LEP.....................Limited English Proficiency
MAP....................Math
NGA....................National Governor's Association
NEA....................National Education Association

PISA....................Program for International Student Assessment
RTT.....................Race to the Top
SAIL.................... Intervention Referral
TPS....................Toledo Public Schools